IMAGES
of America

SARANAC LAKE

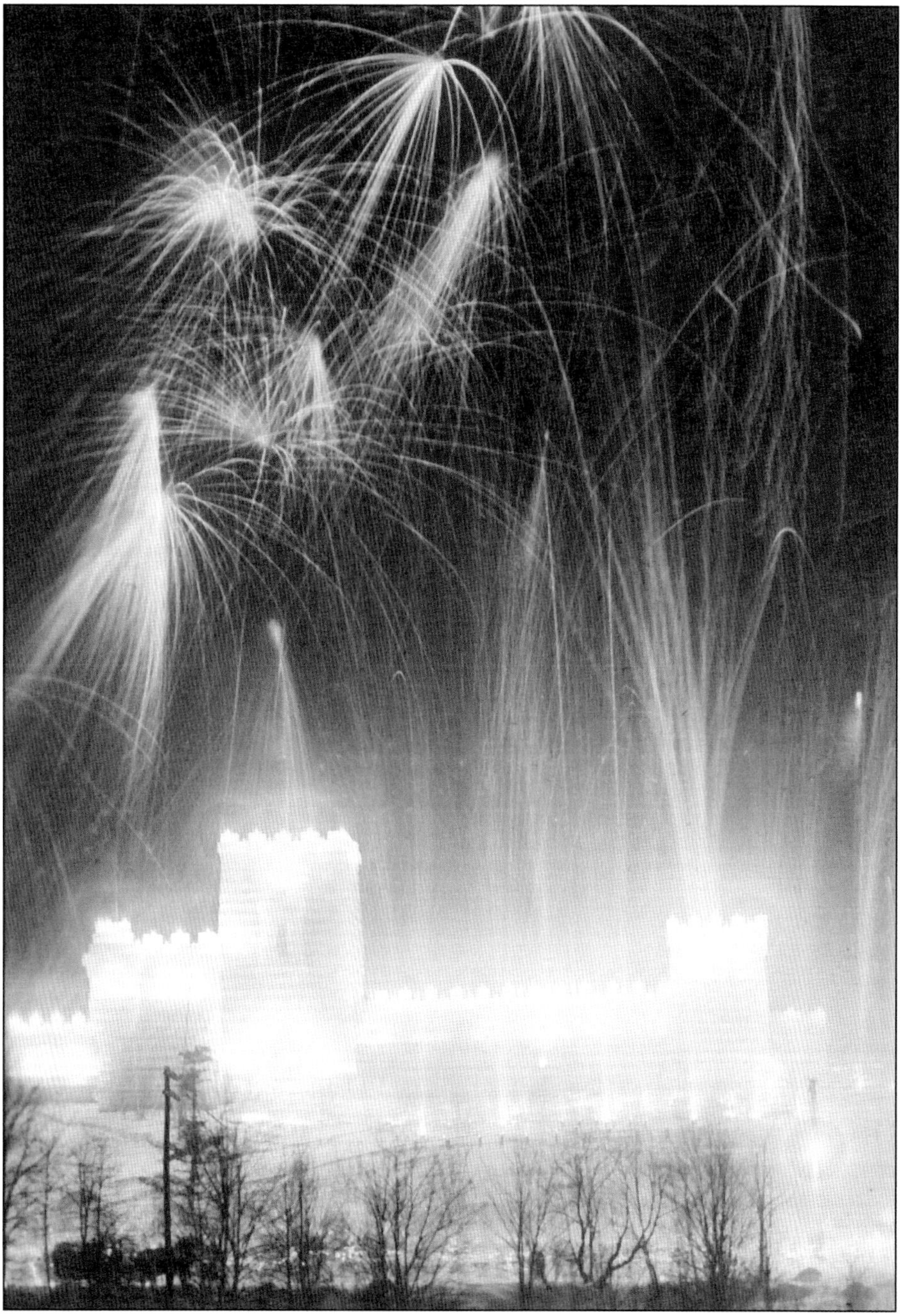

The Winter Carnival was established in 1897 and, with few exceptions, has been one of the biggest events of the year in Saranac Lake. The event draws thousands of visitors to the village, and the Ice Palace is the symbol and focal point of the festivities. This image depicts the fireworks show over the 1920 palace. (Courtesy of the Saranac Lake Free Library.)

On the Cover: This view of Main Street in Saranac Lake is looking toward the Berkeley House in 1907. (Courtesy of the Saranac Lake Free Library.)

IMAGES
of America

SARANAC LAKE

Neil Surprenant

ARCADIA
PUBLISHING

ISBN 978-1-4671-2100-2

Published by Arcadia Publishing
Charleston, South Carolina

Printed in the United States of America

Library of Congress Control Number: 2013945353

For all general information, please contact Arcadia Publishing:
Telephone 843-853-2070
Fax 843-853-0044
E-mail sales@arcadiapublishing.com
For customer service and orders:
Toll-Free 1-888-313-2665

Visit us on the Internet at www.arcadiapublishing.com

To my sons, Nathan, Daniel, and Colin Surprenant. They take a little bit of Saranac Lake with them wherever they go.

Contents

ACKNOWLEDGMENTS

Both individuals and organizations need to be thanked for their help in putting this book together. Foremost among them is my primary partner in this project, the Saranac Lake Free Library. Library director Peter Benson, members of the library board, and especially Adirondack Room curator Michelle Tucker all have my deepest thanks. Michelle helped me day after day with so many things. There would be no book if not for her and the resources of the library. The images from this point forward in this book that do not have a courtesy line attached come from the Saranac Lake Free Library. In other words, 95 percent of the images in this book belong to the library. My other partner is Historic Saranac Lake. Amy Catania and Libby Clark opened their vaults and provided great help.

Thank you—to my wife, Randy Lewis, who came up with the idea for this project and helped with editing and so many other things, and to Natalie Leduc for letting me look through her personal collections, for her knowledge of local people, and for her great stories. Thank-yous go to Mary Hotaling for her encouragement, advice, and for correcting some of my mistakes, as well as to Mark Wanner for the work he has done on the Historic Saranac Lake Wiki—this community should be proud to have its history preserved with the dedication and expertise that he has put into that resource. When (HSLW) is in a caption, it means that the information in that caption was taken entirely from the Historic Saranac Lake Wiki. A thank-you goes to Phil Gallos for the incredible research document he created on the history of the downtown buildings in the village. It is a great resource for anyone interested in Saranac Lake history and it is available in the Saranac Lake Free Library. Finally, thank you, to my employer, Paul Smith's College, for granting me the sabbatical that gave me the time to devote to this project.

INTRODUCTION

In 1819, Jacob Moody became the first settler on the land that would later become part of the Village of Saranac Lake. Many of the early settlers came to the Adirondacks in the 19th century to make their living by harvesting the virgin forests that surrounded their homes. Saranac Lake became a hub for the lumber industry. It had its own sawmill, but it was also a place where loggers came in from their camps to spend their money and have a good time. It was such a lawless town that one hotel owner was gunned down on the porch of his establishment after refusing service to a drunk patron.

By the 1870s, the clean air, beauty, and terrific hunting and fishing of the Adirondacks were discovered by wealthy city people. Hotels sprang up on the Saranac Lakes and in every community from Paul Smiths to Bloomingdale. Saranac Lake became the center for this tourist trade and the village grew in response to the new economy.

The event that really started the development of the modern village—and brought together the elements that would create the character of Saranac Lake that makes it different from any other community in the Adirondack Park—was the establishment of the Adirondack Cottage Sanitarium by Dr. Edward Livingston Trudeau in 1884. Over the years, his first building, Little Red, grew into a medical facility where hundreds of patients could come to be treated for tuberculosis. Even more important to the village were the cure cottages and institutional sanatoria that were created to house the large numbers of patients who came to Saranac Lake to be cured of tuberculosis at what became America's "Pioneer Health Resort." As their numbers continued to grow through the early 1900s, the impact of the "tubers," as local residents sometimes called the patients, grew. The patients and the people who came for the newly created economic opportunities and jobs wanted stores, restaurants, theater, increased exposure to the arts, excellent medical care, and library services. All of these amenities and more were developed and the village prospered.

In the years after World War II, drugs were developed that ended the need for the kinds of tuberculosis treatments patients received in Saranac Lake. This resulted in a slow decline in the curing industry, and hard times came to village. An economic revival came as America's rise in middle class prosperity in the postwar years led to an increase in mass tourism. Motels, cabin colonies, and restaurants were built across the region to meet the demands of the new car-based tourists. Second-home buyers also came into the Adirondacks, and what were once backcountry lakes and ponds saw a construction boom as seasonal residents built new homes and camps.

Other postwar events helped diversify the local economy and bring new residents to the area. Education became important as Paul Smith's College and North Country Community College were opened and brought faculty and staff jobs as well as thousands of students over the years. The Trudeau Sanatorium evolved into the Trudeau Institute and the village became the home to a premier medical research facility. The American Management Association took over the former Trudeau buildings and became a major employer. In addition, government jobs became important as the State of New York established regional headquarters for the Department of

Environmental Conservation, the Adirondack Park Agency, and the New York State Police. All of these institutions together created a more diversified economic base than that of any other community in the Adirondack Park. The diversified interests of these residents also helped to create the spirit of community and volunteerism that helped to get Saranac Lake designated an All-America City in 1998.

This book attempts to show what the world was like for people who lived here 50, 70, or 125 years ago. How did they dress? What were the buildings like that they entered and exited, and how do they compare to buildings today? How did they get around on horses, wagons, and sleighs, or the old cars and trucks that were part of their lives? This book will try to tell a story in pictures of the everyday lives of the people who lived in this village. Instead of movers and shakers, there are human impressions of life in this small town in the Adirondacks. A bartender at his bar or a group of firemen after a hard battle with a fire show the real faces of old Saranac Lake. Young athletes proud of their teams, people out on the streets going about their business, local residents having a parade, or workers installing water mains are the true faces of old Saranac Lake.

Local historian Mary Hotaling gives her readers the then-and-now angle in her weekly Pictures from the Past feature in the *Adirondack Daily Enterprise*. This book will follow her example and compare the past and present as much as possible. This way, people can get some perspective on how the area has changed over the years. What is amazing is how much of the village has been preserved in our fast-changing world.

Saranac Lake is very fortunate to have some resources in the community that made this approach possible. There have been some excellent photographers who have recorded its daily history over the years. Taken together, the work of George Baldwin, William L. Distin, and especially William Kollecker cover village history from the 1880s through the 1940s. The fact that so much of their work has been preserved in the collections in the Adirondack Room of the Saranac Lake Free Library is particularly fortunate. Another valuable resource for community history is Historic Saranac Lake. Its exhibits and collections are in its building on Church Street, and its wiki is at hsl.wikispot.org. Bunk's Place (www.bunksplace.com) is also a valuable resource. Some might call Bunk's Place the keeper of the people's history of Saranac Lake. Both of these websites are a must-see for anyone interested in village history.

At the core of all of the coming and going of people through history is Saranac Lake's location in the Adirondack Mountains. The forests, the rivers, the lakes, the wildlife, the winters, and all of the other aspects of being in the mountains combine to make life in the Adirondacks different from anything else in the eastern United States. The environment of the mountains drives more of what goes on here. Whether it's hunting, fishing, skiing, canoeing, snowmobiling, hiking, or any other outdoor pursuits, environment drives much of the recreation. The long winters can make travel difficult, so there can be a feeling of isolation. Even today, you hear people talking about cabin fever when winter lasts too long for their tastes. No matter what locals do for fun, how they feel about winter, or what they do for a living, they have the secret knowledge that they get to live where other people come for their vacations. That is why most residents would agree that Saranac Lake is the coolest place in the Adirondacks.

One

Making a Living

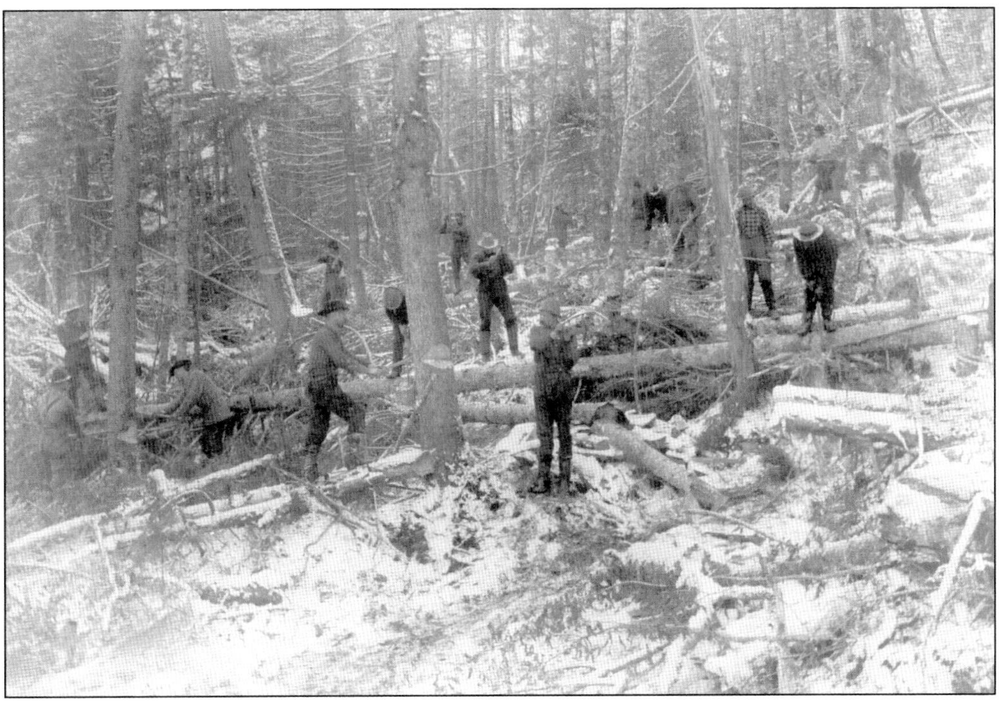

The title on the back of this 1888 image of loggers at work is *The Choppers*. Logging was one earliest ways of making a living that brought settlers to the Adirondacks. The methods have changed, but lumbering continues to be a contributor to the local economy in the 21st century.

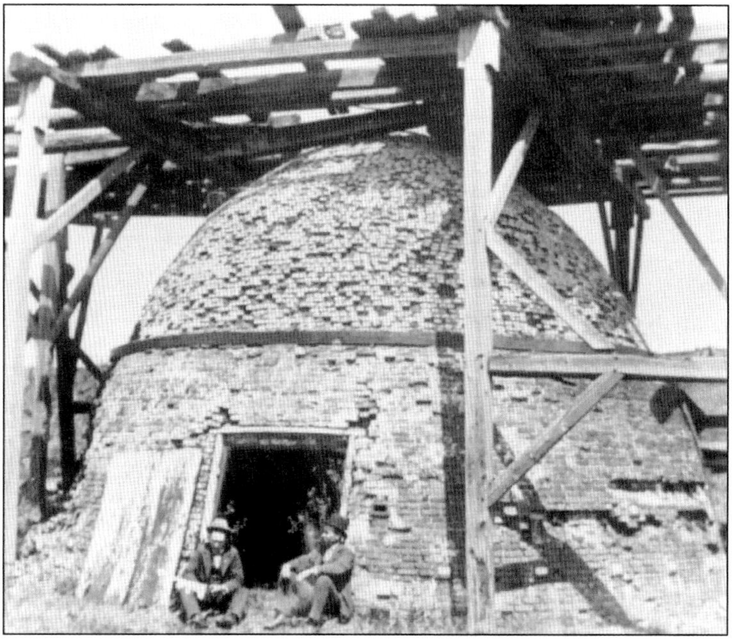

This is a charcoal kiln. The charcoal industry was a huge employer in the 19th-century Adirondacks. While the softwoods were used for lumber in the various mills in the region, the hardwoods—maple, birch, and beech especially—were used to make charcoal. Between 1873 and 1903, the Chateaugay Ore & Iron Company alone used over 1.5 million cords of Adirondack hardwoods for charcoal.

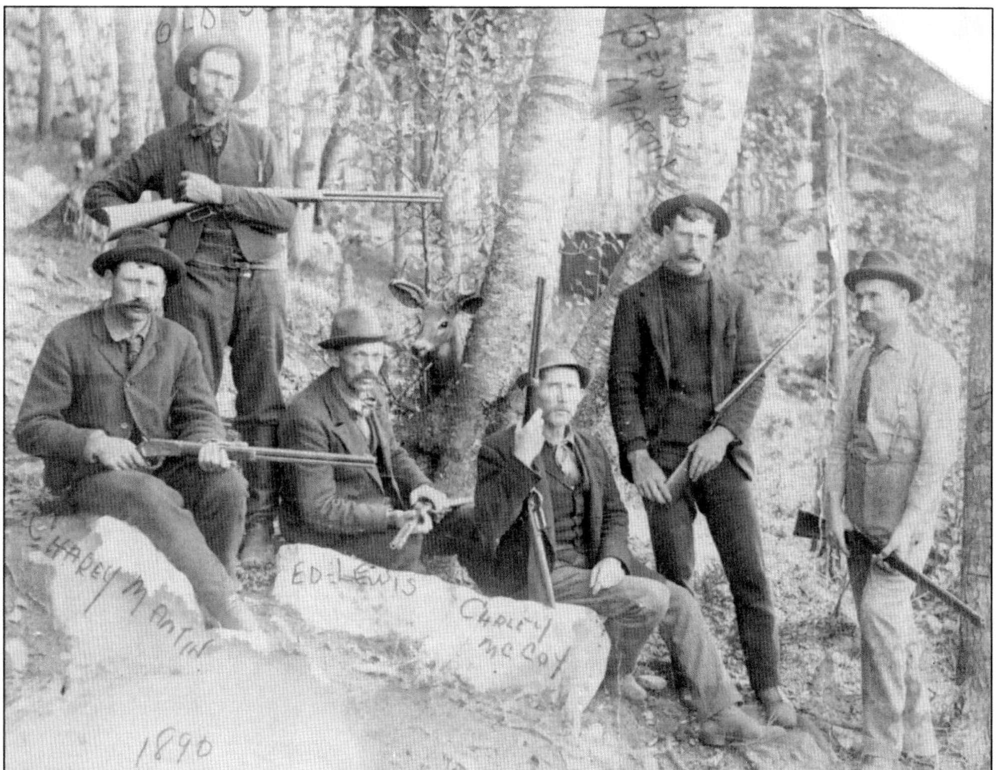

Many locals made a living by guiding vacationing sports. "Sports" was the name locals used for tourists in the 19th century. These Saranac Lake guides are posing in 1890. They are, from left to right, Charley Martin, "Old" Jack Davis, Ed Lewis, Charley McCoy, Bernard Martin, and Bob King.

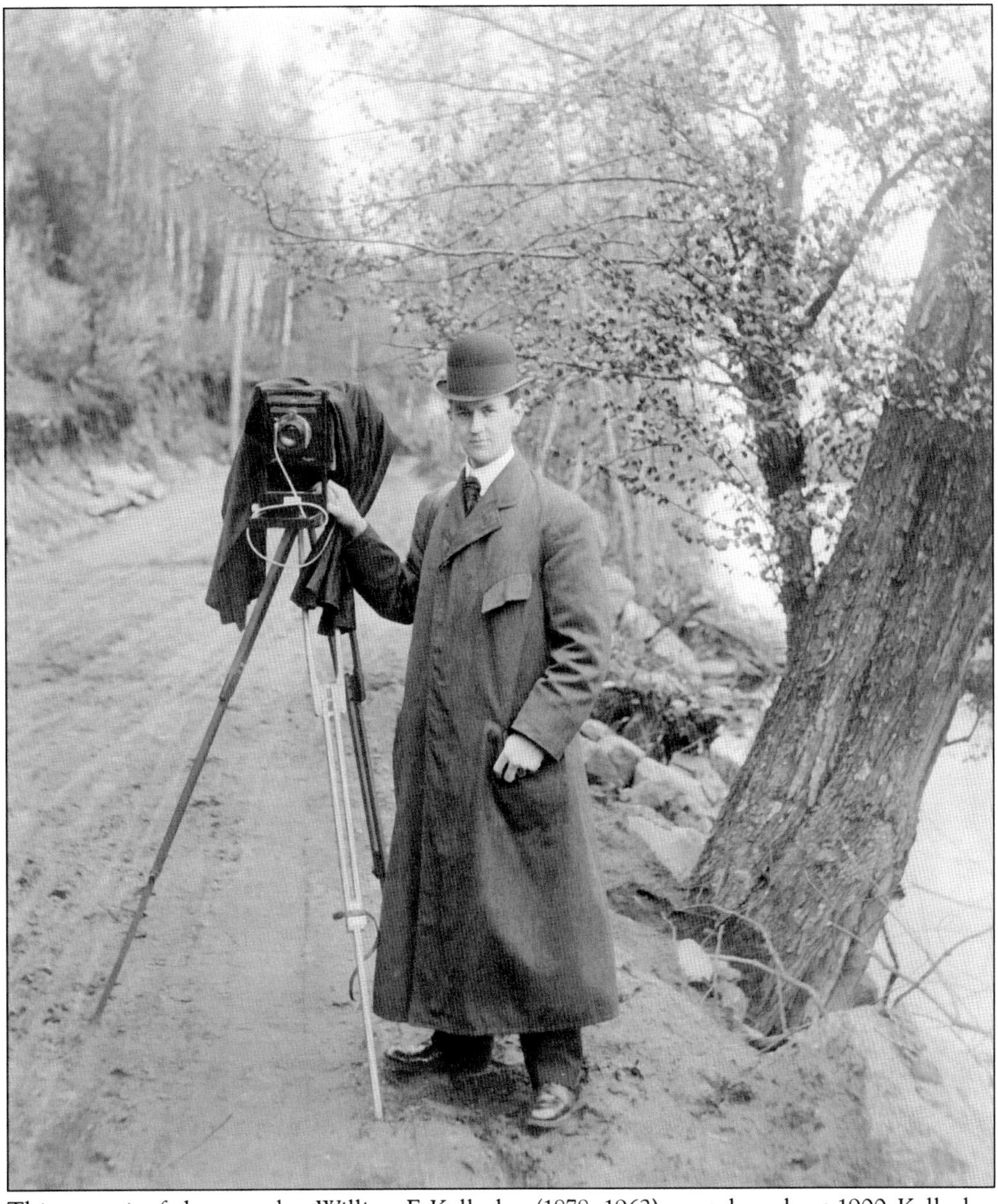

This portrait of photographer William F. Kollecker (1878–1962) was taken about 1900. Kollecker had a photography shop on Main Street where he recorded the history of Saranac Lake for many years. Some of his photographs survive in the Saranac Lake Free Library and have been used in this book.

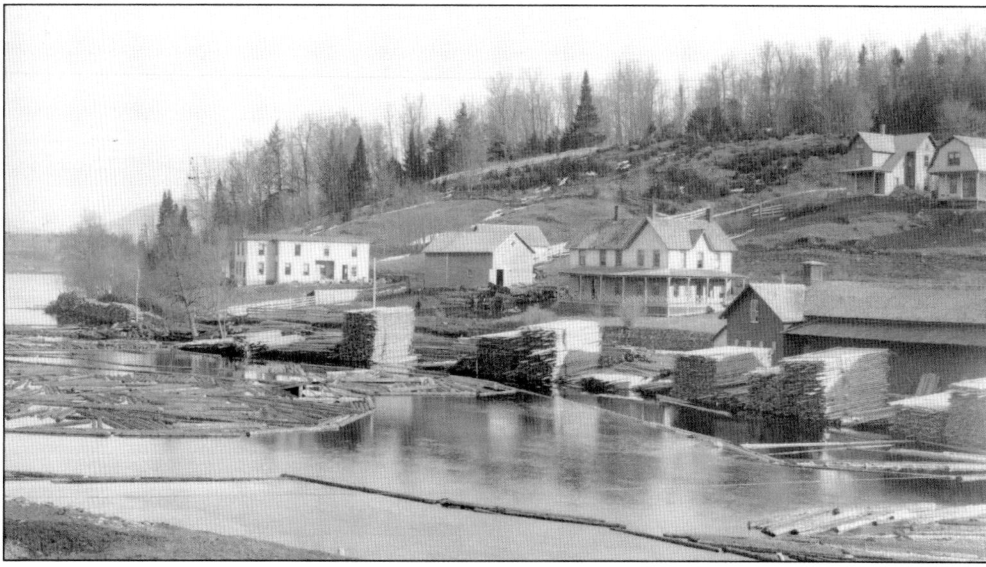

Steve Merchant's Lumber Mill was located at the foot of Lake Flower around the dam site on Main Street. In the early 1890s, Merchant operated the mill that had been established by Pliny Miller in 1827. The site was sold to the Saranac Lake Electric Company in 1894 (HSLW). Logs were floated or dragged by barge from upstream on the Saranac River to be processed and sold at the mill.

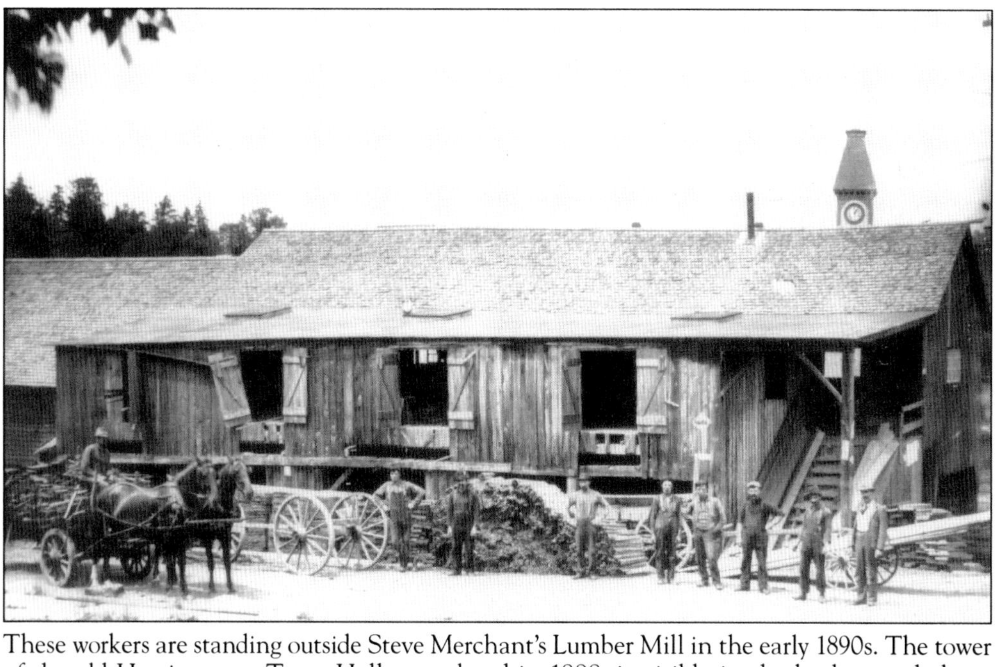

These workers are standing outside Steve Merchant's Lumber Mill in the early 1890s. The tower of the old Harrietstown Town Hall, completed in 1888, is visible in the background above the mill.

The Adirondack National Bank was organized May 3, 1897. The beautiful headquarters was built between 1906 and 1907. The new owner, Marine Midland Corporation, decided to modernize this beautiful building in 1962. Onlookers walking down Main Street look at the bland brick covering of the First Niagara Bank building and remember that this historic front hides beneath it.

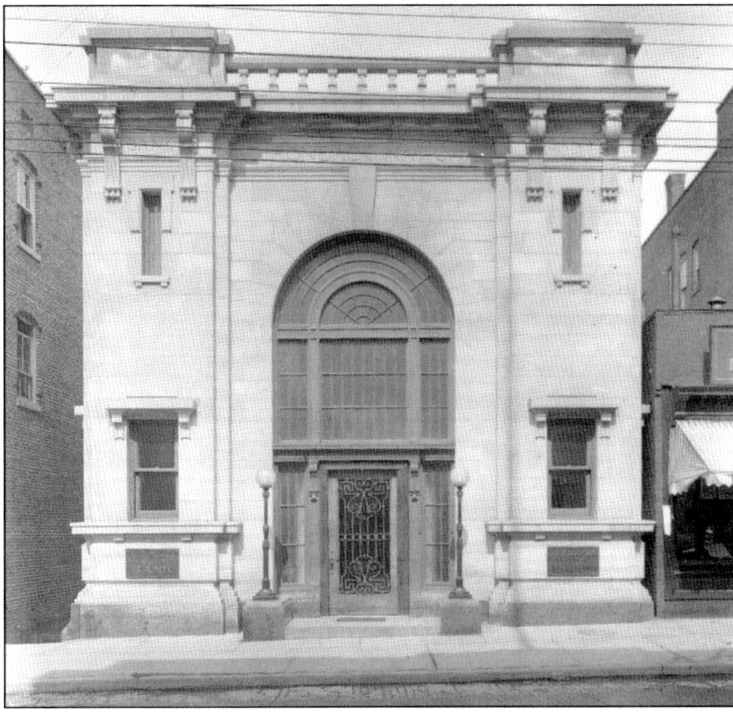

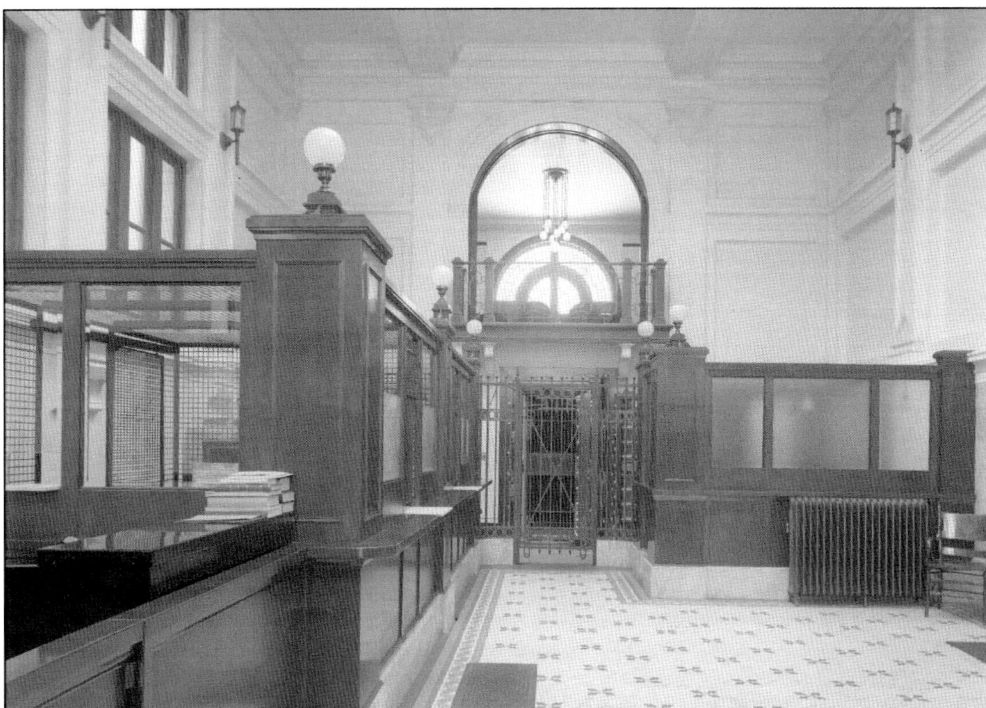

This was the interior of the Adirondack National Bank; this view looks toward the vault. In 1962, the Marine Midland Bank Corporation gutted this historic building and replaced it with the Corporate Modern interior that is still present today.

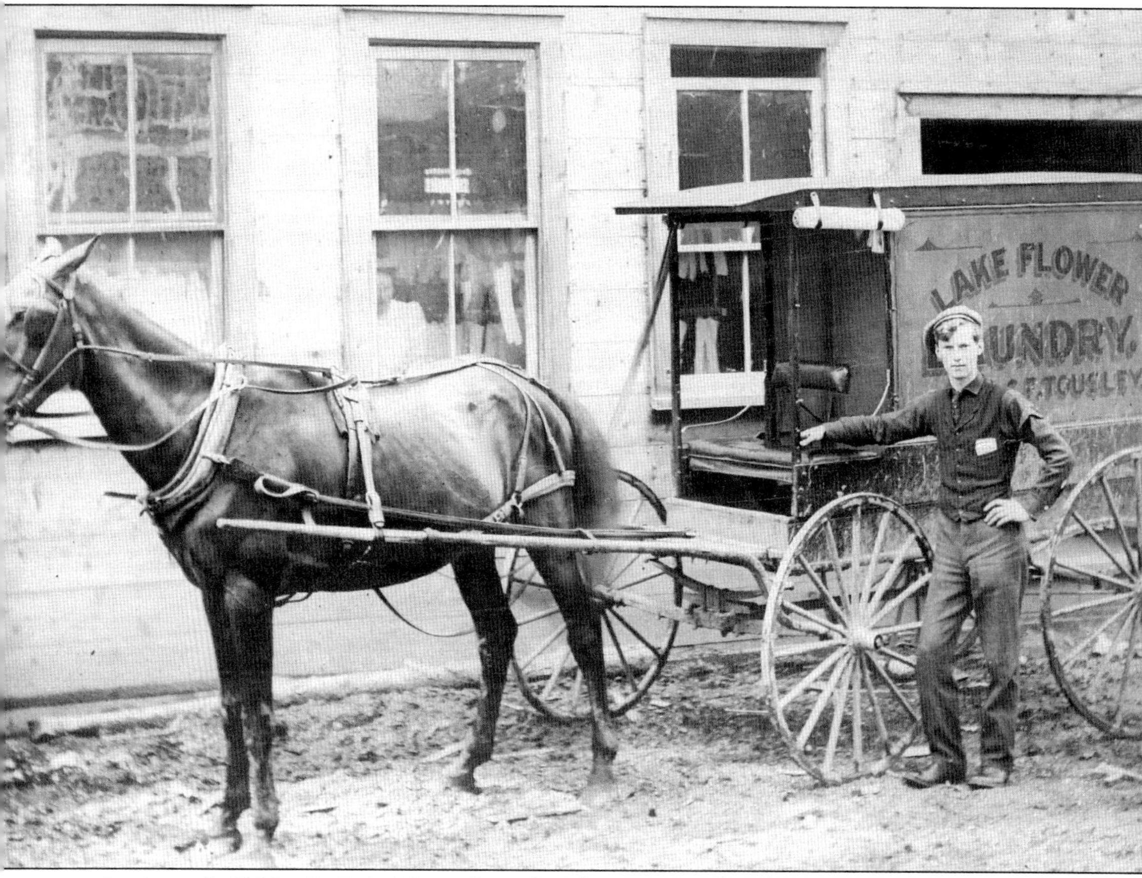

In the early 1900s, the Lake Flower Laundry's location was listed at 21 River Street. Today, that is part of Riverside Park.

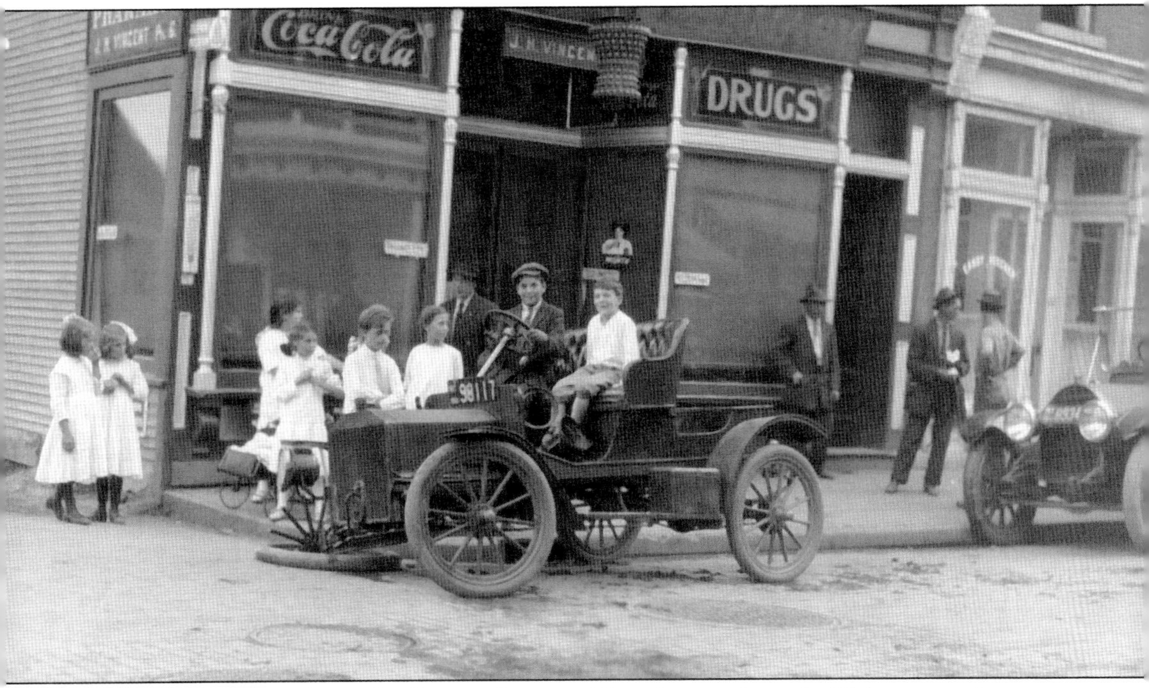

Vincent's Pharmacy was located at Dorsey Street and Broadway early in the 20th century. It must have had a soda fountain, because the signs out front advertise ice-cream sodas, egg drinks, and Moxie. Moxie was one of the first mass-produced soft drinks in the United States. In this 1908 image, the car out front with the broken wheel has drawn the attention of the neighborhood children.

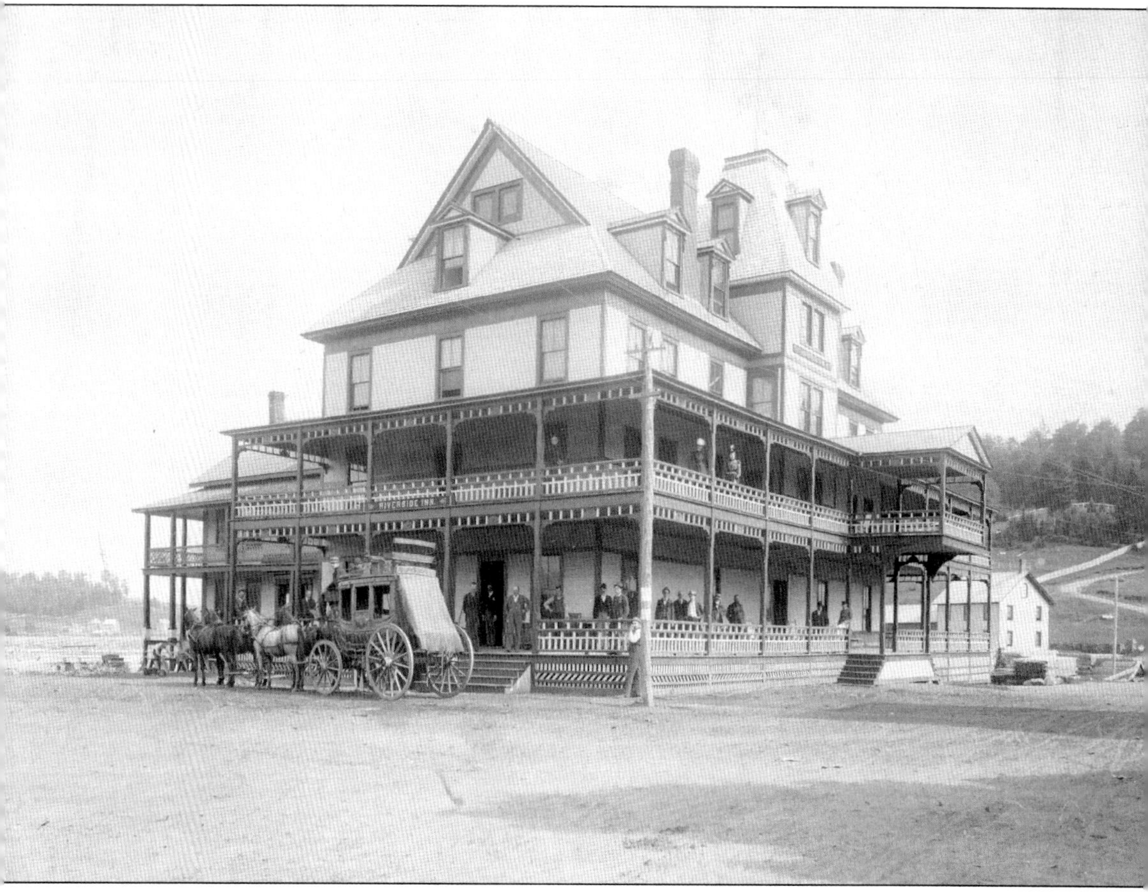

Orlando Blood opened Blood's Hotel on July 4, 1860. He later purchased the Main Street building and the 80 acres around it from John J. Miller in 1865 for $2,115. Blood ran the establishment until 1883 when he leased it to Charles H. Kendall. Kendall then subleased it to George Berkeley, who ran it until he was killed there in 1888. A guide named Charles Brown shot and killed Berkeley while he was standing on the hotel porch. The drunken Brown was refused service, and was then thrown out of the hotel bar. Brown threatened to shoot Berkeley and made good on his threat.

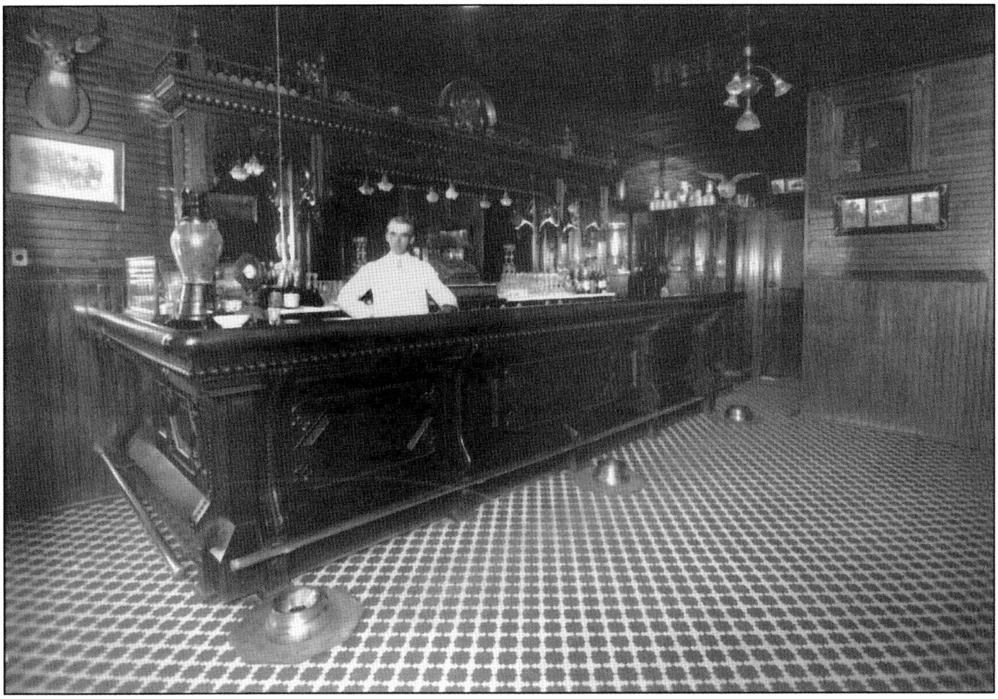

Here is the bar at Blood's Hotel. In the early days, the hotel was famous for the balls it put on for the community. The name of the hotel was later changed to the Riverside Inn, and Riverside Park now incorporates the site of this old inn.

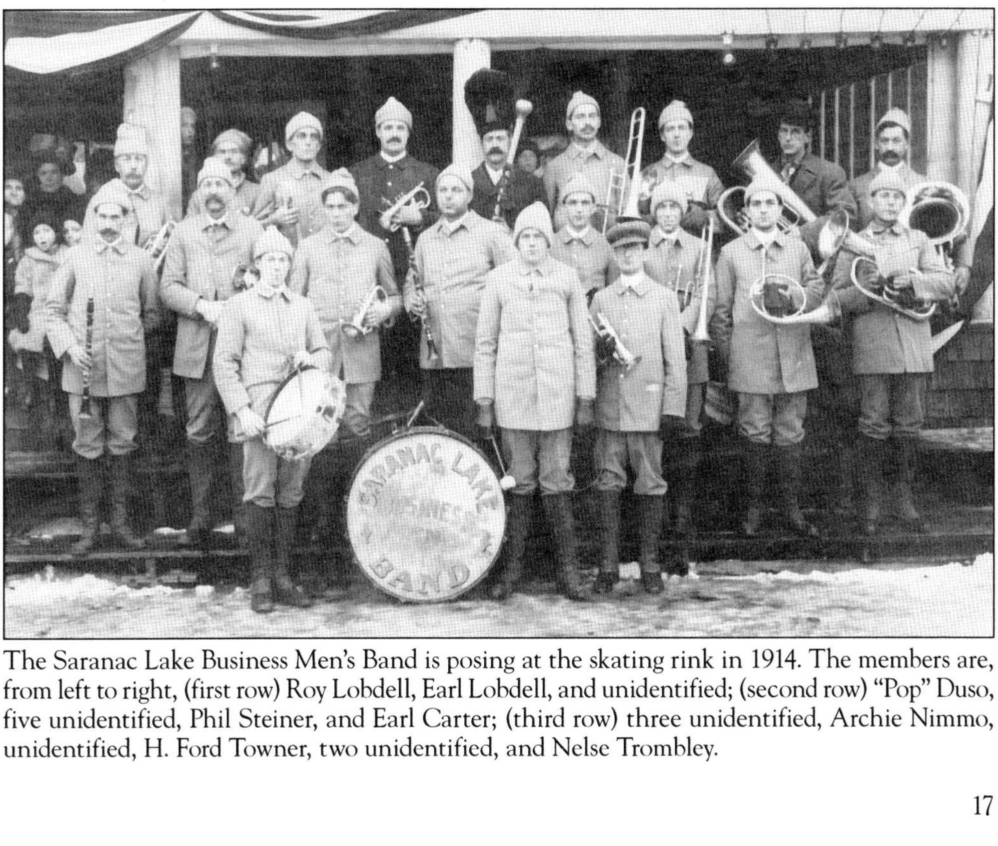

The Saranac Lake Business Men's Band is posing at the skating rink in 1914. The members are, from left to right, (first row) Roy Lobdell, Earl Lobdell, and unidentified; (second row) "Pop" Duso, five unidentified, Phil Steiner, and Earl Carter; (third row) three unidentified, Archie Nimmo, unidentified, H. Ford Towner, two unidentified, and Nelse Trombley.

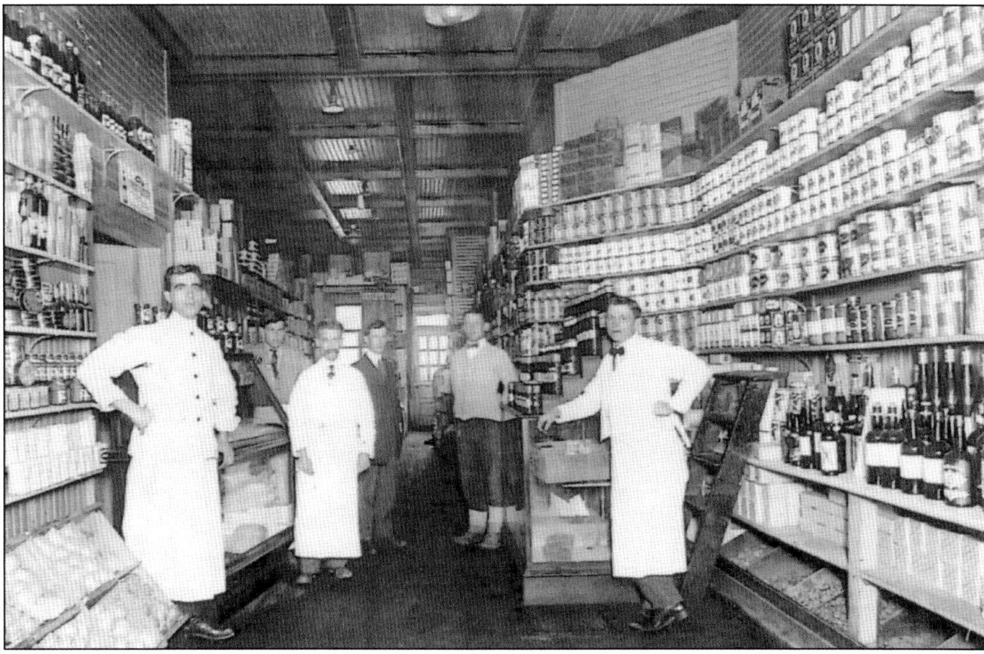

This is the interior of Munn's Grocery on Main Street. The Munn brothers—Will, Bert, and Matt, all in white—ran their store in the Fowler Block from 1909 to 1925.

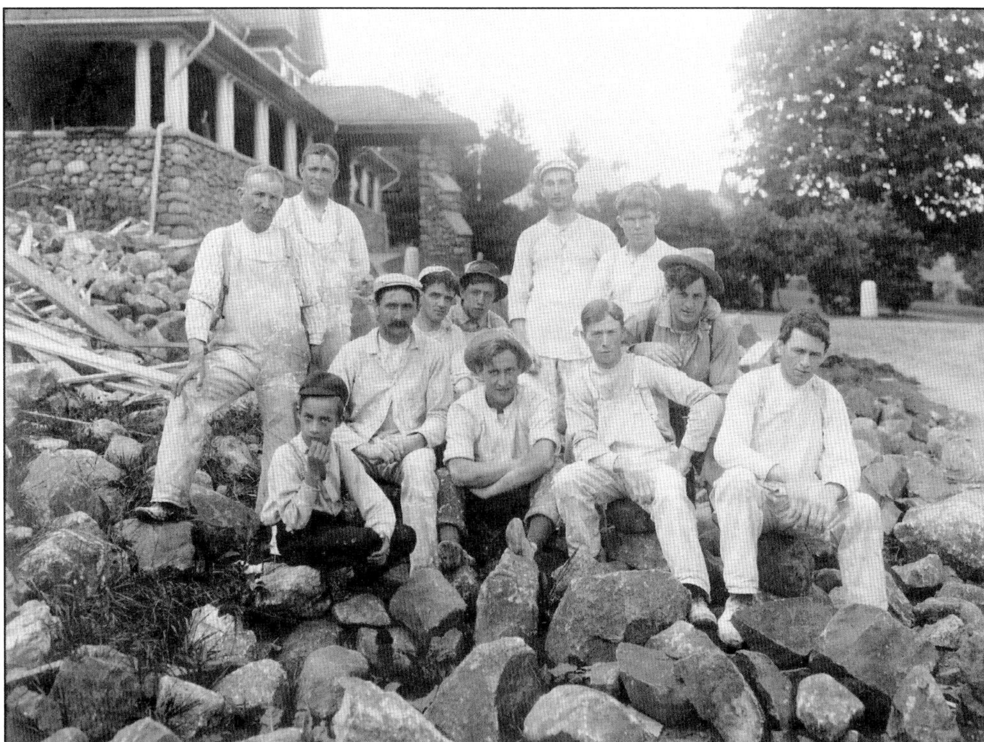

This painting crew is taking a break from work on the Trudeau Sanatorium.

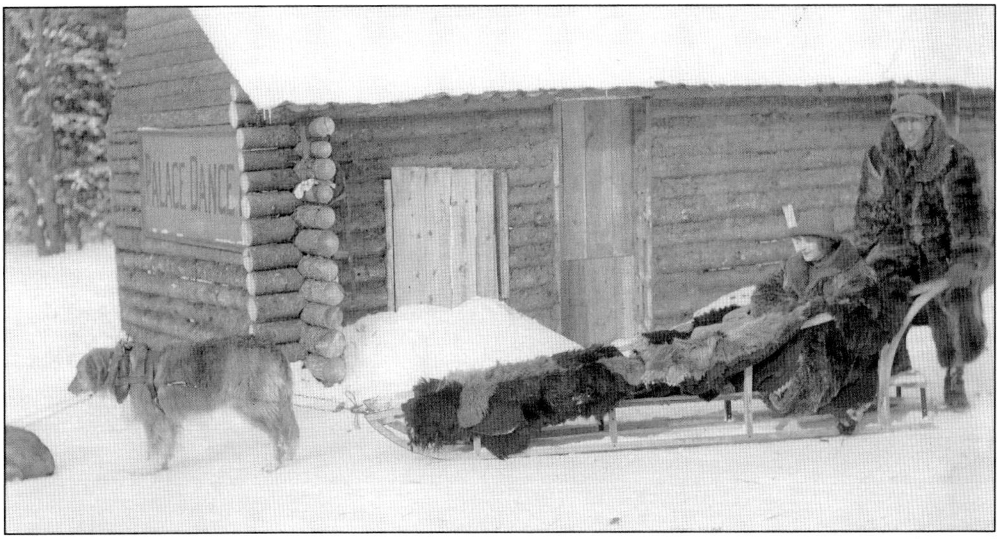

In 1913, William F. "Caribou Bill" Cooper set up a Klondike gold rush silent-movie set on Edgewood Road. Here are two of his actors, Walter Weir and Renee Davis, in front of one of the movie set's fake buildings.

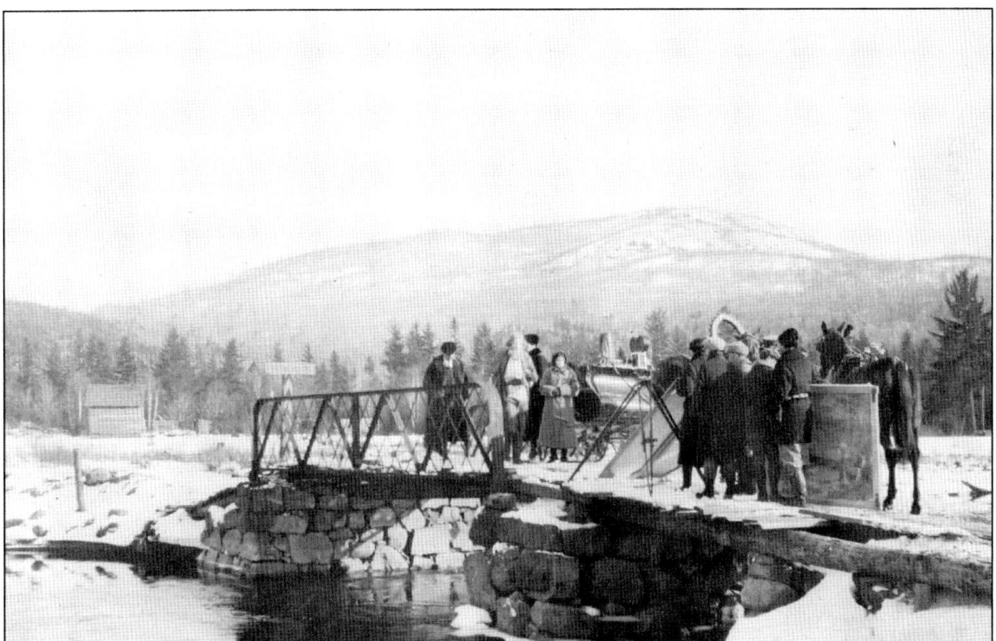

Saranac Lake was the location for quite a few silent films in the early days of moviemaking. Stars Norma Talmadge and long-whiskered Marc McDermott are shooting the final scene of the film *The New Moon: A Select Production of Powerful Contrasts in the Red Rule of Russia* in 1919. (Courtesy of Historic Saranac Lake.)

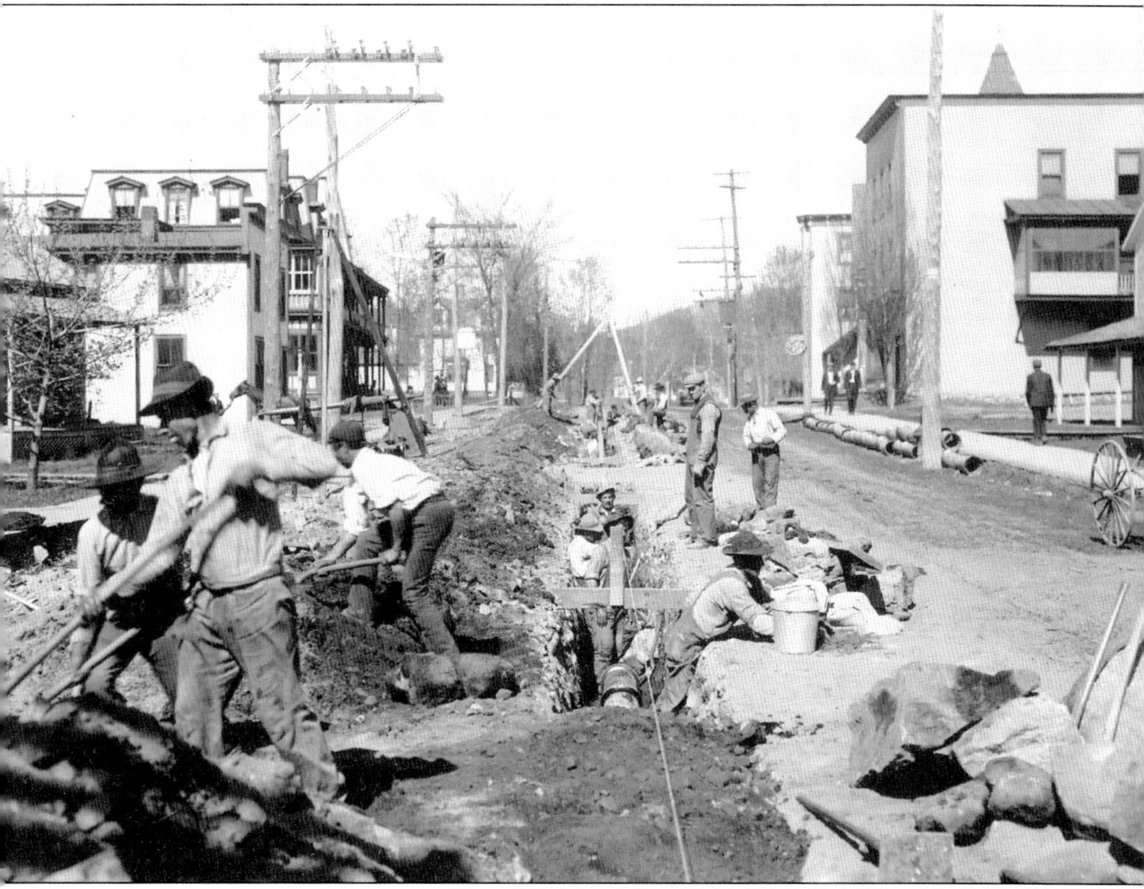

These men are digging a trench for the installation of water mains on Bloomingdale Avenue. McKenzie Pond supplied the village with the water supply that was pumped through these pipes for many years.

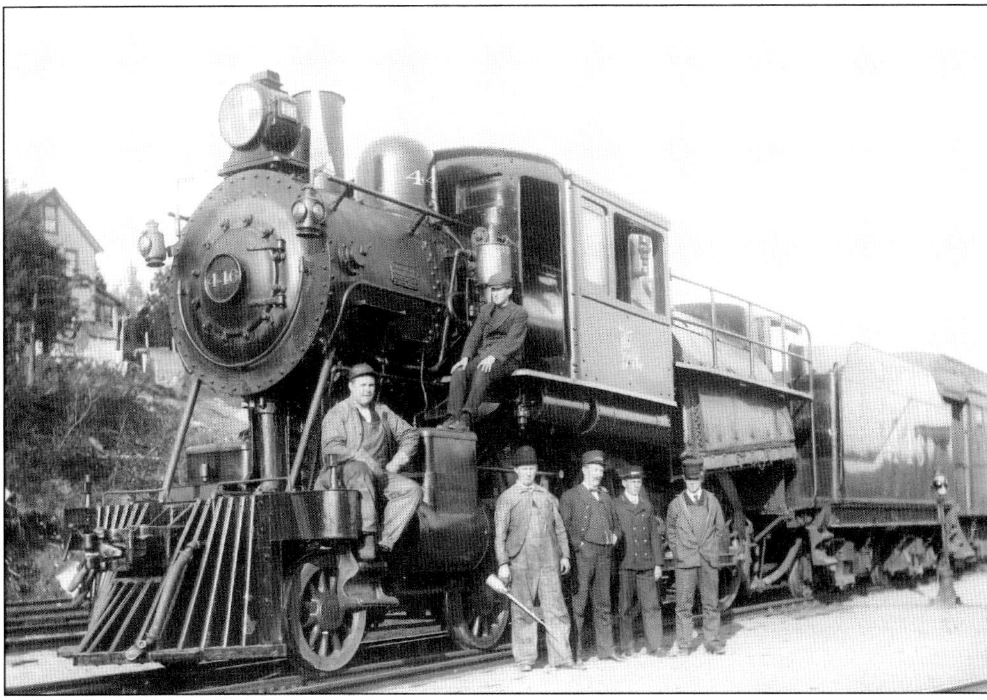

A train crew poses with Delaware & Hudson engine No. 446.

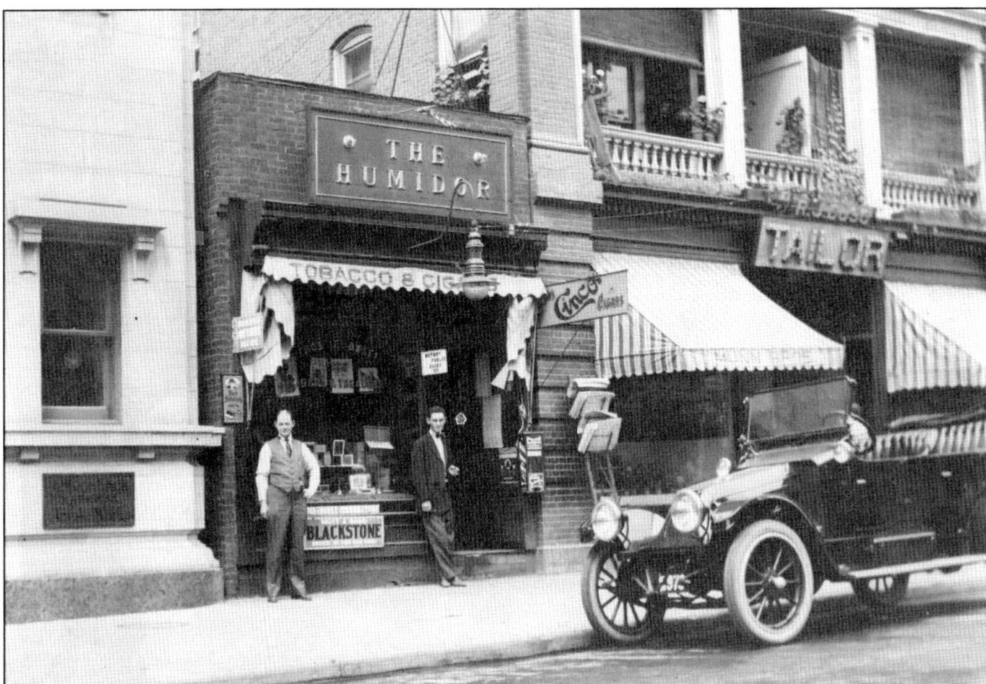

The Humidor was located at 75 Main Street between the Adirondack National Bank and the Munn brothers' store in the Fowler Block. This local tobacco store was built by Patrick J. Daley prior to 1908 and was run for many years by his son Tommy. The location is now the aluminum-and-glass entrance to the First Niagara Bank.

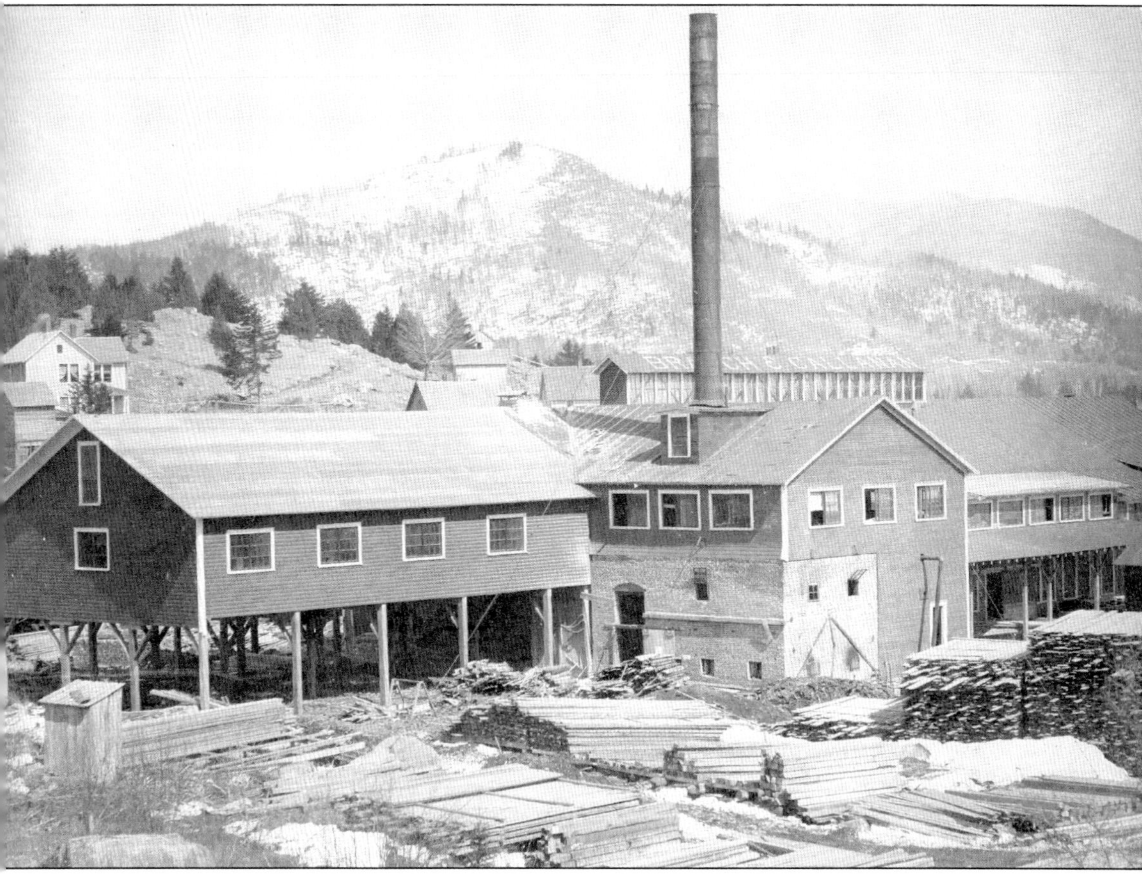

The Branch and Callanan Mill was located along the railroad at the end of Depot Street. In addition to constructing many of the finest buildings in the area, the company had this mill that produced doors, window sashes, and other woodwork for its projects as well as the projects of other regional contractors. Much of the mill burned in 1930.

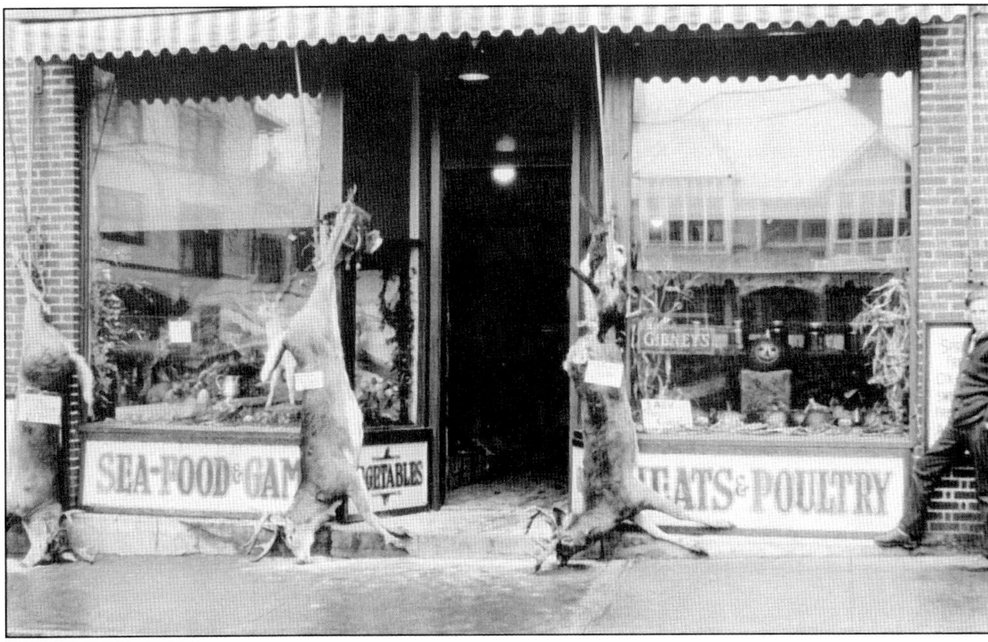

Gibney's Market was located at 52 Main Street. This meat market specialized in high-end meat, and wild game was a specialty, as the sign behind the middle deer suggests. Its heyday was the 1920s. The building was sold in 1936 after the market went bankrupt (HSLW).

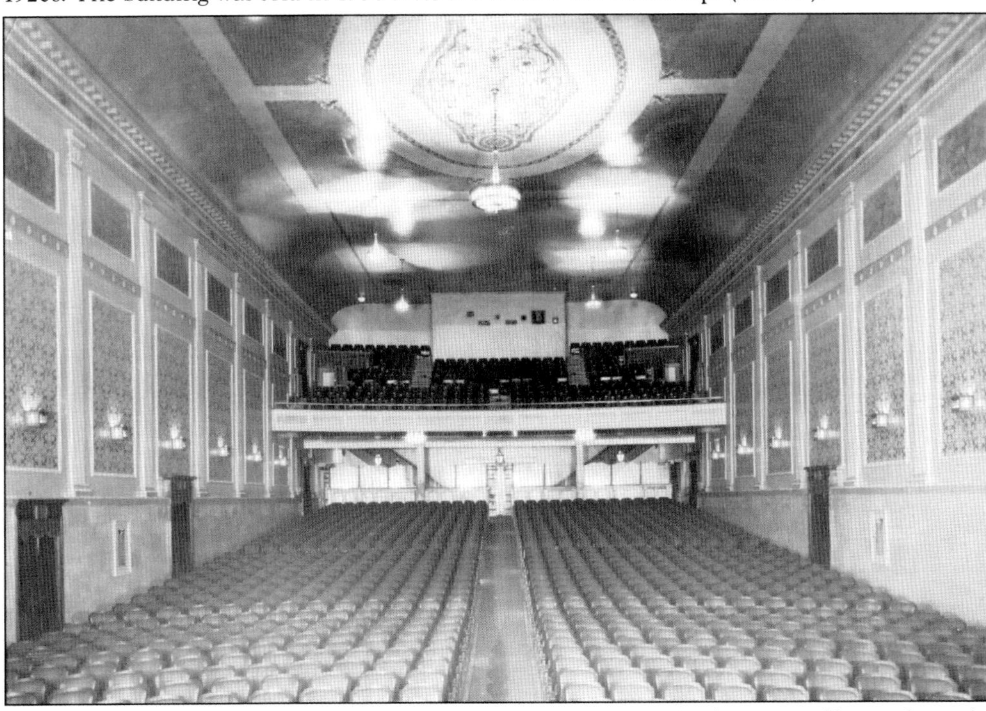

The Pontiac Theatre was built in 1917. Movies and live shows were both presented here. This is the interior as seen from the stage in 1928. Al Jolson, Sophie Tucker, and Ray Bolger, the Scarecrow in the movie *The Wizard of Oz*, are just a few of the stage acts that performed at the Pontiac. It burned on December 19, 1978, and today the site is the parking lot below the Berkeley Green.

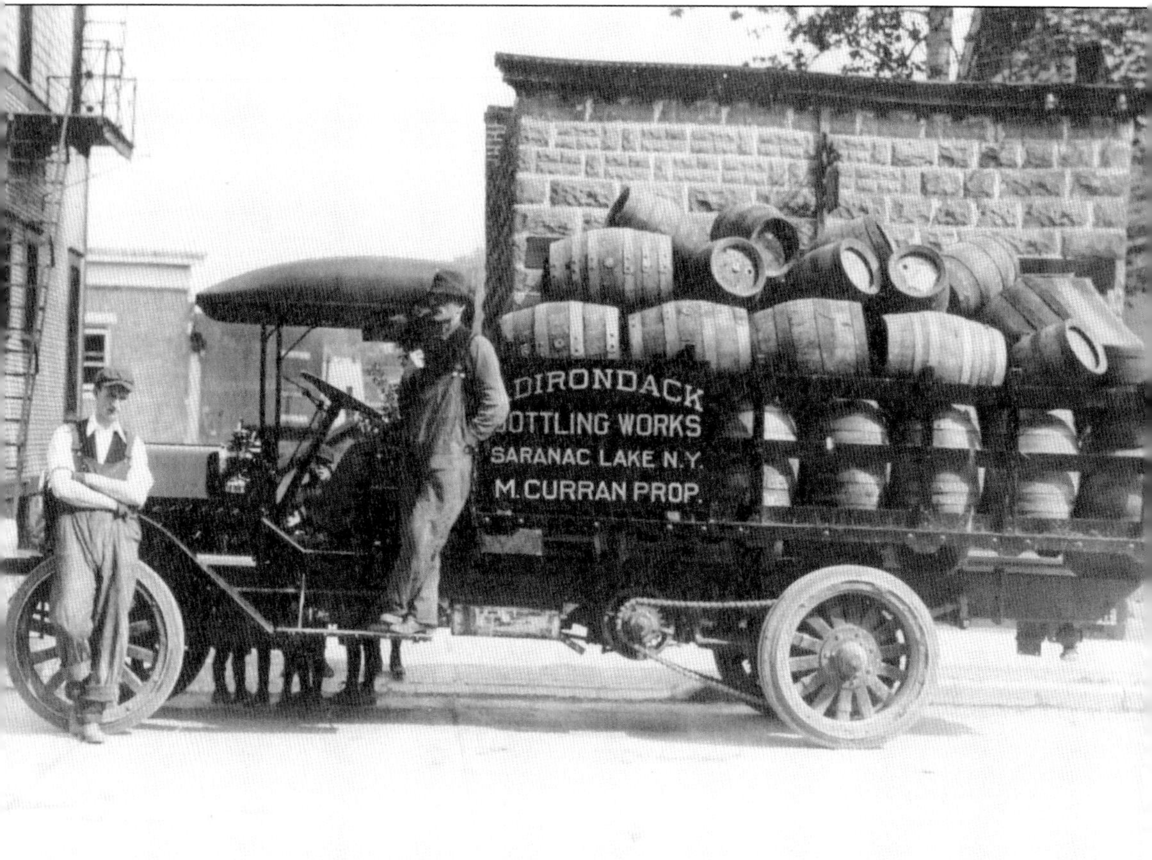

The Adirondack Bottling Works was located along the river behind 16 Main Street where the right-of-way for the LaPan Highway is now. It had contracts to bottle Pabst beer, Feigenspan's Ale and Porter, as well as soft drinks. Its building burned in 1958 (HSLW). Note the chain drive on the truck and the neighborhood kids peeking through the cab opening to get their picture taken.

Chance's Restaurant was built at 97 Main Street in the 1930s and went out of business in 1937. The space was reopened in 1938 by O.M. Sanborn and Meta J. Bofinger as the Blue Gentian. This successful restaurant continued into the 1970s. After a series of other restaurants came and went in the location, the Community Store took over the building in 2011.

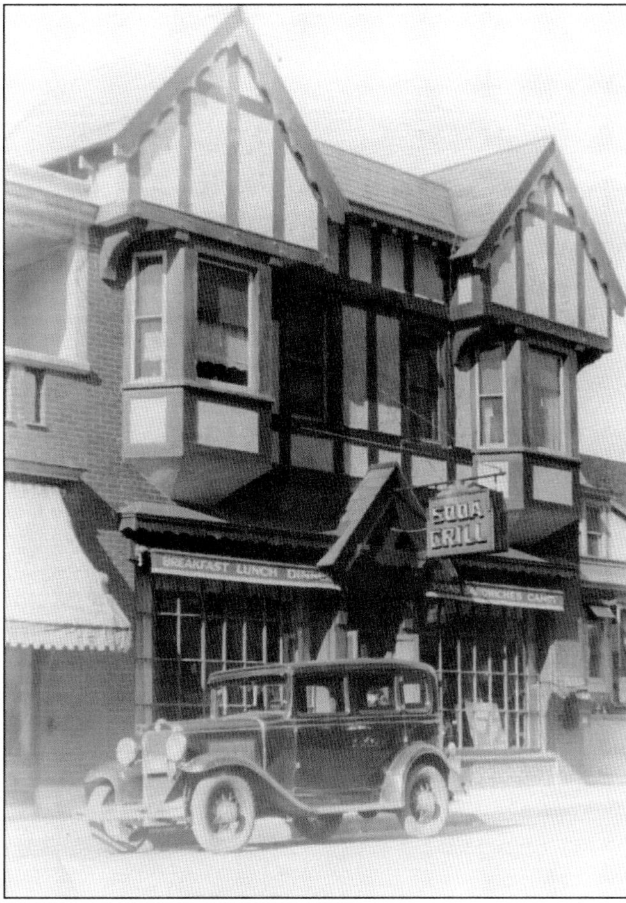

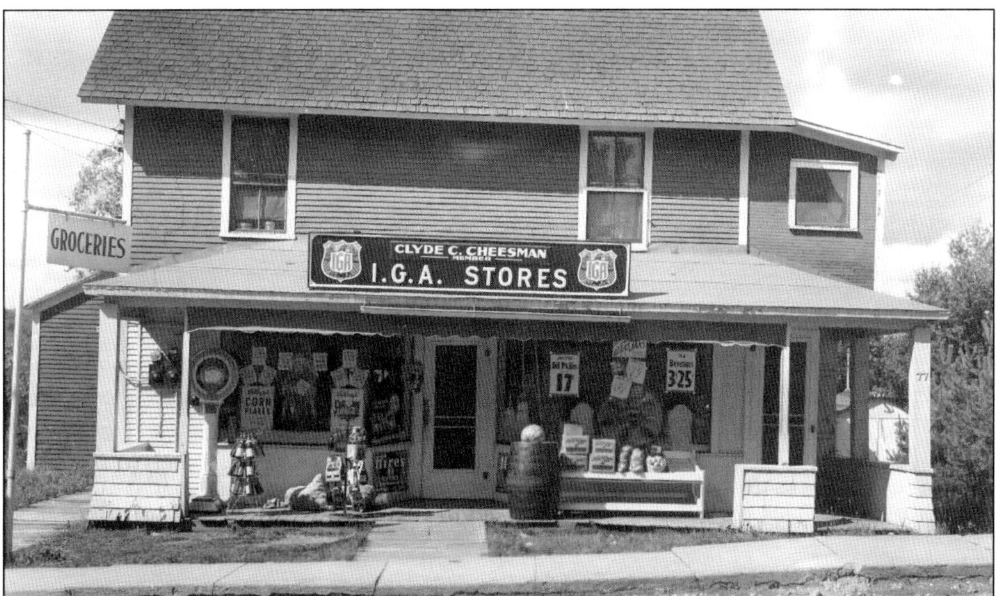

This is the Clyde Cheesman's store in 1939. It was located on Lake Street.

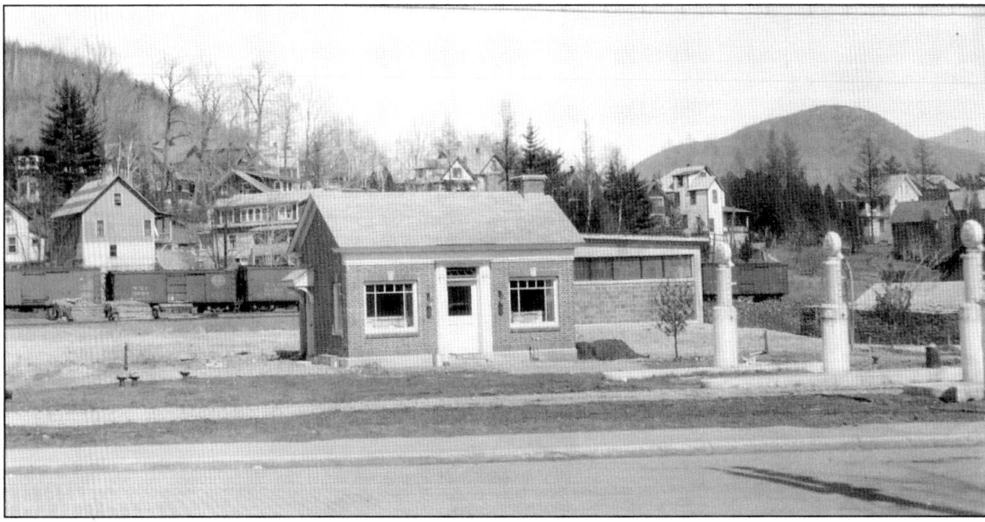

The Broadway Garage was located where the Hyde Fuel mini-mart is located today. Notice the early fuel pumps out front. Before metered pumps, gasoline pumps had a calibrated glass cylinder on top. The desired quantity of fuel was pumped up into the cylinder as indicated by the calibration. Then the pumping was stopped and the nozzle was opened to let the gasoline flow down and out into the customer's tank by gravity.

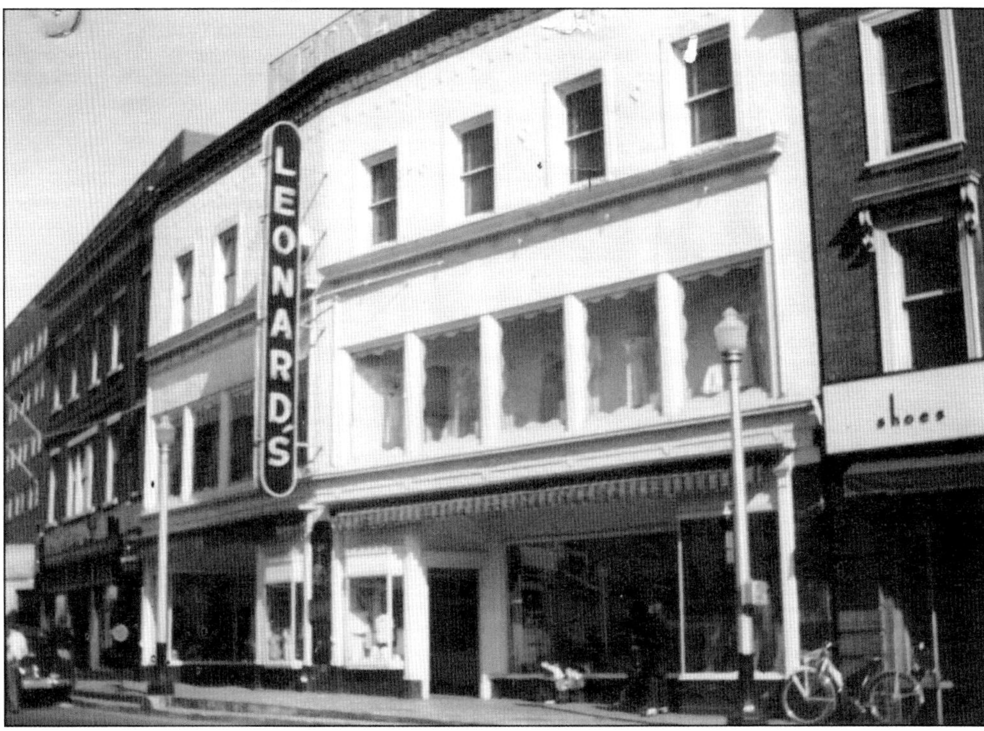

William C. Leonard built the first department store in Saranac Lake in two parts. The first was constructed in the late 1890s, and the second was built in 1905 at what is today 86 Main Street. The structure was equipped with a pneumatic tube system for moving paperwork and money throughout the store. Beginning in March 1966, the National Army Store took over the building, which currently houses Surgical Eye Care.

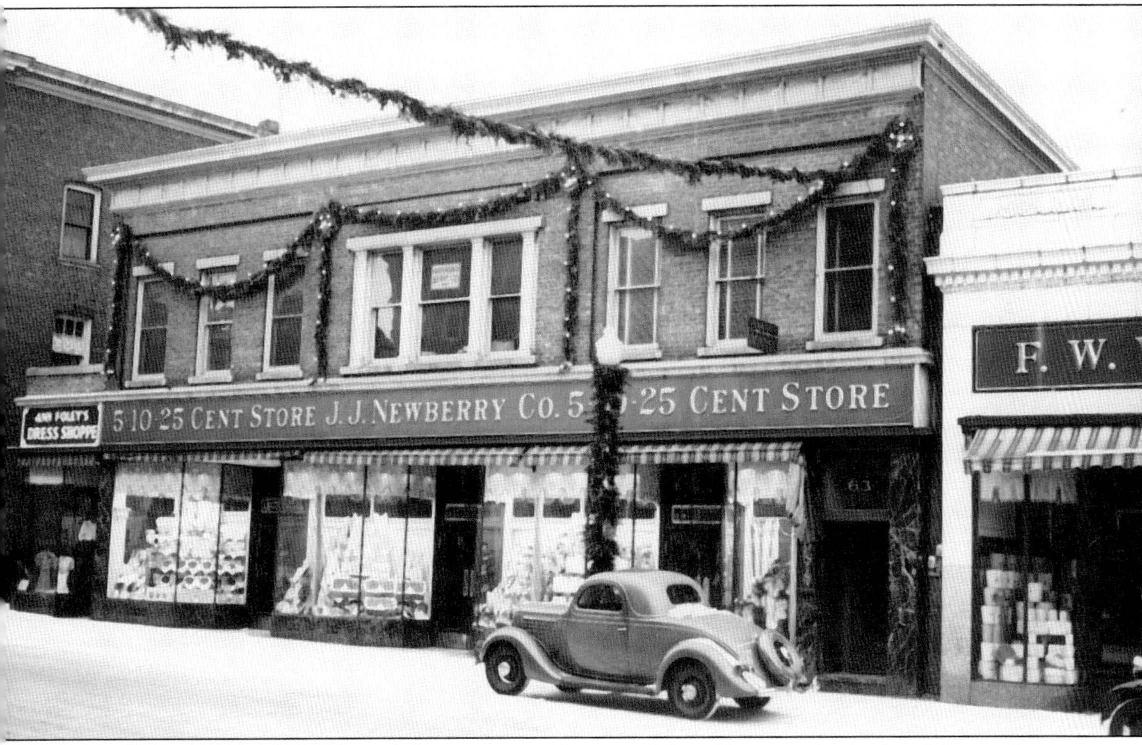

This 1941 view shows Newberry's Department Store on Main Street with the brick front that was covered over in the early 1960s. Next door is the F.W. Woolworth's store. The department stores competed side by side until Woolworth's closed down in 1959. Newberry's took over the space, remodeled, and combined the two stores into one. Out front is a 1935 Ford three-window coupe.

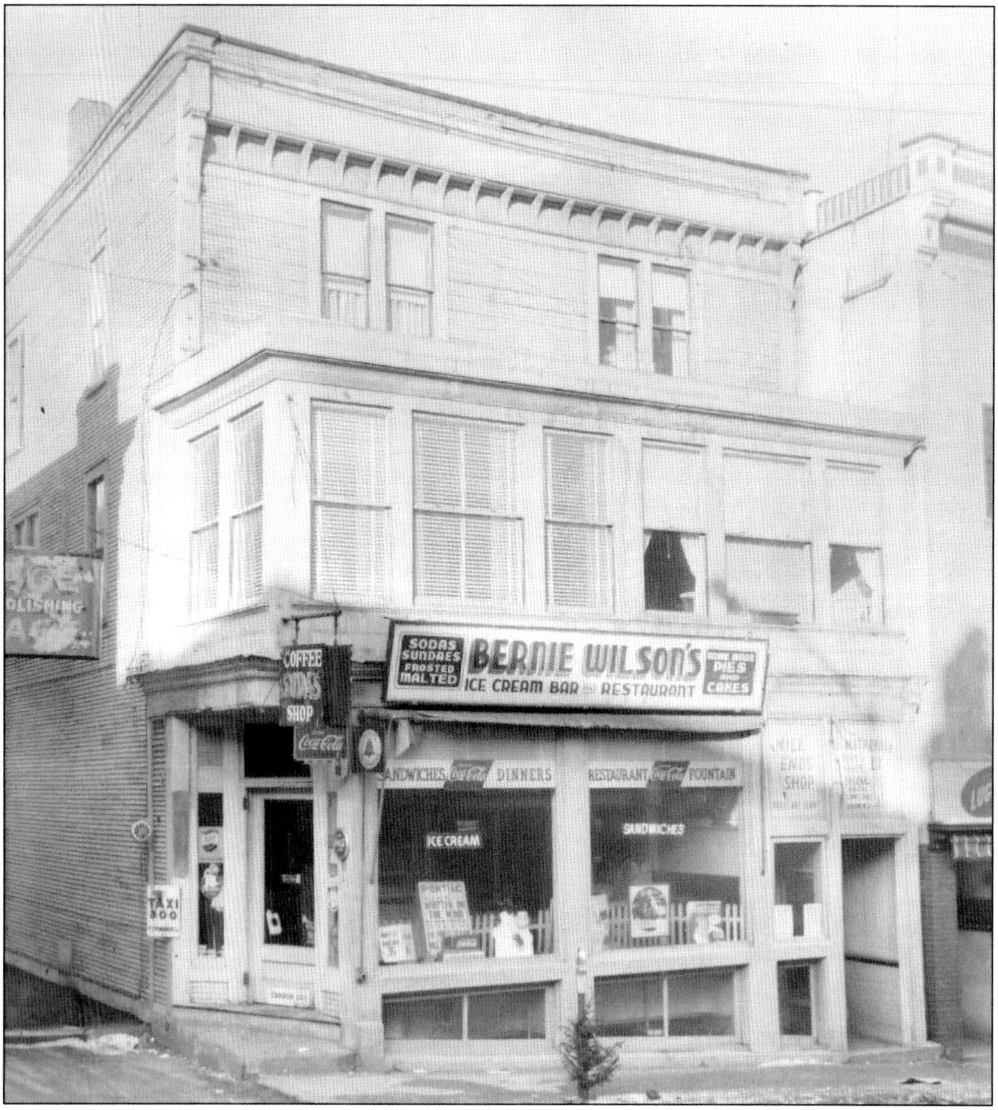

Bernie Wilson's Restaurant was located at 5 Broadway from the 1940s to the early 1960s. It was a hot spot for generations of high school students. It operated as Betty's Restaurant from 1965 until 1975. It then became Alice's until that diner closed in 1991 (HSLW). The building was the home of the women's clothing store Pink in the early 2010s.

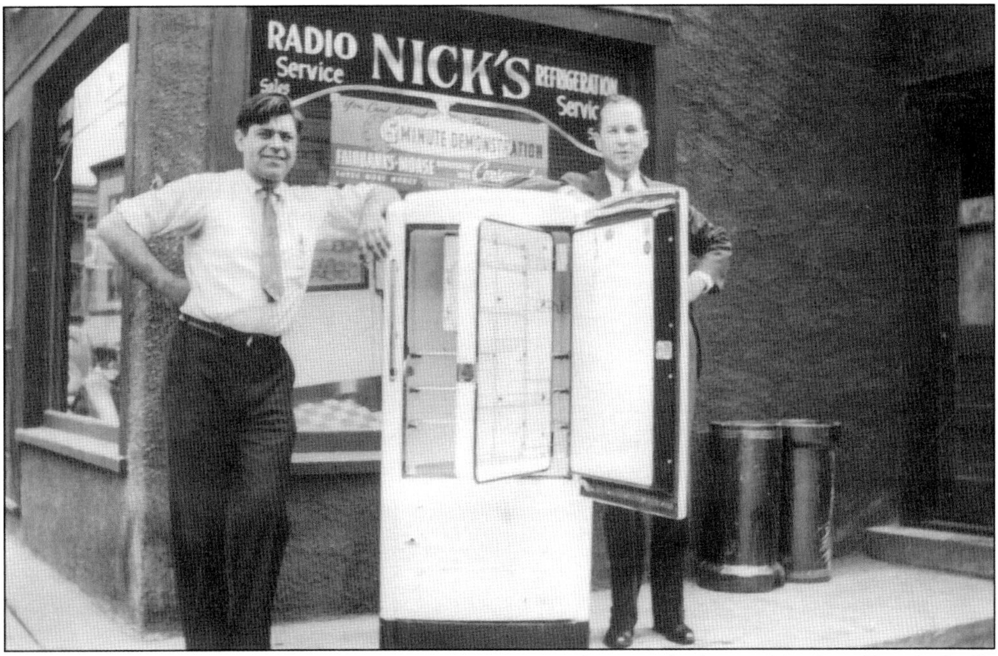

Nick Tartaris opened his first appliance store at 33 Broadway in the late 1930s. Dew Drop's Grille occupied that building in 2013. Tartaris later moved his appliances to 65 Broadway, which became Captain Cook's. Here he is, on the left, showing off his newest refrigerator in 1950.

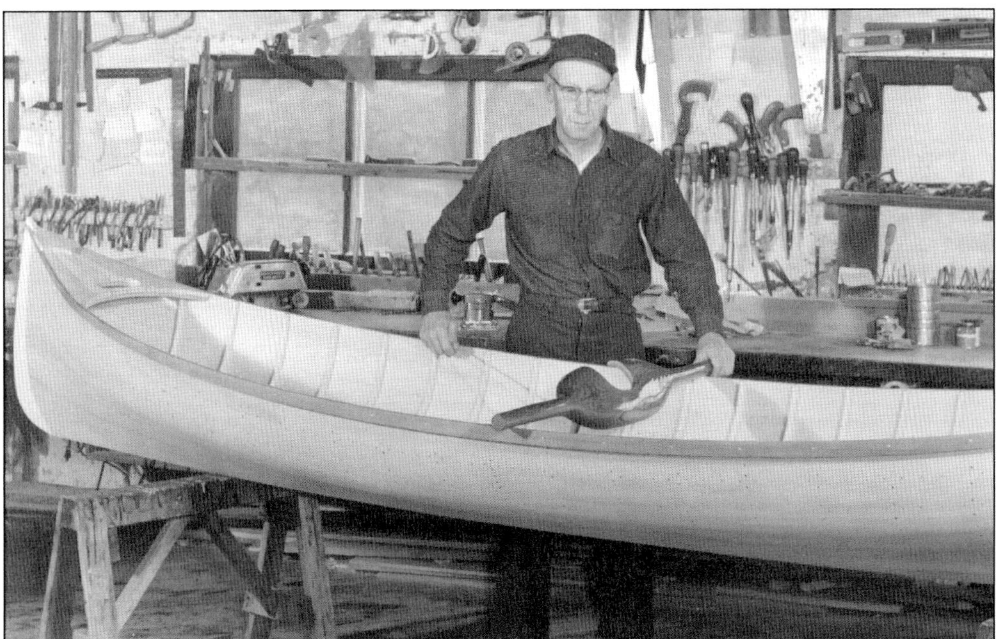
Willard Hanmer is at work in his boat shop. Hanmer was one of the premier guideboat builders in Adirondack history. His business was taken over by Carl Hathaway and later purchased by Chris Woodward. Woodward operates it today in the same location at 3 Hanmer Avenue, and the Hanmer Guideboat Races honor Willard's memory every summer.

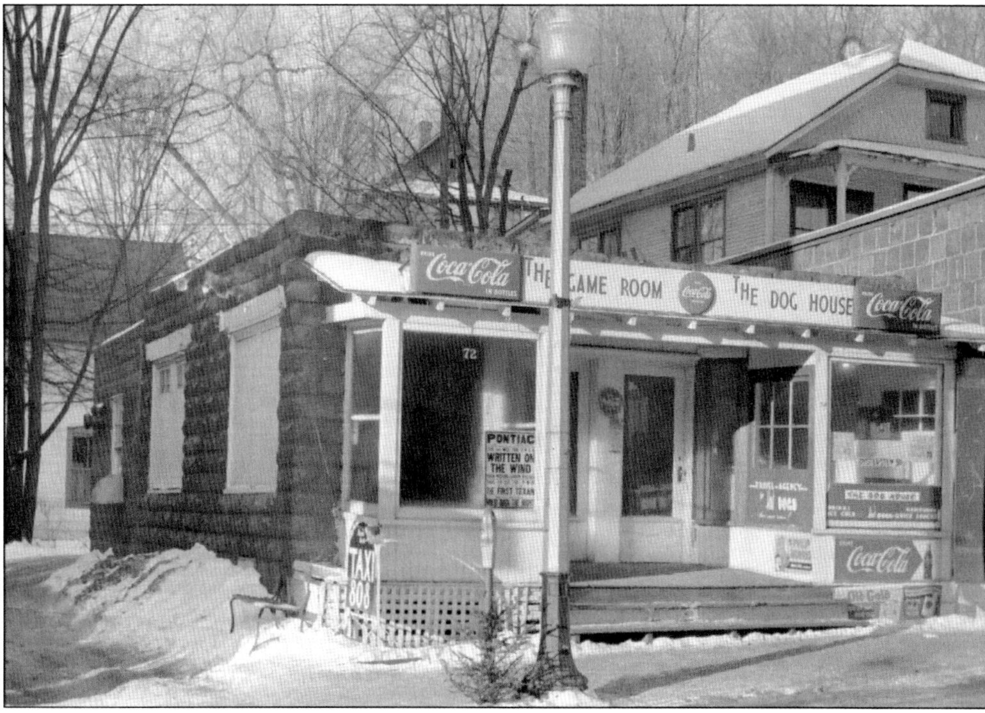

The Dog House was located on Broadway at what is now the site of the parking lot next to the Masonic lodge.

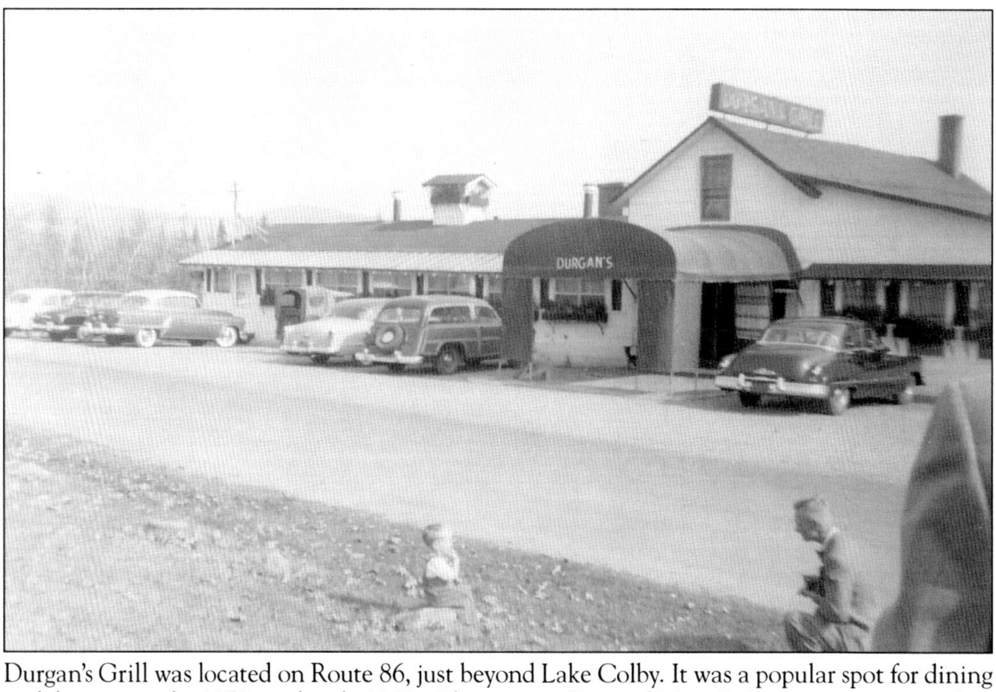

Durgan's Grill was located on Route 86, just beyond Lake Colby. It was a popular spot for dining and dancing in the 1950s and early 1960s. The owners, Bea and Mose LaFountain, were jazz fans who brought in some of the best talent in the country. The building later became Muldowney's Steak House, then the Club 86. Today, the site is the home of Tissot Construction (HSLW).

Two

America's Pioneer Health Resort

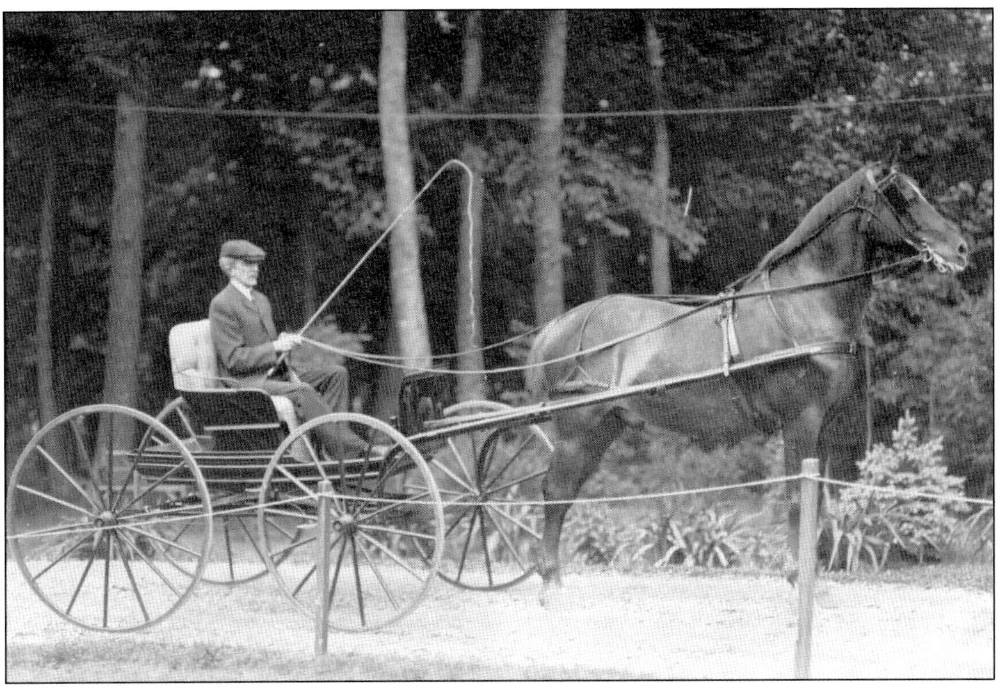

It can be argued that no man in village history was more important to the growth and prosperity of Saranac Lake than Dr. Edward Livingston Trudeau. He founded the cure industry that brought in thousands of patients and led to the building of the many cure cottages, sanatoriums, and hospitals as well as creating jobs for the people who were needed to care for the patients.

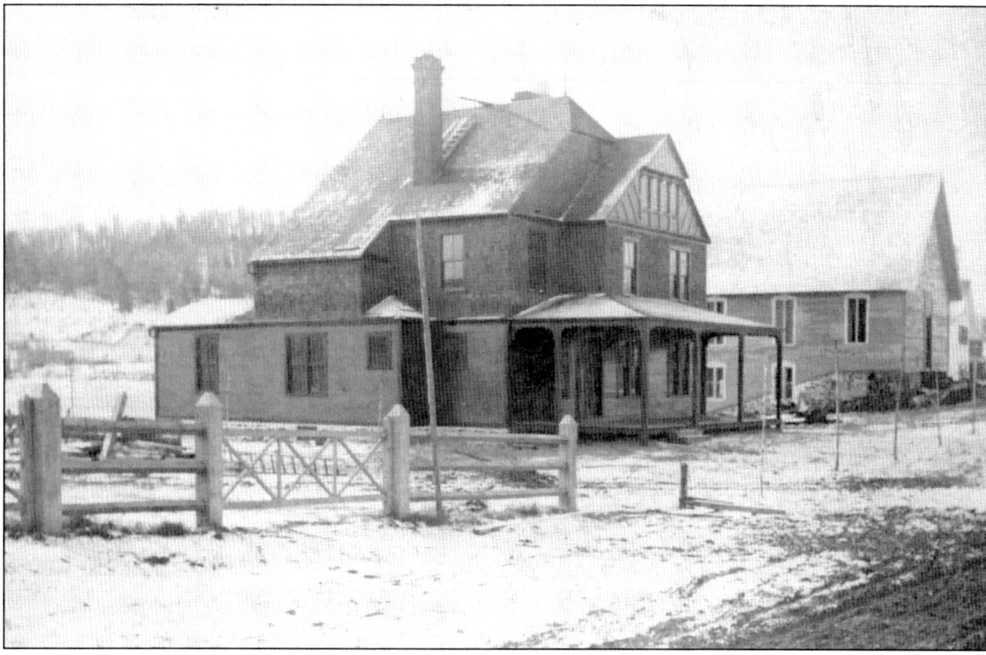

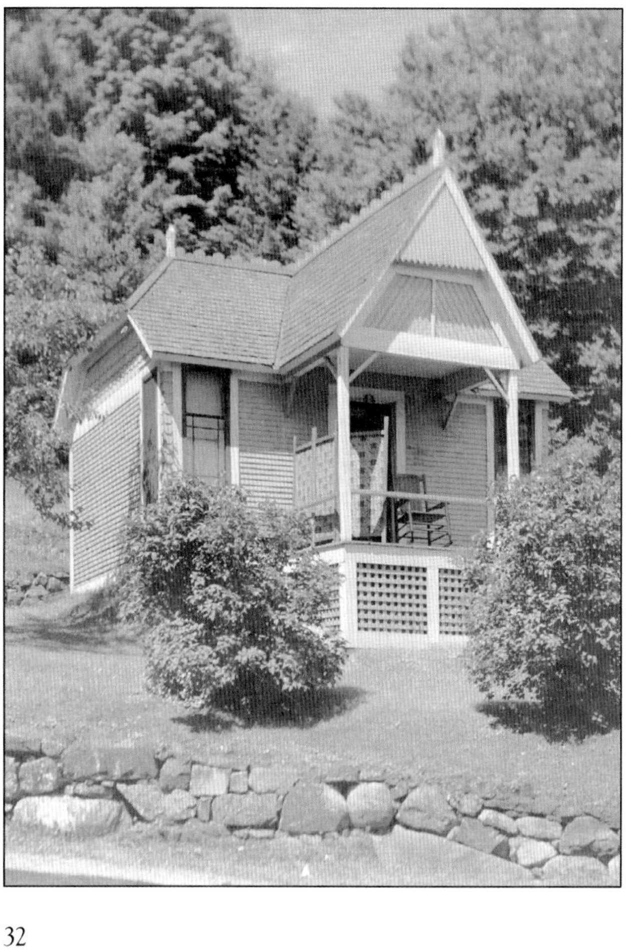

This was Dr. Trudeau's first home and laboratory in Saranac Lake, about the time it was built in 1884. It was located on the corner of Main and Church Streets. The house burned in 1894, but his new home was built on the same spot. It became the home of Medical Associates of Saranac Lake.

Dr. Trudeau started the first tuberculosis curing hospital, the Adirondack Cottage Sanitarium, in Saranac Lake in 1884. This building, Little Red, housed his first two patients. Over the years, the patients coming to be cured became the major commercial force driving the economy of the village.

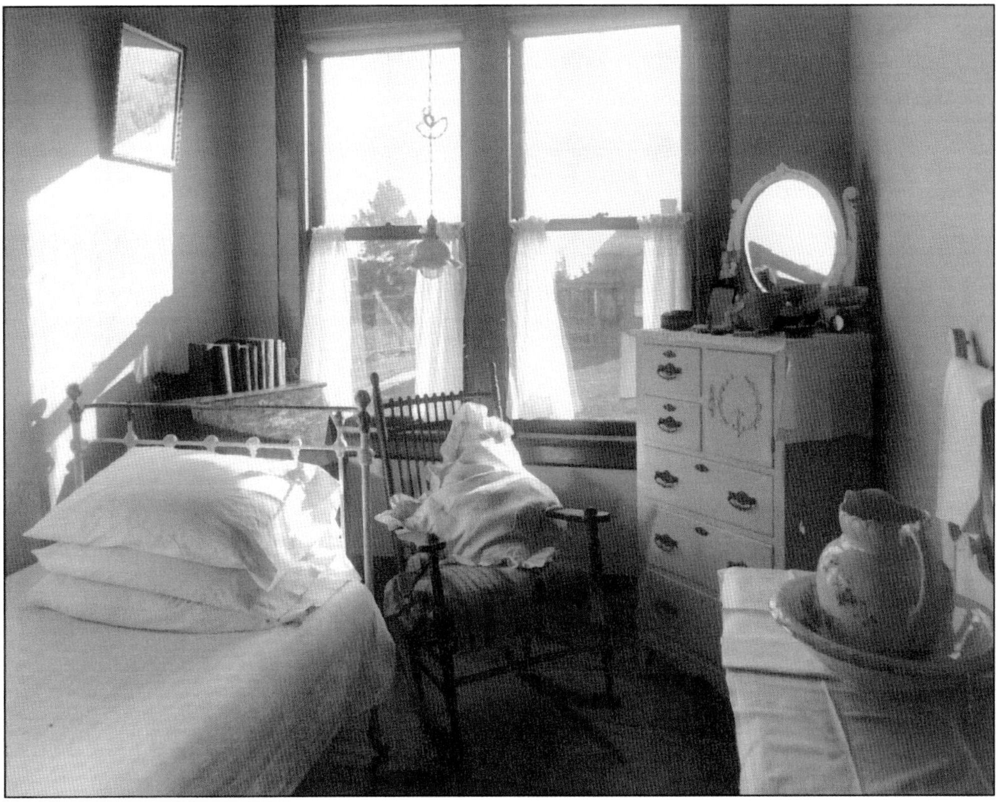

This is what a typical 19th-century cure cottage room looked like. Most were not fancy, and this one had a pitcher and bowl instead of running water.

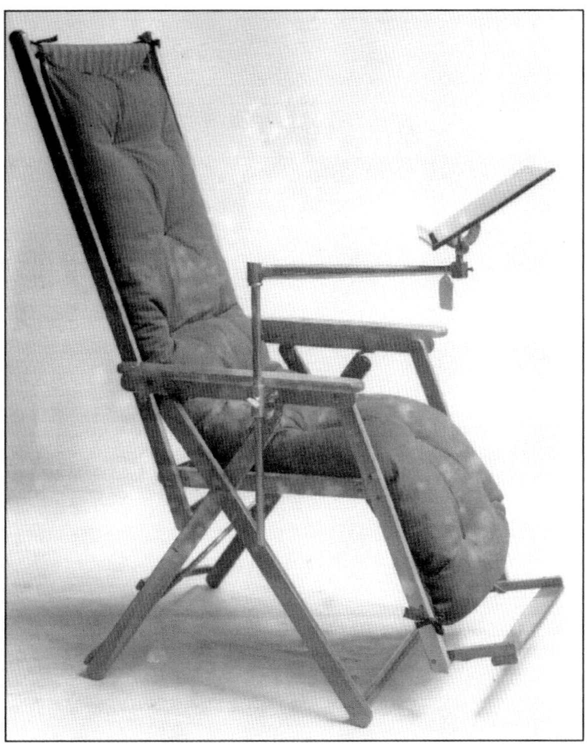

This is an early cure chair. As time went on and the cure industry became more sophisticated, equipment improved and chairs became more comfortable.

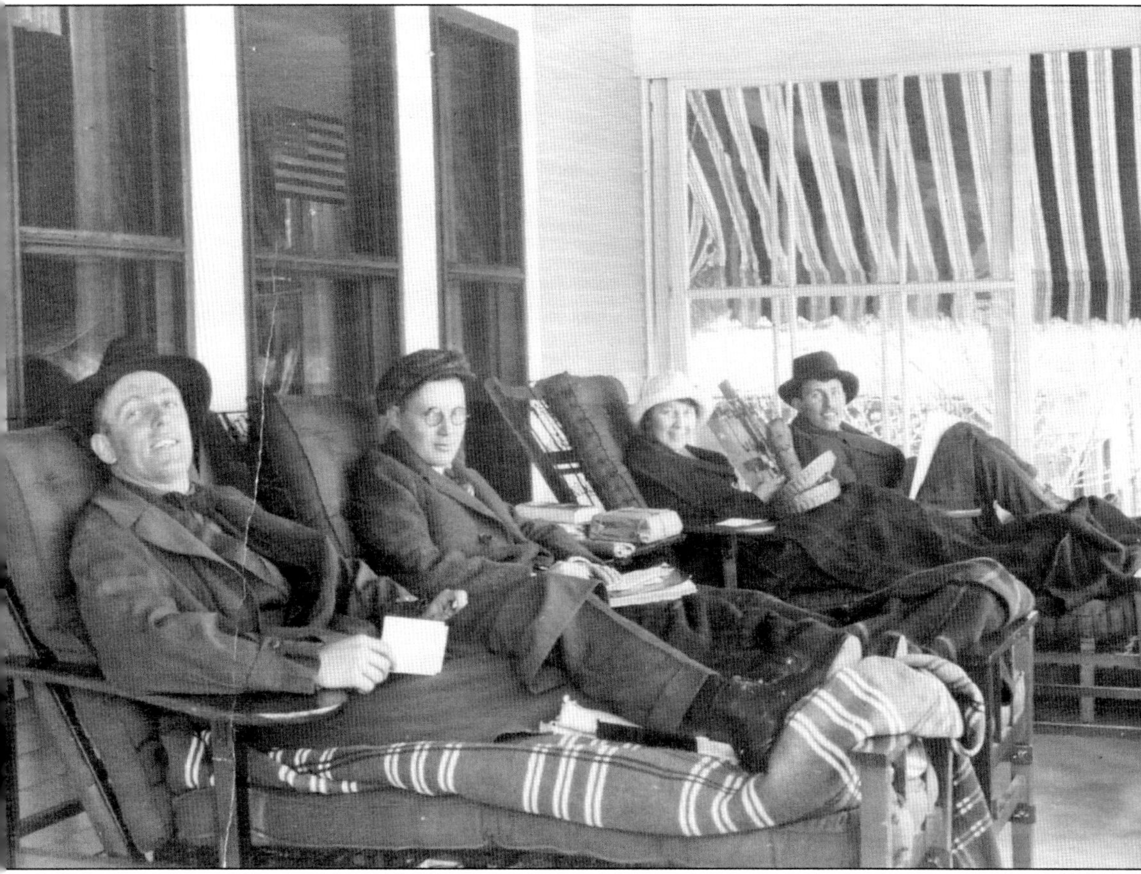

Patients curing in Saranac Lake were supposed to rest, eat the proper diet, and most importantly get a lot of fresh air. This photograph shows how the fresh air cure meant sitting out on the cure porches in all temperatures. These patients are taking the cure in 1919 in the classic cure chairs, which could be custom-made at Stark's Hardware on Broadway.

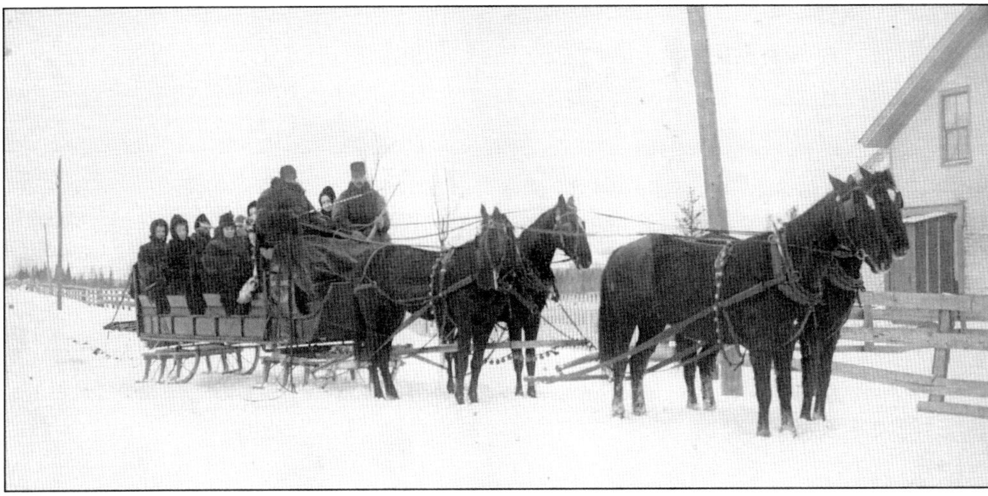

Once the bed rest phase of the cure was over, patients were cleared for moderate exercise. These Trudeau patients are out for a sleigh ride in 1890.

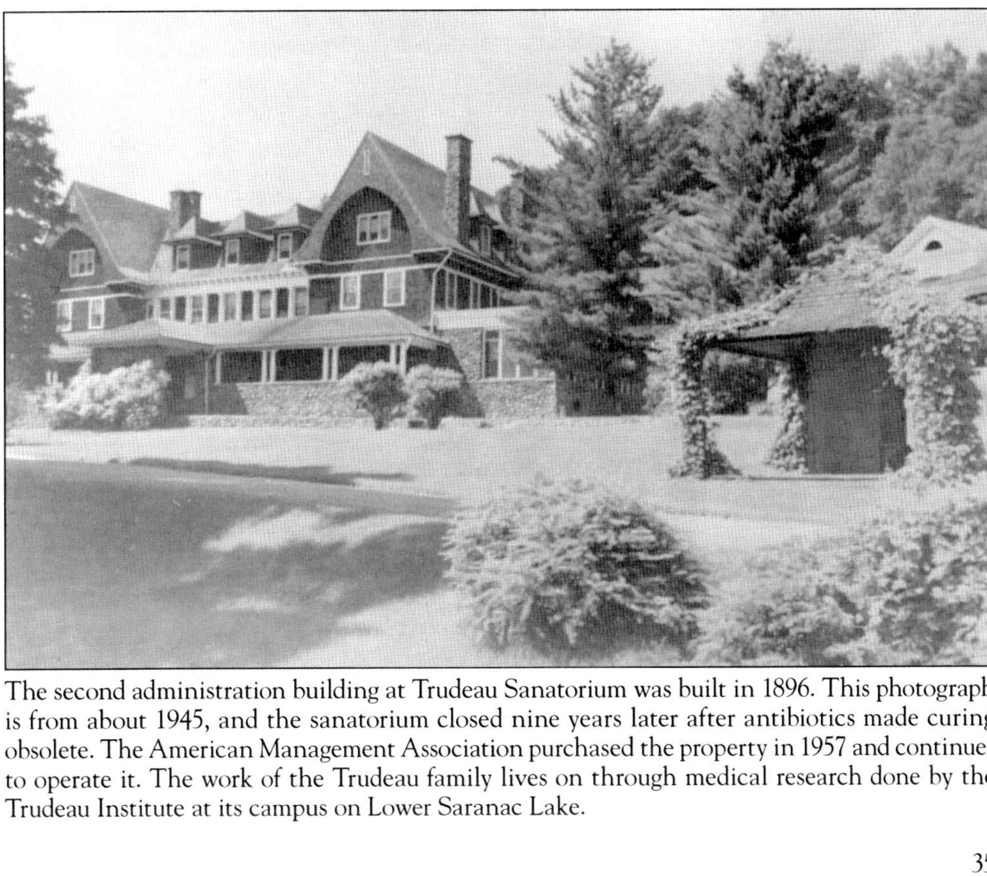

The second administration building at Trudeau Sanatorium was built in 1896. This photograph is from about 1945, and the sanatorium closed nine years later after antibiotics made curing obsolete. The American Management Association purchased the property in 1957 and continues to operate it. The work of the Trudeau family lives on through medical research done by the Trudeau Institute at its campus on Lower Saranac Lake.

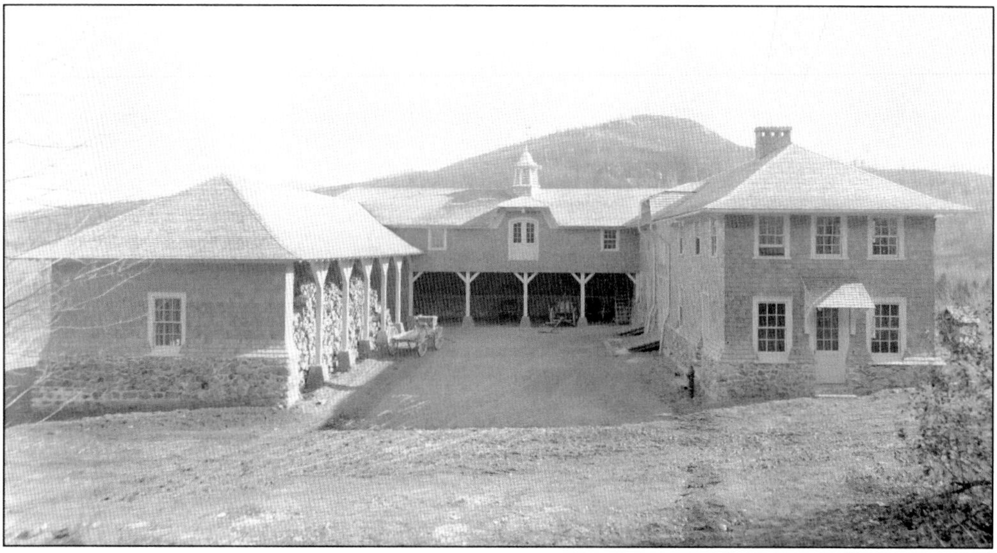

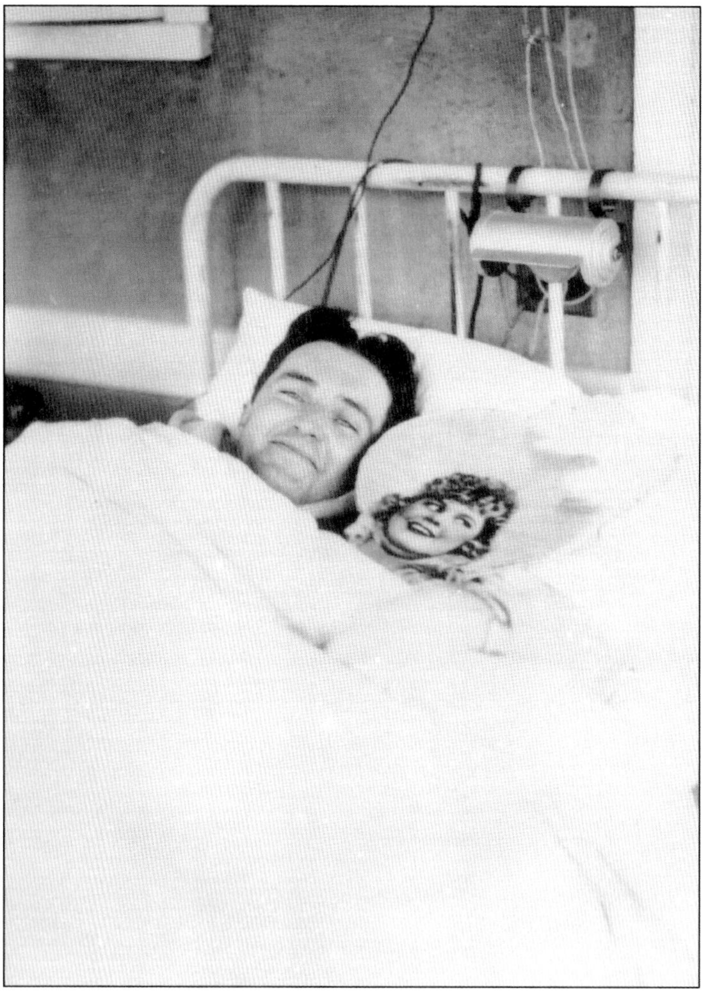

The McGibbon Stable at the Trudeau Sanatorium was built in 1909. It included a woodshed and housing for male workers.

Life in the mountains could be pretty lonely for some patients. This patient went to creative lengths to find a friend.

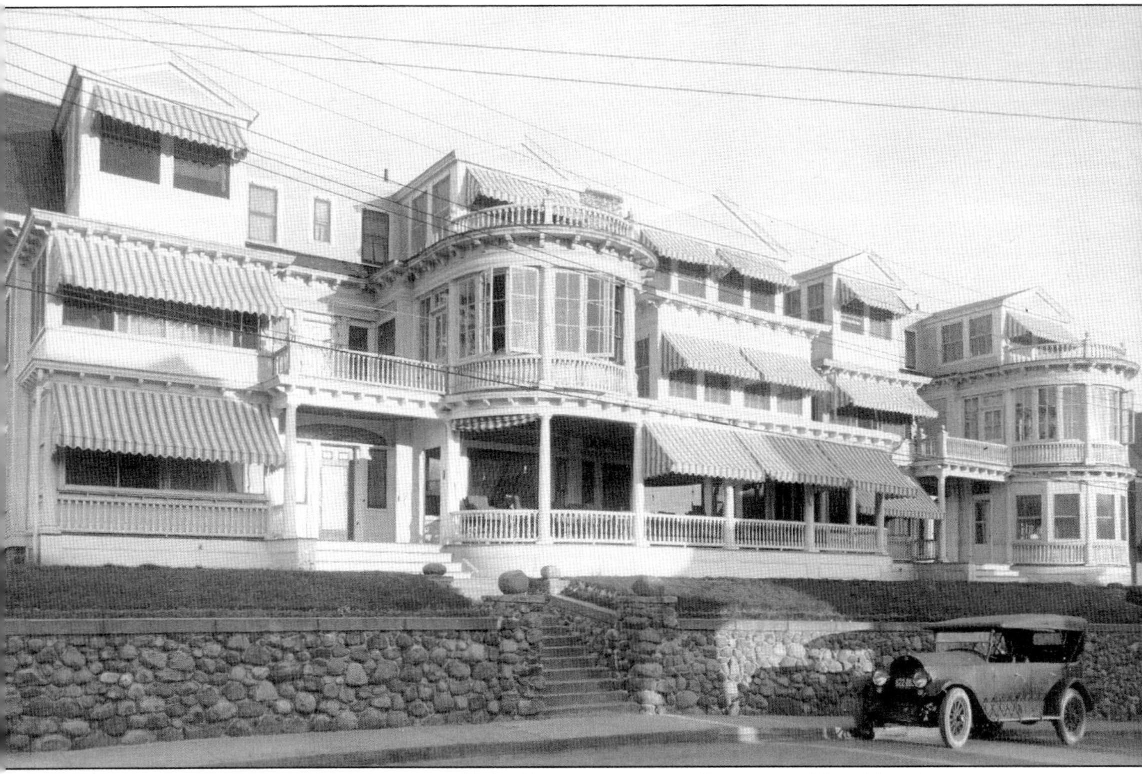

The Alta Vista cure cottage was originally built as two separate houses on Franklin Avenue prior to 1902. About 1924, they were converted to one building, which burned in 1959 (HSLW).

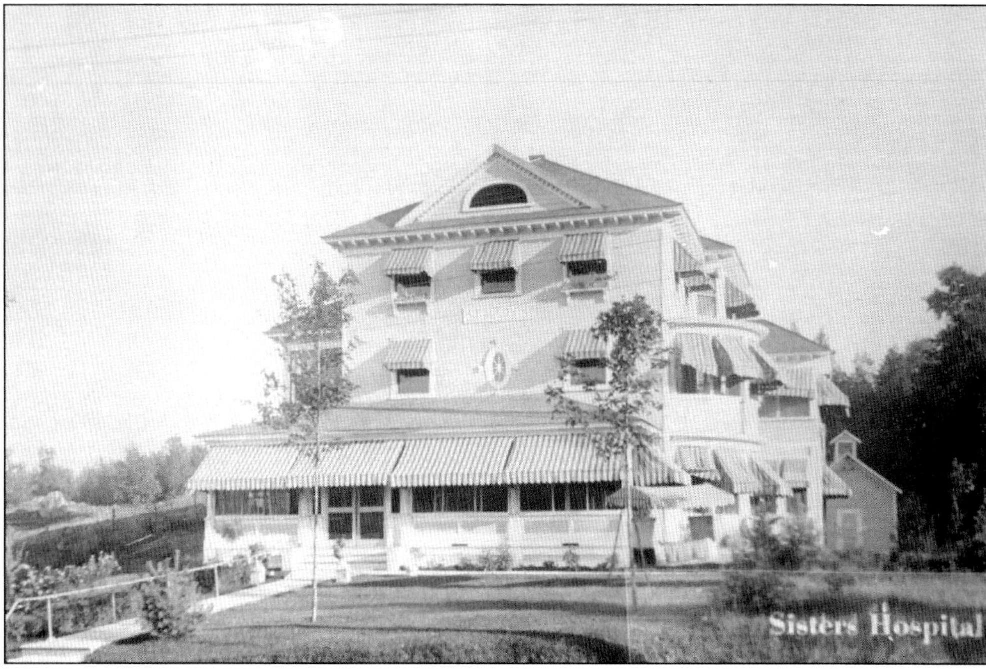

The Sisters of Mercy Hospital was located at 144 Ampersand Avenue. It first served as a sanitarium for patients with advanced cases of tuberculosis. From 1941 to 1951, Sisters Hospital was a home for nuns who were aging and ill. It has since been torn down (HSLW).

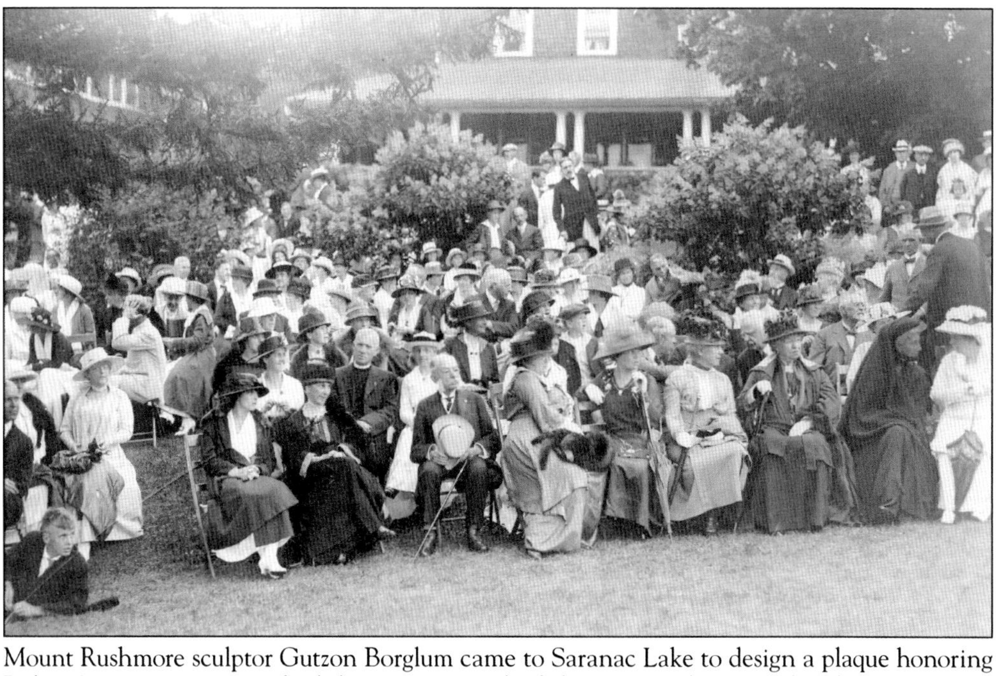

Mount Rushmore sculptor Gutzon Borglum came to Saranac Lake to design a plaque honoring Robert Louis Stevenson and, while visiting, met the failing Dr. Trudeau. Borglum later designed a memorial statue of Dr. Trudeau that stands on the grounds of the Trudeau Institute. Here, people are awaiting the dedication of that statue. Second from the right in the first row is Dr. Trudeau's widow, Charlotte, clothed completely in black.

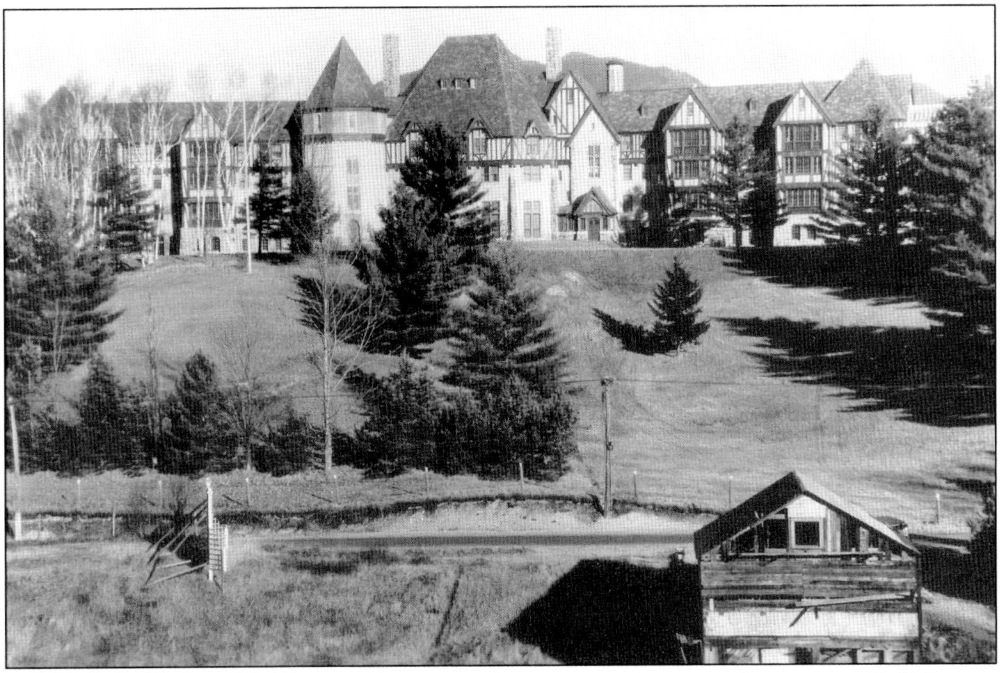

This is an early view of the hospital later named in memory of stage-and-screen star Will Rogers. It was opened in 1930 by the National Vaudeville Artists to care for ill and aging performers. The hospital closed in 1975 and went through several owners until its new life as a retirement community named Saranac Village at Will Rogers.

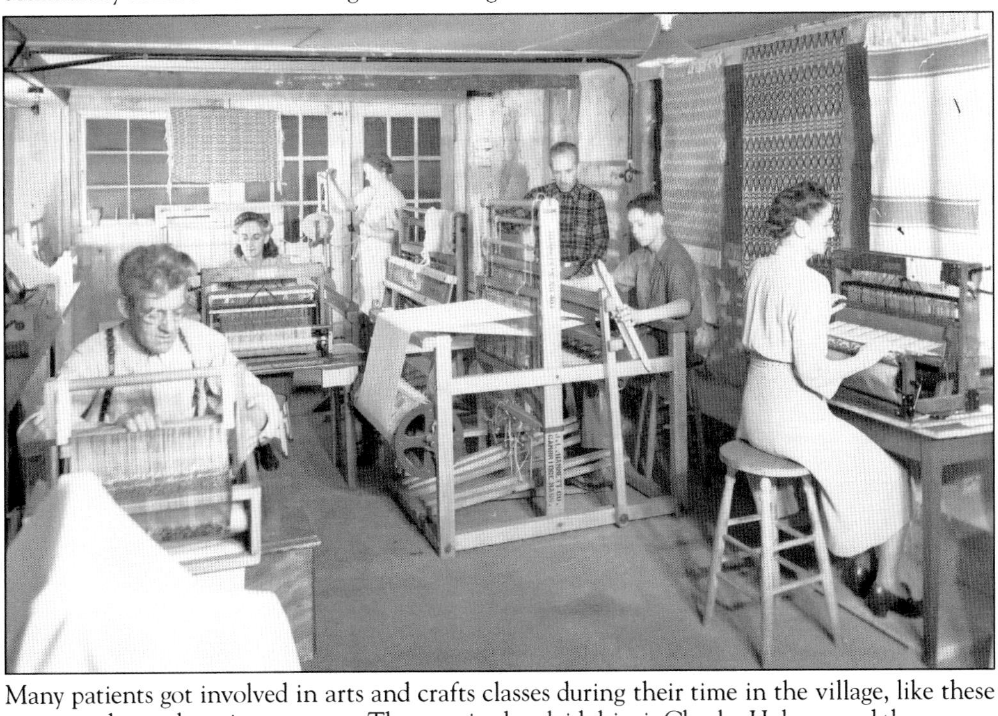

Many patients got involved in arts and crafts classes during their time in the village, like these patients who are learning to weave. The man in the plaid shirt is Charles Holmes, and the woman standing in back is Millie Holmes.

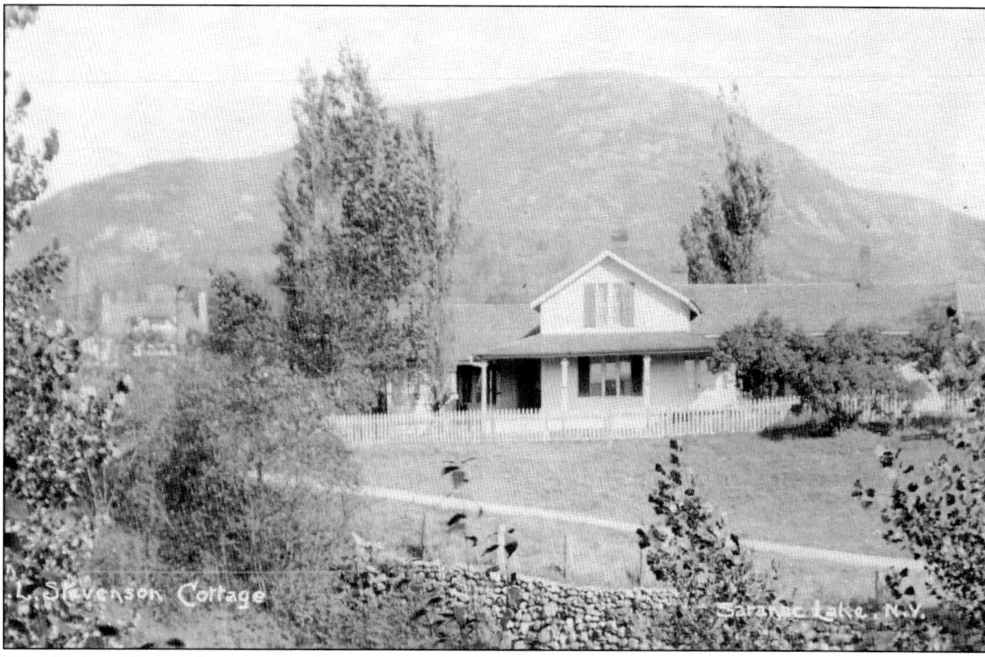

The Robert Louis Stevenson Cottage was built between 1865 and 1866 by guide Andrew Baker (HSLW). It got its name because Stevenson cured there from October 1887 to April 1888. During his stay, he worked on a series of essays for *Scribner's Magazine* and the novel *The Master of Ballantrae*. This historic site is open for public tours at 44 Stevenson Lane.

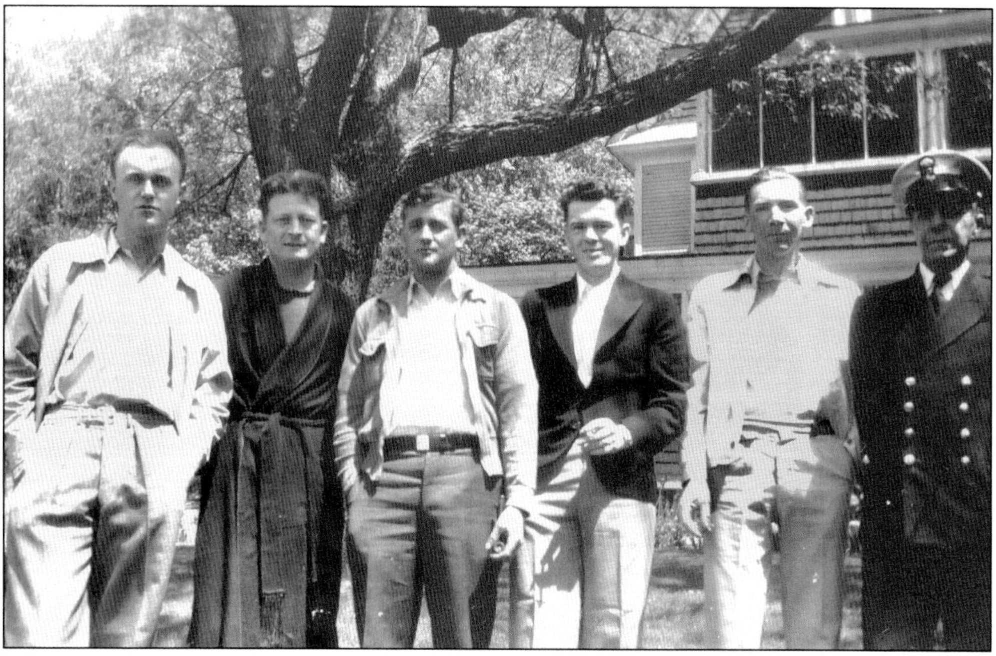

When the Nazis invaded Norway in April 1940, many Norwegian merchant seamen were at sea and came to the United States hoping to join the war effort. A number were found to be suffering from tuberculosis and several came to Saranac Lake hoping to cure. Sixteen Norwegians died and are buried in a special section of Pine Ridge Cemetery. The image depicts six of those sailors.

Three

Downtown

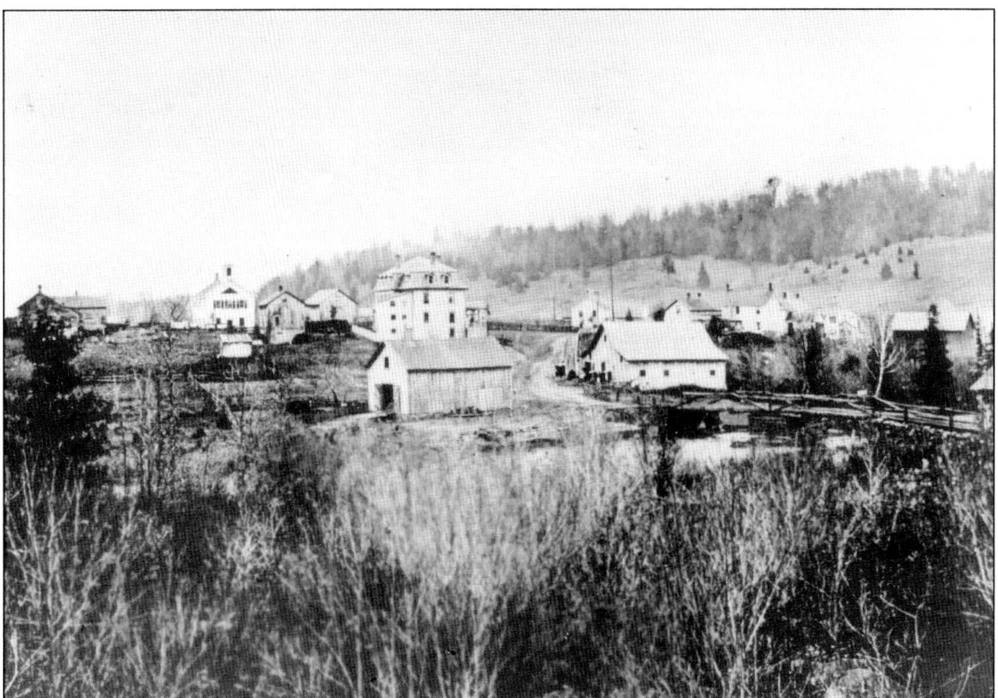

The note on this photograph in the Saranac Lake Free Library says that this 1877 view up Broadway is the earliest known image of Saranac Lake. In the center, with the mansard roof, is the Berkeley House. To its left, the building with the steeple is an early school building. In 1890, this was replaced by a new high school that is now the site of the Hotel Saranac.

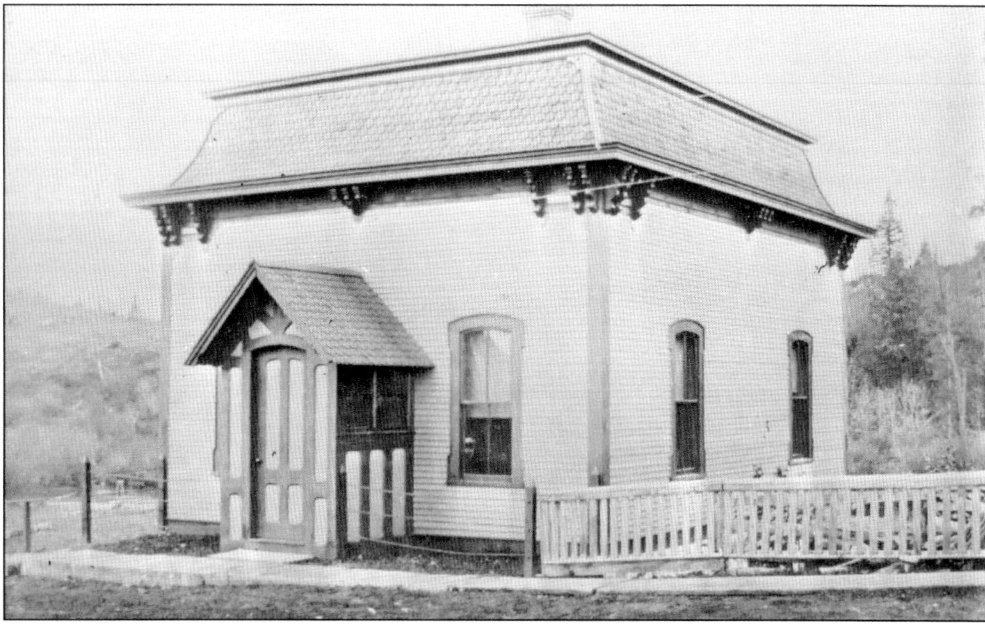

This is one of the oldest buildings in downtown Saranac Lake. It housed the first library in the village, which was founded in 1880 as the Franklin County Library. After that, it housed a series of businesses including Gibney's Market. It later became the home of the Post Office Pharmacy. Beginning in 1949, it was operated by Carl Bevilacqua, and today his son Jim carries on the family tradition.

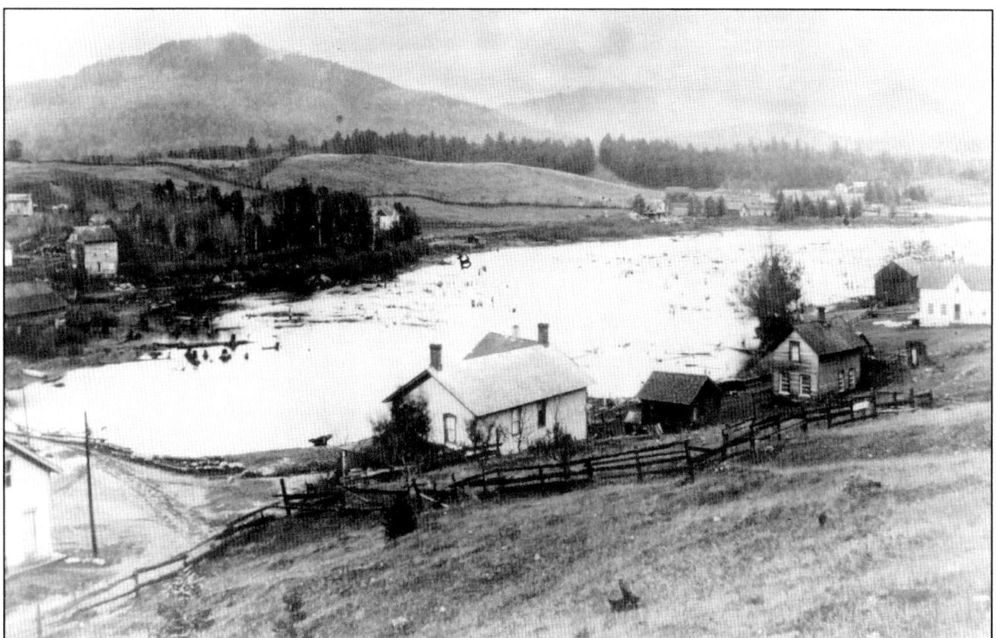

In this view of the Saranac River, stumps are visible in the water from the trees that were cut down before the dam was built. Most of the stumps were finally removed in 1910. The resulting body of water was named Lake Flower, in honor of New York governor Roswell P. Flower, the man who provided state funds to clear out the tree stumps.

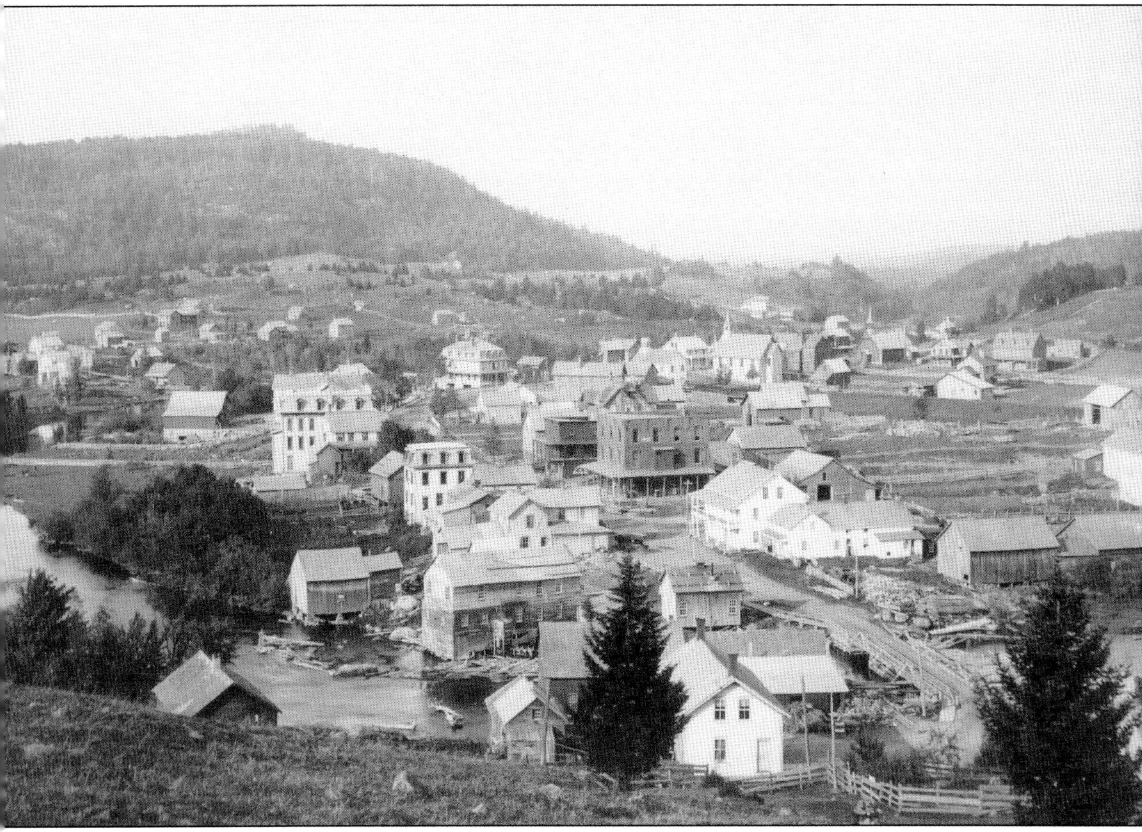

The village is pictured here around 1887. (The Harrietstown Town Hall was finished in 1888, and that tower is nowhere in sight in this image.) St. Luke's Church was built in 1878, and the first Methodist church, also shown, was completed in 1886 on Main Street. Note the church spires above the center of the picture and a little to the right.

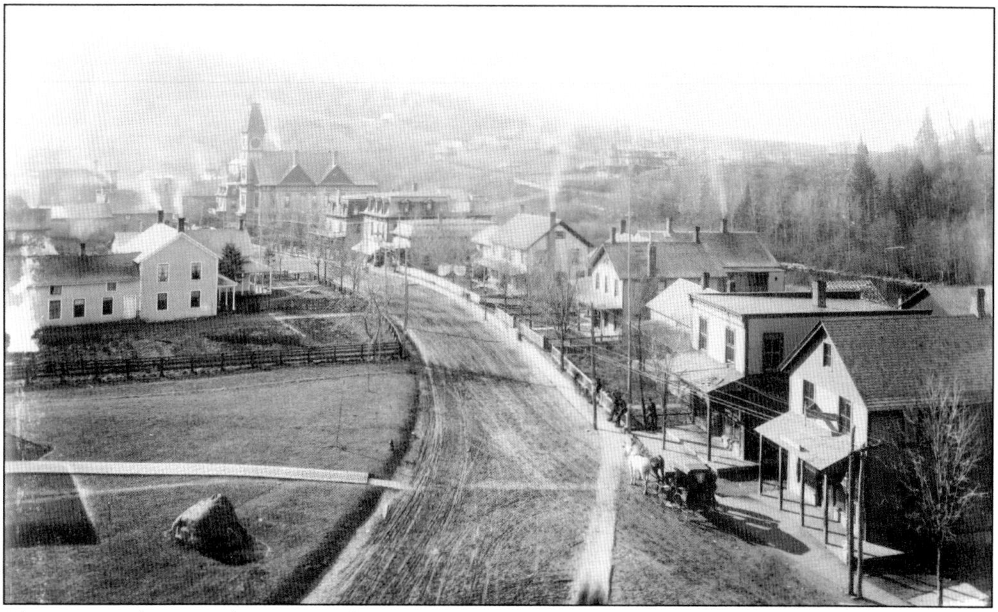

This is an early view of an unpaved Main Street, looking toward the old Harrietstown Town Hall, which is on the right. It would have to date from after 1888, when the town hall was finished and before 1905 when the brick paving of the downtown village streets started (HSLW).

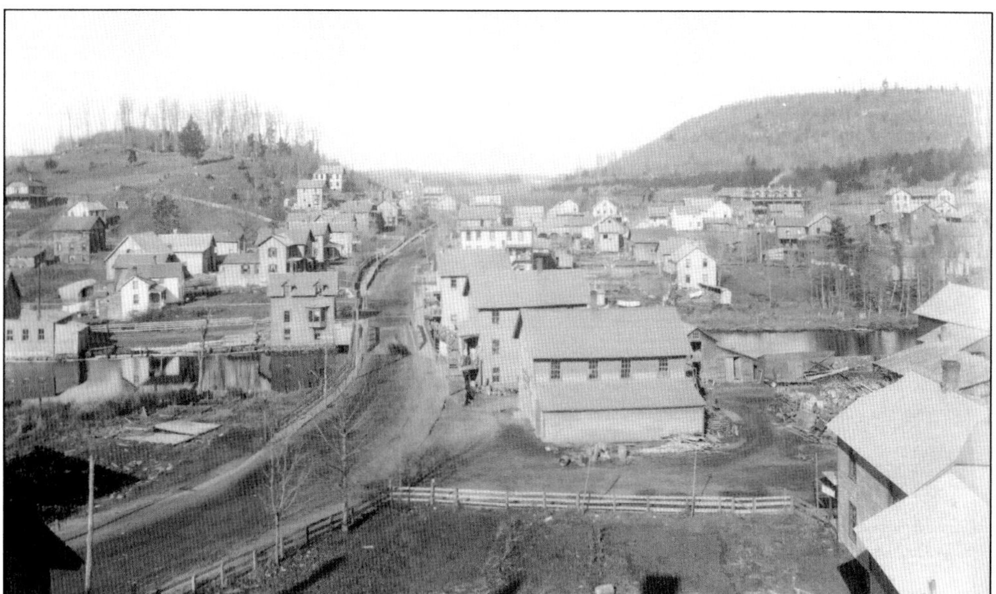

Here is a scene of Broadway from before 1900, probably from high in the Berkeley House. The bridge over the Saranac River is visible, but most of the familiar and contemporary buildings have not yet been built.

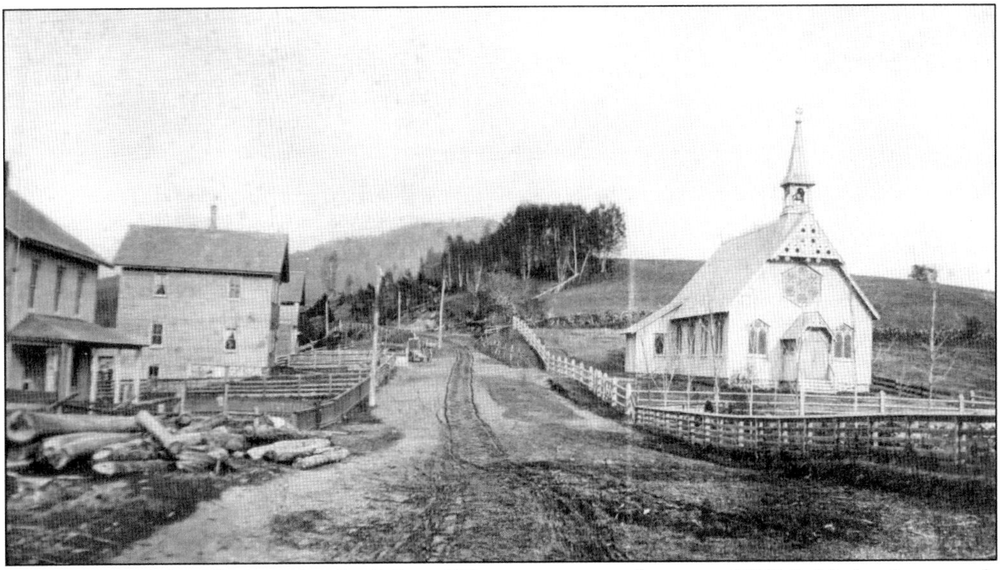

The Episcopal church, St. Luke the Beloved Physician, is seen here in a G.W. Baldwin photograph from around 1880. The church was built in 1878. The architect Richard Michell Upjohn donated the building plans to the community. There are houses on the left side of Main Street, as the Church Street extension would not be built there for a long time.

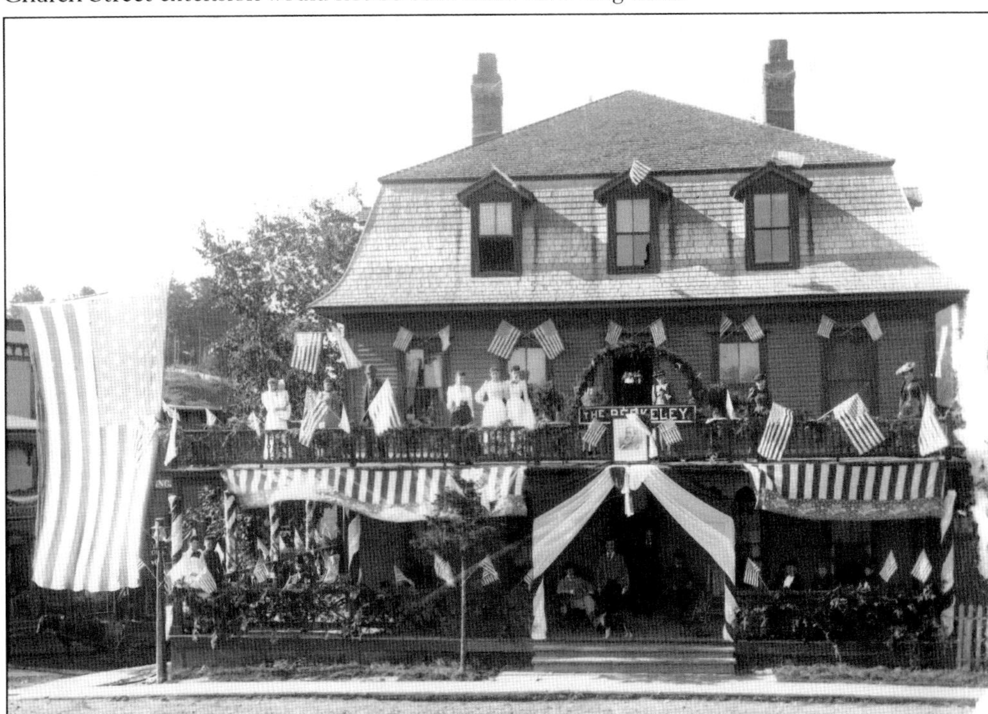

Pres. Benjamin Harrison was a native of Ohio but enjoyed visiting the Adirondack region. The Berkeley House is decorated for Harrison's visit to Saranac Lake in 1890. The president was here to dedicate the new high school, which was built across Main Street from the Berkeley. Harrison came back to the area in 1892 to stay at the Loon Lake Inn.

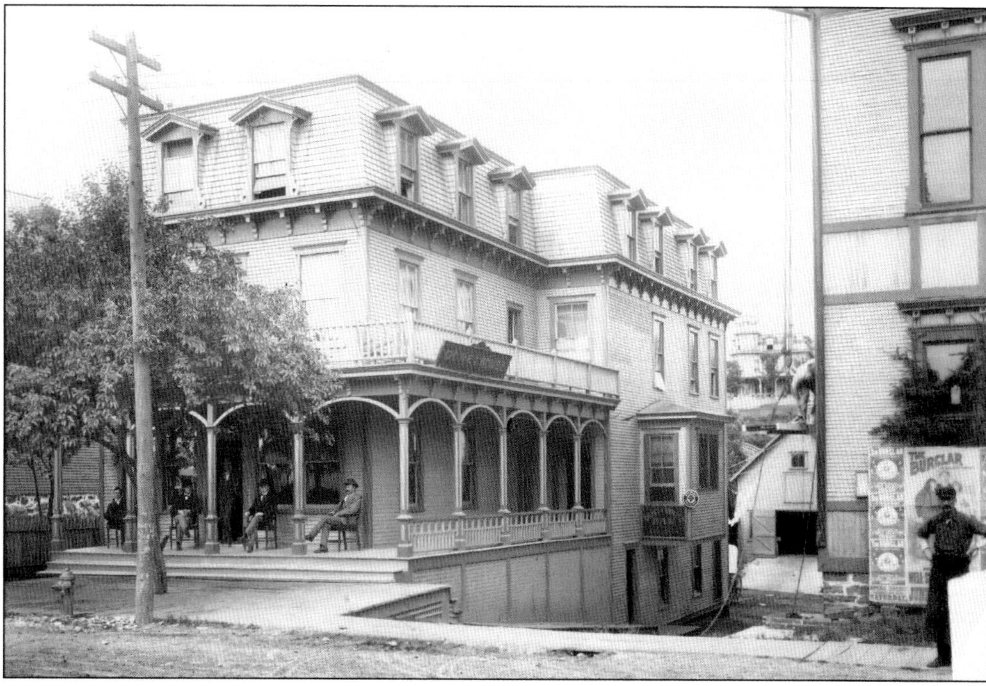

This photograph of the Dewey House was taken in 1895. The Dewey House was located on Main Street to the left of the Harrietstown Town Hall. The Dewey was also named the St. Nicholas Hotel at one time. In 1899, the name was changed to the Empire Hotel. It was torn down in 1927 during the construction of the new Harrietstown Town Hall after the 1926 fire destroyed the old town hall.

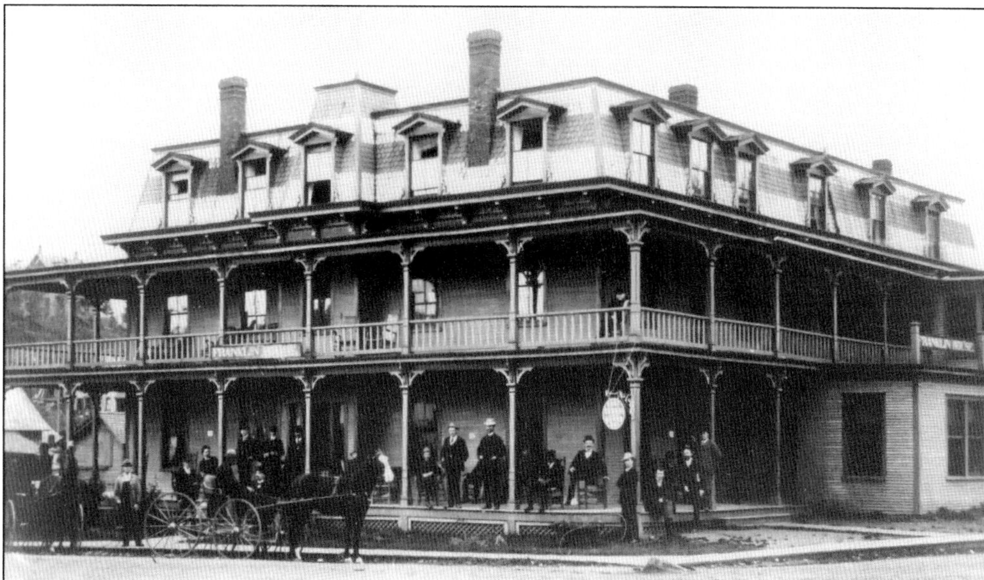

The Franklin House was built at the corner of Depot Street and Bloomingdale Avenue in 1891. The name was later changed to the Grand Union Hotel. In 1907, Michael Morgan & Son sold it to Harmon & Disco, proprietors of the Central Hotel on Broadway, for $23,000. Stewart's Shop now occupies the site where the Franklin House burned down in 1926 (HSLW).

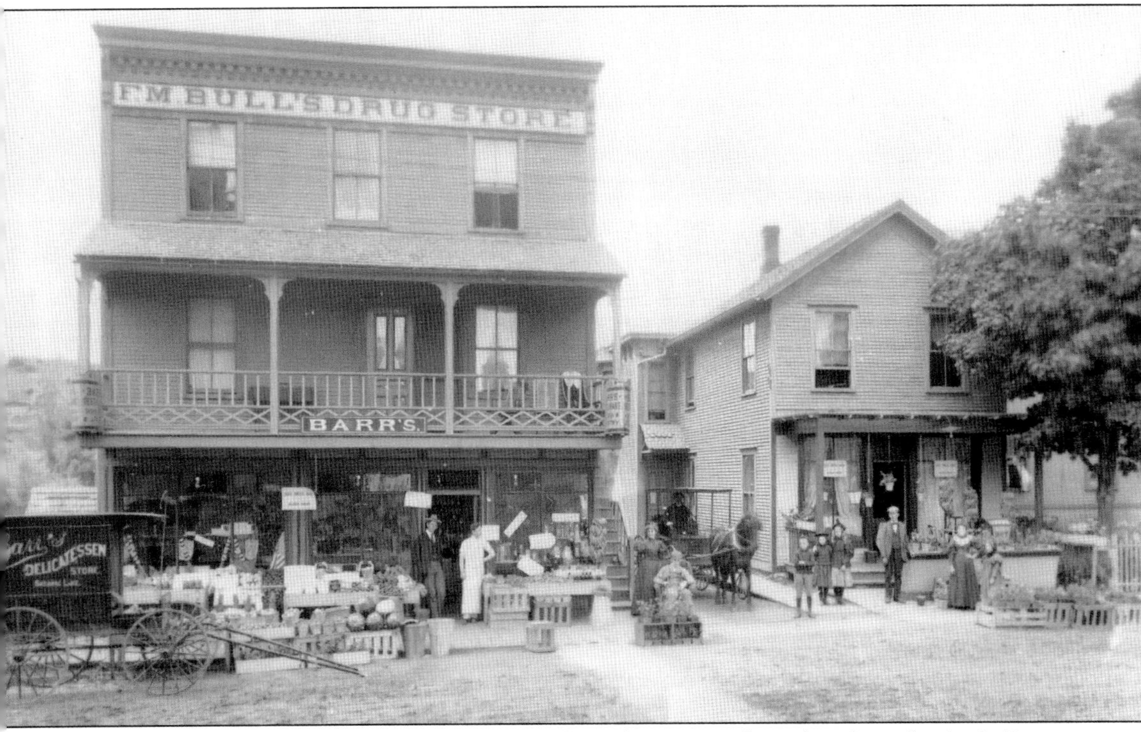

Barr's Delicatessen on 18 Main Street was located in what is now the right-of-way for the LaPan Highway. The various signs in this June 1897 photograph indicate that in addition to the food items on display, Barr's was also a restaurant, a bakery, and a pastry shop. The business occupied the former home of Bull's Drug Store.

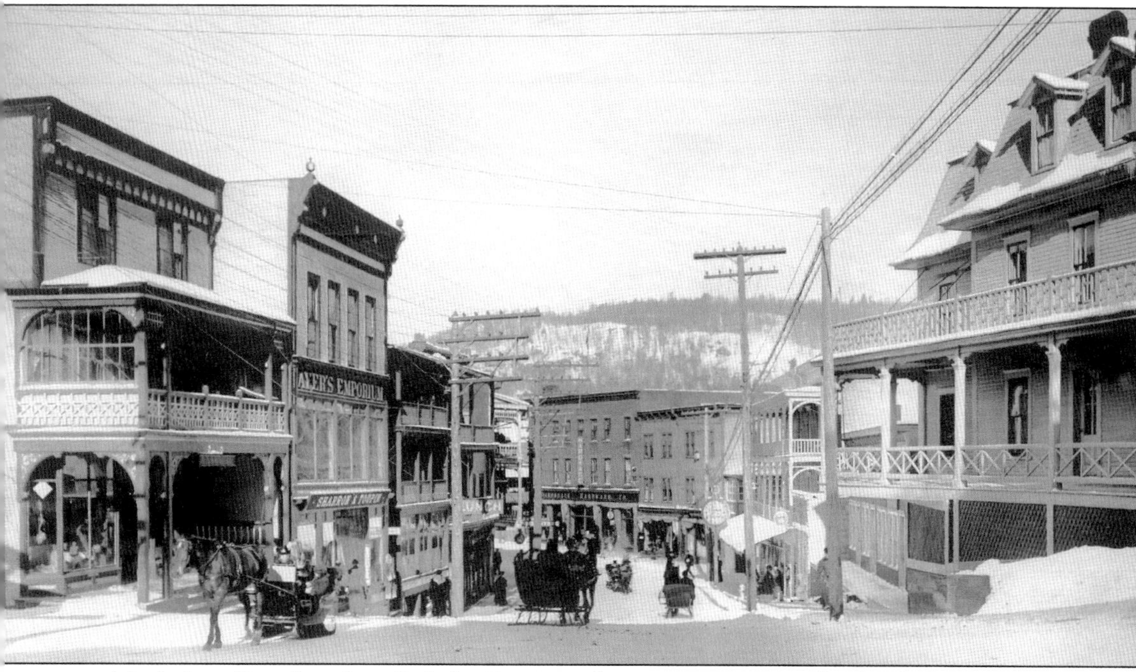

A look down Broadway from Berkeley Square in this winter scene—in the days before cars—shows the Berkeley House on the right. The view from the top of the hill today is remarkably similar, except that Berkeley Green has replaced the hotel and sleighs are a rarity on village streets.

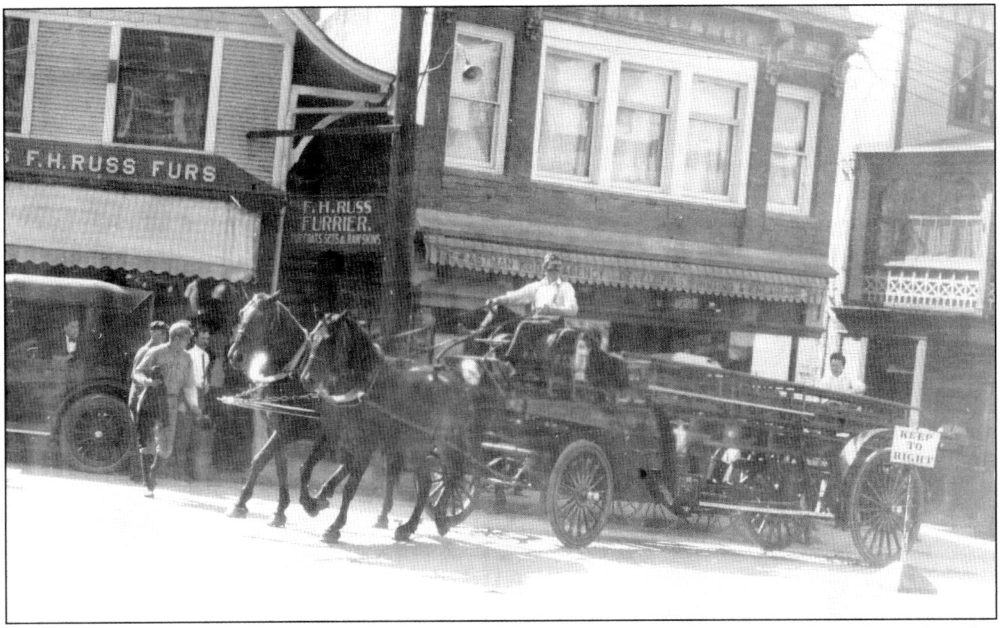

From the way the driver appears to be working the reins as this fire department wagon makes the turn from Broadway onto Main Street, he must be on the way to a fire. The man in the baseball uniform in front of the wagon seems to be running in the same direction. Maybe the ballplayer's game was interrupted by a fire call.

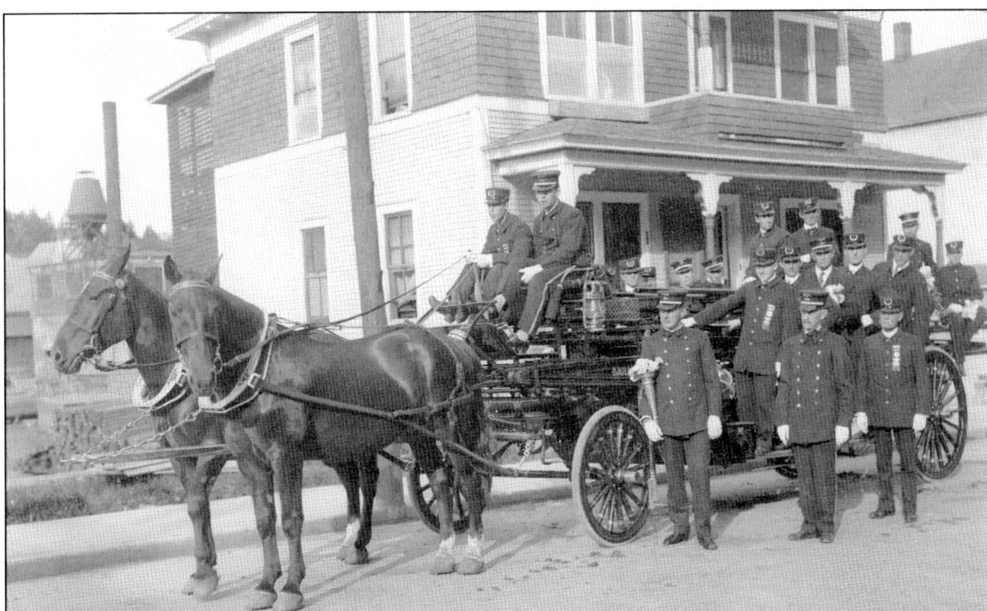

This looks like the same fire department wagon, but with the firemen posing in a calmer moment.

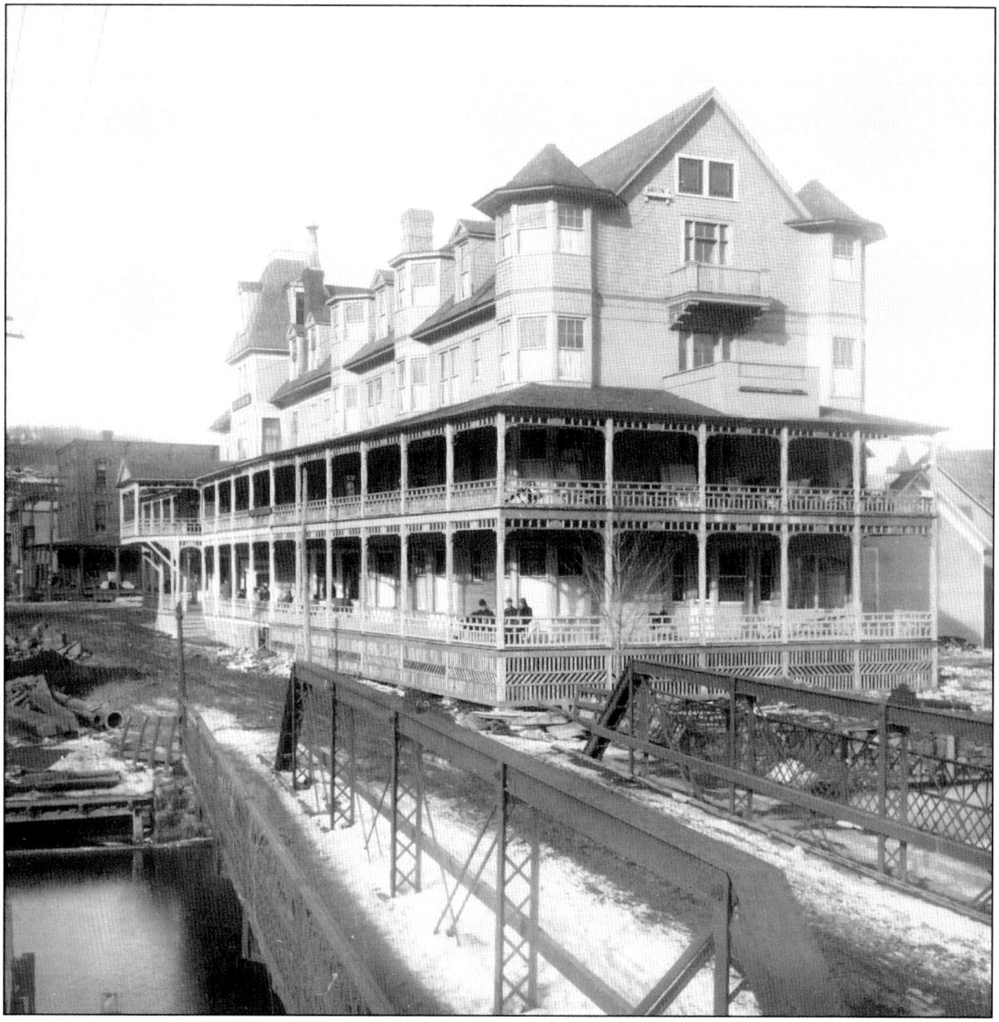

This view of the Riverside Inn is looking down the unpaved Main Street from the bridge at the outlet of Lake Flower. After the murder of George Berkeley at Blood's Hotel, Wallace Murray ran it for years. Around this time, the name was changed to the Riverside Inn. It kept this name until it was torn down in the mid-1930s. Riverside Park marks its former location.

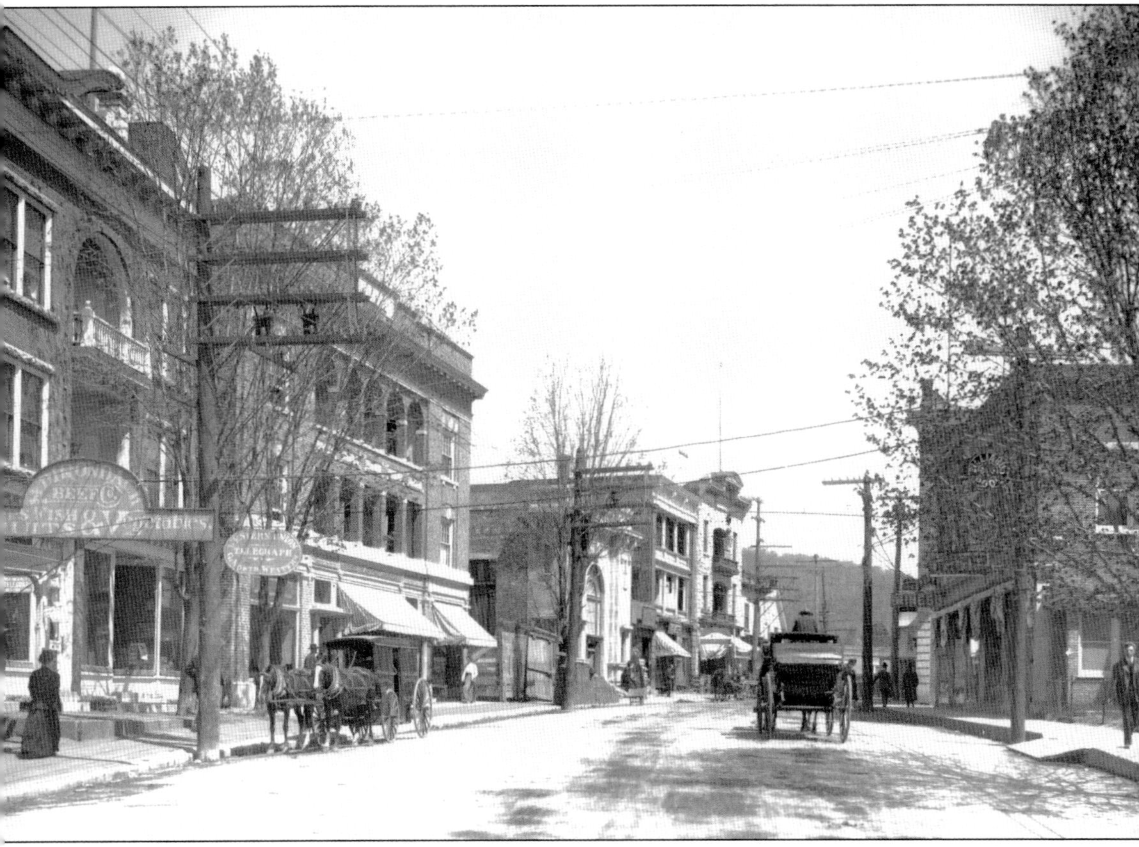

This is Main Street in 1907. The buildings are much the same as today, but the businesses have changed. The first sign on the left hangs off of the Post Office Pharmacy building, which is just out of frame. It reads "Adirondack Beef Company – Meat/Fish/Fruits & Vegetables." The next sign reads "Telegraph – Western Union/Great North Western." Just beyond, above the striped awning, is "Haberdasher," and on the right is "Fruit" on one sign, then "Wine," and a dentist just beyond, while on a second floor is "Billiards/Pool."

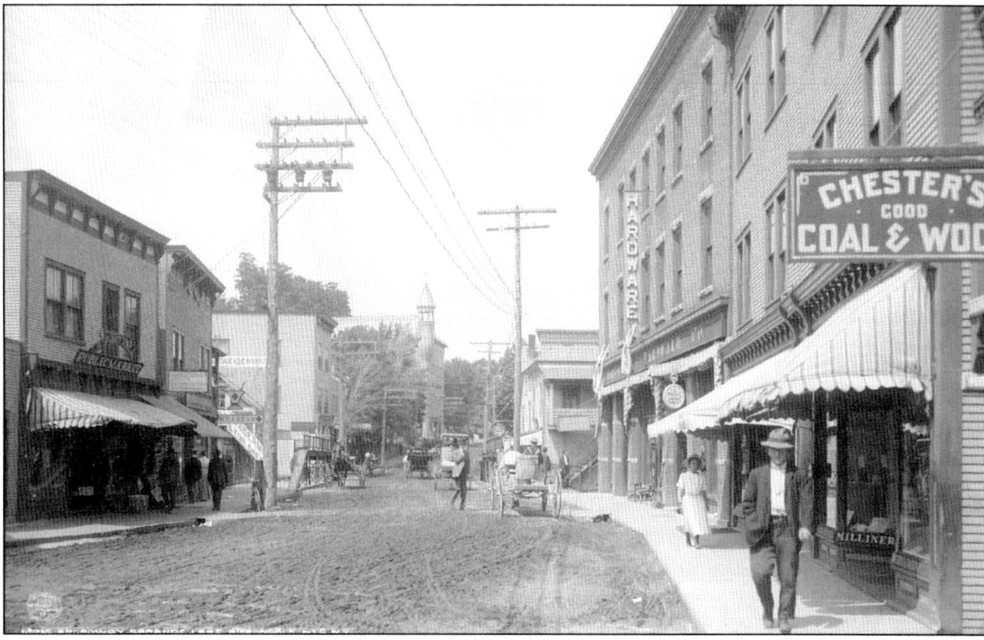

This photograph of Broadway was taken before 1905, the year they started paving the downtown streets with bricks. A. Fortune's Public Market, on the left, occupies the site of White Pine Designs today. On the right is Stark's Adirondack Hardware, which later became Aubuchon's. Today, the Upscale Resale antique shop occupies the building. The tower in the center was part of the still-standing Masonic Temple until it was removed.

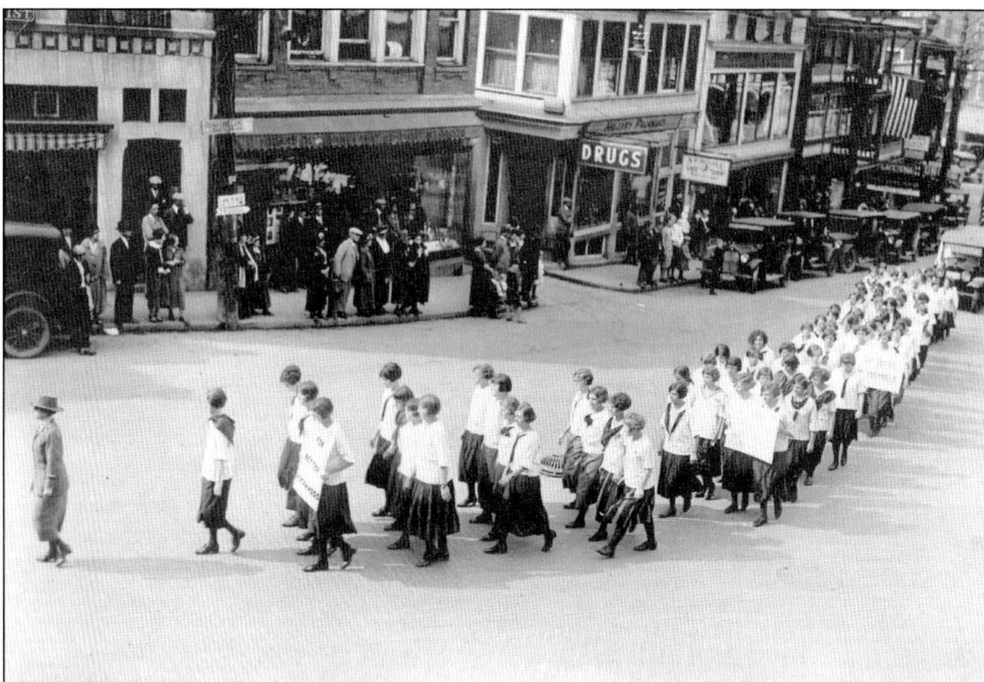

Local young women march at Broadway and Main Street in a late 1910s parade in support of women's suffrage.

The first Methodist church was completed in 1886. When the new church was built on Church Street in 1927, the Independent Order of Odd Fellows took over the building as its meetinghouse. Later, it was used for summer theater shows. Finally, it was purchased by the Hotel Saranac and torn down to make the parking lot that is next to the hotel today.

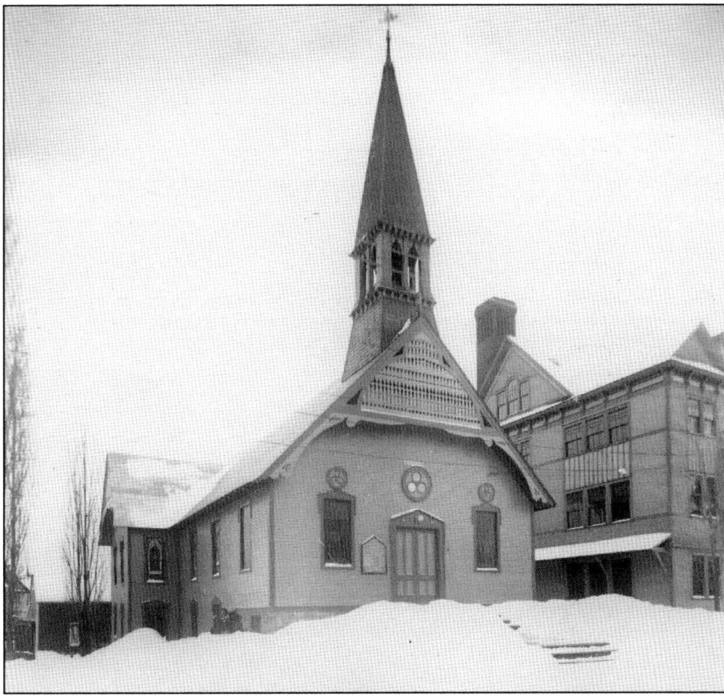

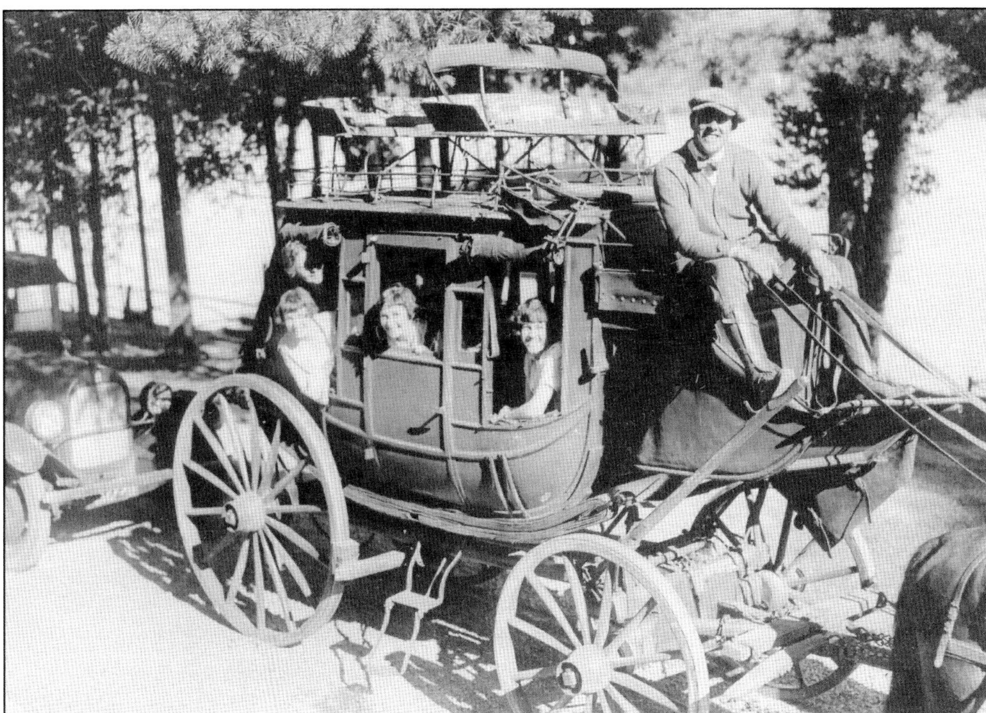

Police chief Walter Weir is seen here driving the 1868 Paul Smith's Hotel stagecoach in a 1915 parade. This coach is owned by Paul Smith's College and was restored through the efforts of former college professors Ruth and Gould Hoyt and many volunteers in the 1980s. It continues to be used in local events and parades.

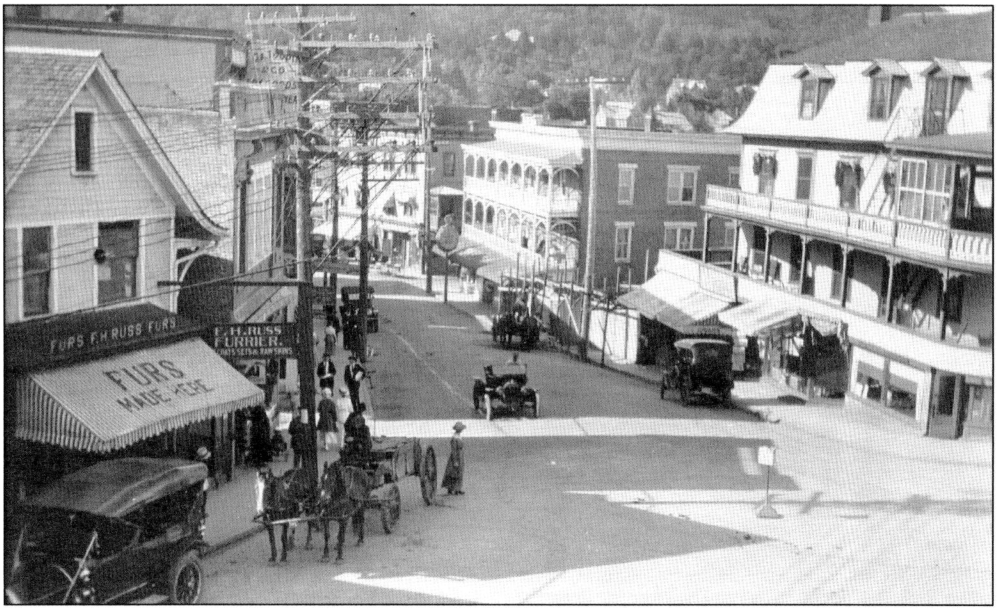

The 1910s were a time of transition between horses and cars. This scene of Broadway in 1916 reflects that era. The message on a postcard written about that time reads, "Dear Mary, I went to Saranac Lake on Saturday. It is a very pretty place. I'm going to try and see all I can before winter comes and I get snowed in here."

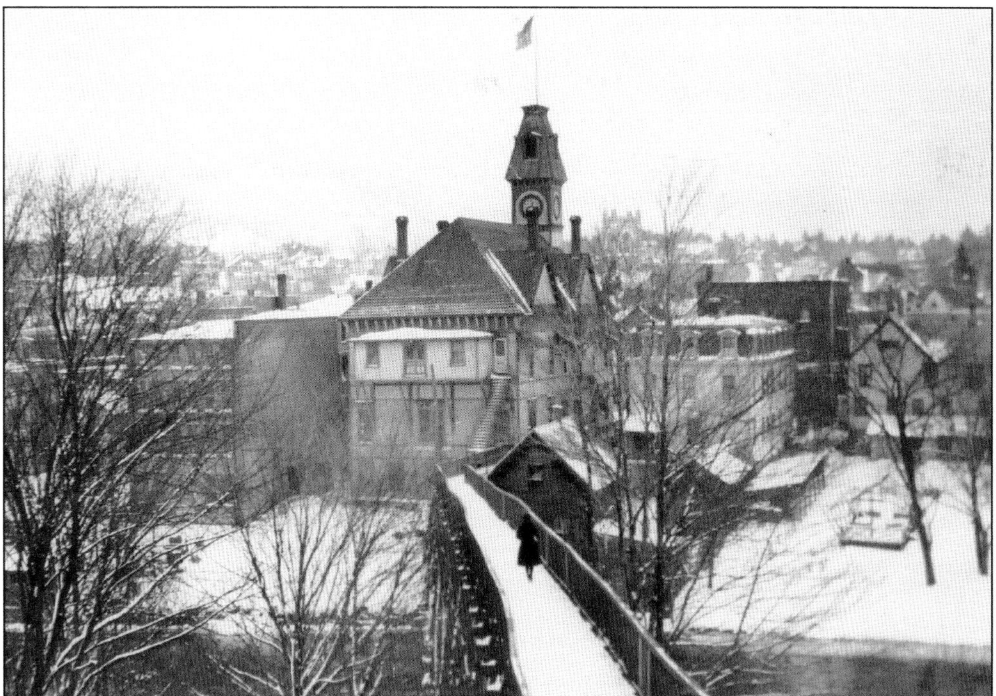

This footbridge behind the old Harrietstown Town Hall used to carry walkers across the Saranac River in the early 20th century. It was on the downstream side of the current Route 3/LaPan Highway Bridge.

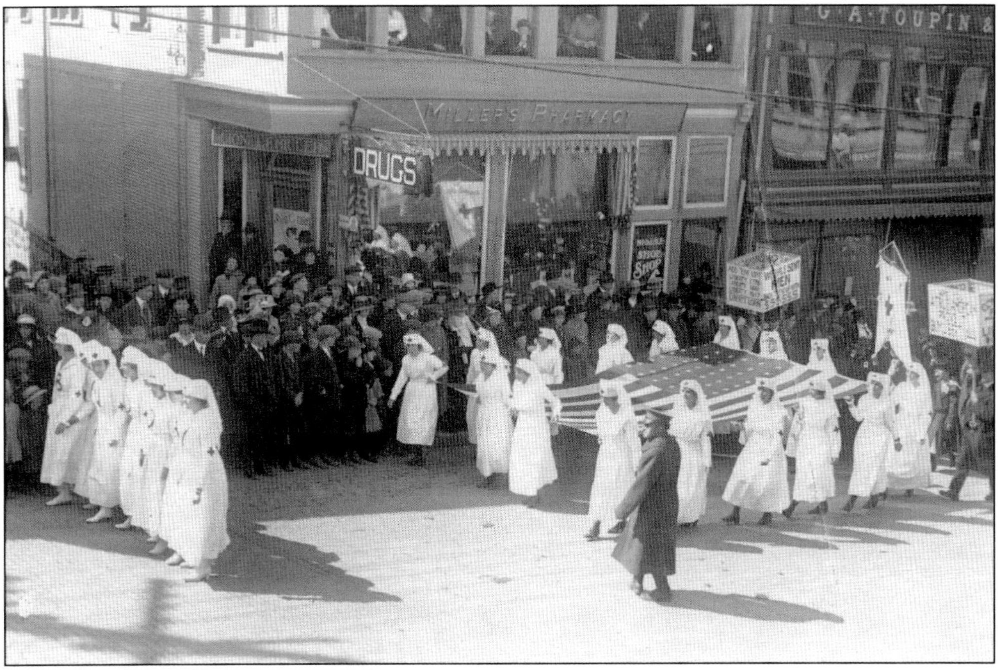

Nurses march up Broadway in this early-1918 World War I war-bond parade. One of the signs reads, "Are You a True American? Prove It – Buy Liberty Bonds." Another says, "We Sent Men – Back Them Up With $$$$$."

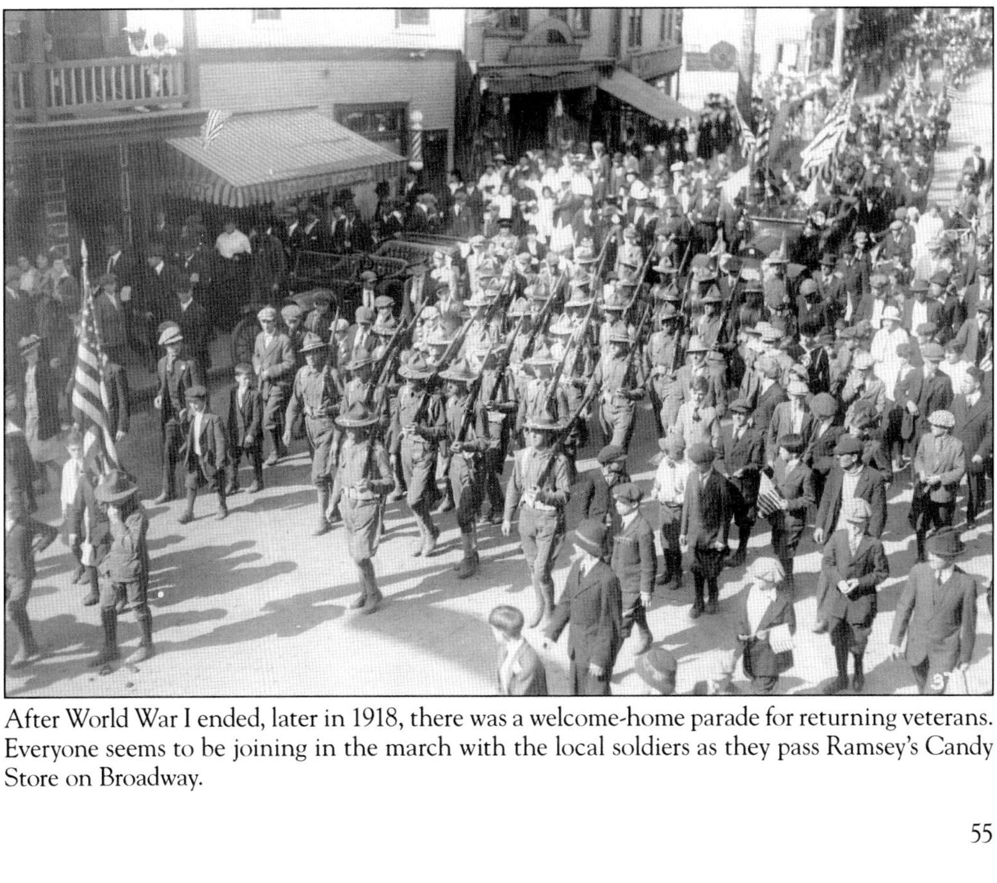

After World War I ended, later in 1918, there was a welcome-home parade for returning veterans. Everyone seems to be joining in the march with the local soldiers as they pass Ramsey's Candy Store on Broadway.

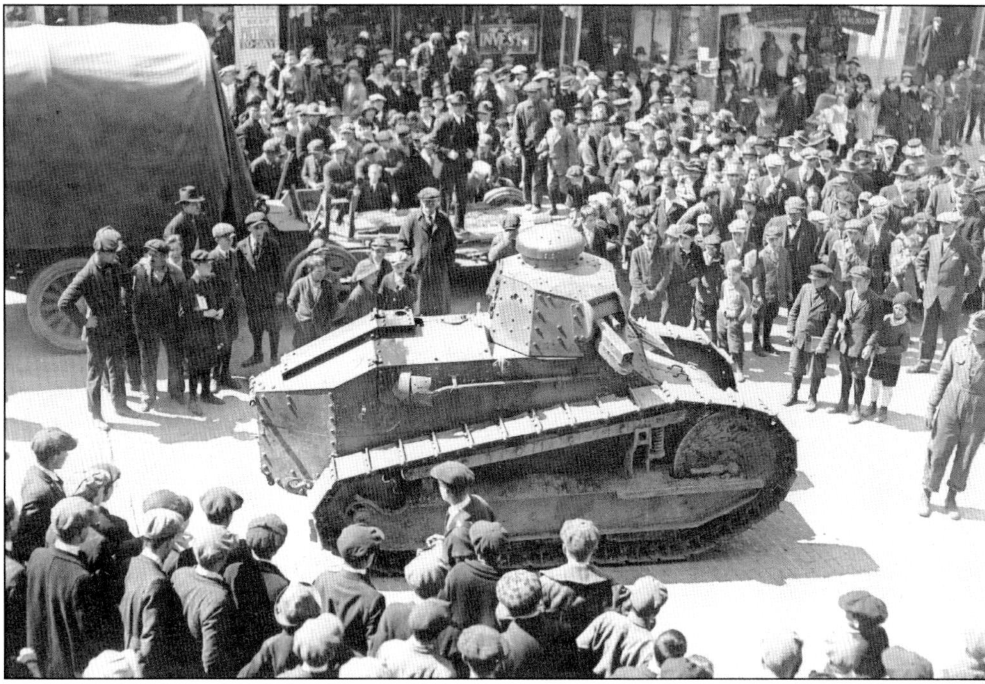

This is an M1917 tank in Berkeley Square after the welcome-home parade. The M1917 was designed for American use during World War I, but by the time enough were built, the war had ended. The M1917's crew consisted of a driver and a gunner and it had a top speed of nine miles per hour, which was very fast for that era. The tank drew a big crowd, even though it never saw combat.

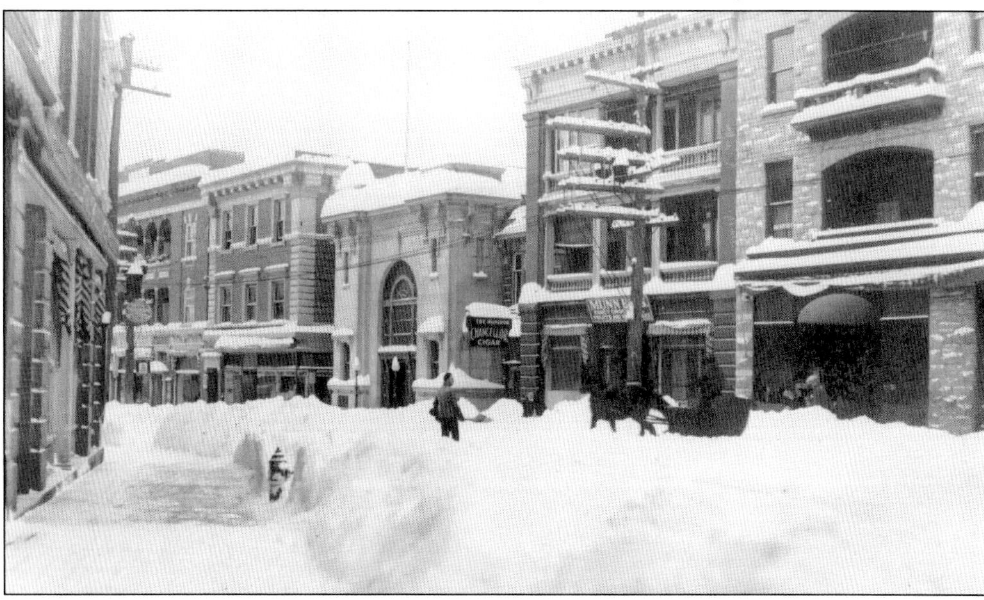

The buildings in this picture of the aftermath of a 1920s snowstorm look very much the same as they do today. This is a tribute to the historic preservation efforts of groups like Historic Saranac Lake in conjunction with local business owners who have a respect for the heritage of their village. The exception in this streetscape is the Adirondack National Bank building in the center, which was covered with bricks in 1962.

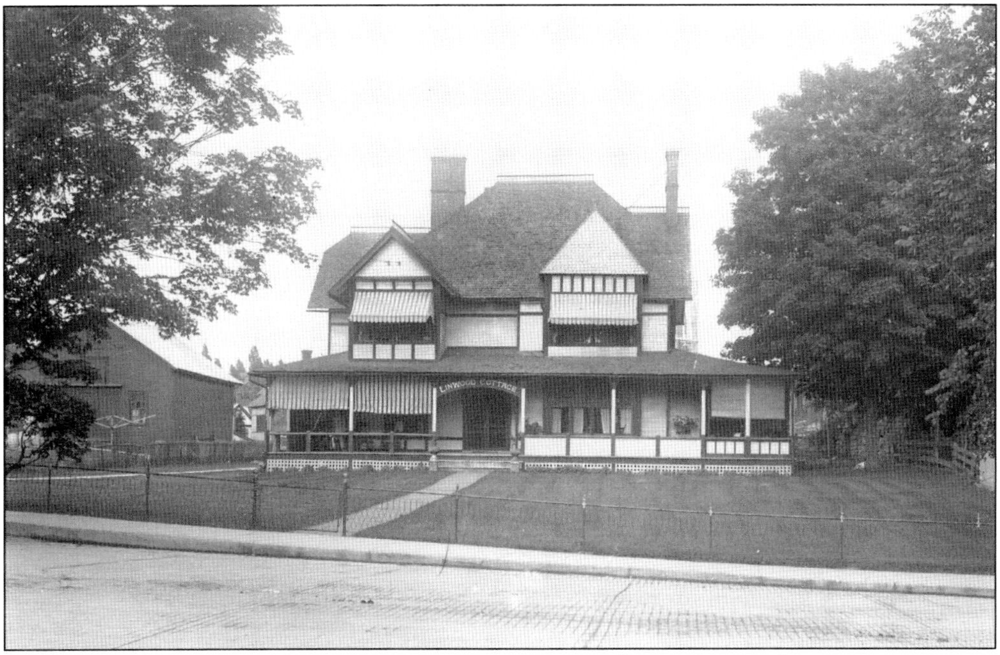

The Linwood Cottage was built on Main Street in 1881 and rented rooms for many years. It was torn down in 1953. The parking lot now next to the Sears store is in its former location.

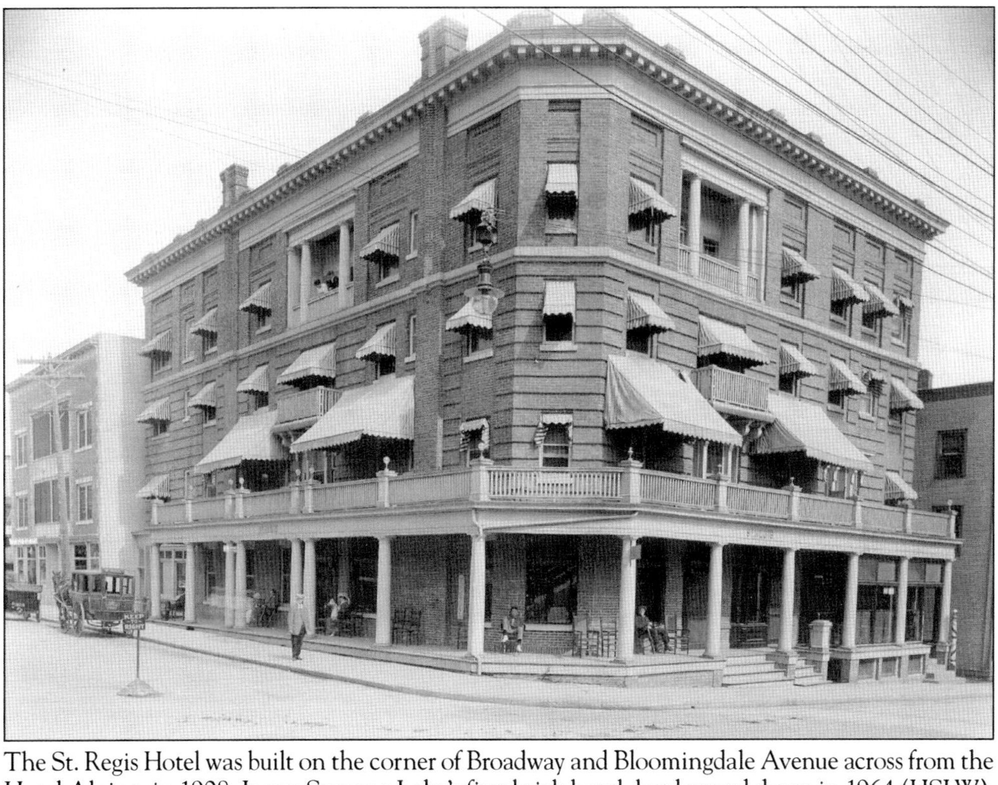

The St. Regis Hotel was built on the corner of Broadway and Bloomingdale Avenue across from the Hotel Alpine, in 1908. It was Saranac Lake's first brick hotel, but burned down in 1964 (HSLW). This photograph was taken about 1920. A parking lot occupies the site today.

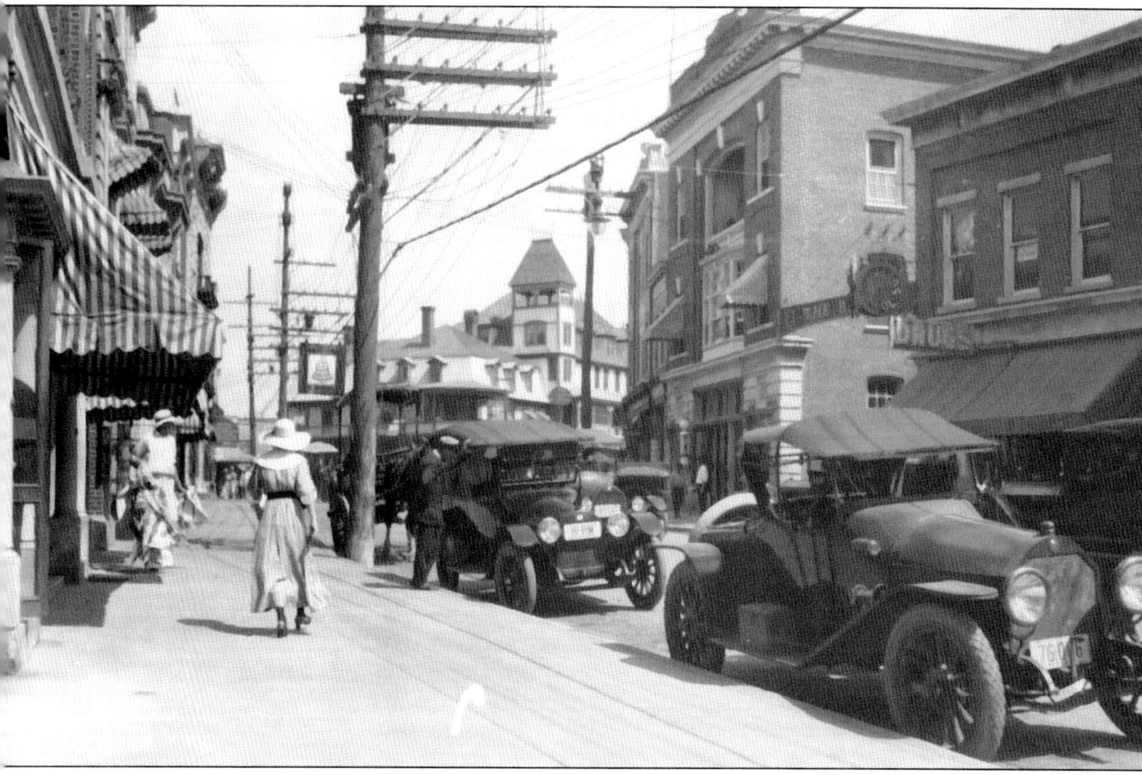

This is a busy day on Main Street in the early 1920s. Cars have not taken over yet. A horse-drawn wagon is parked behind the car in the center of the picture and another is coming up the street in the distance.

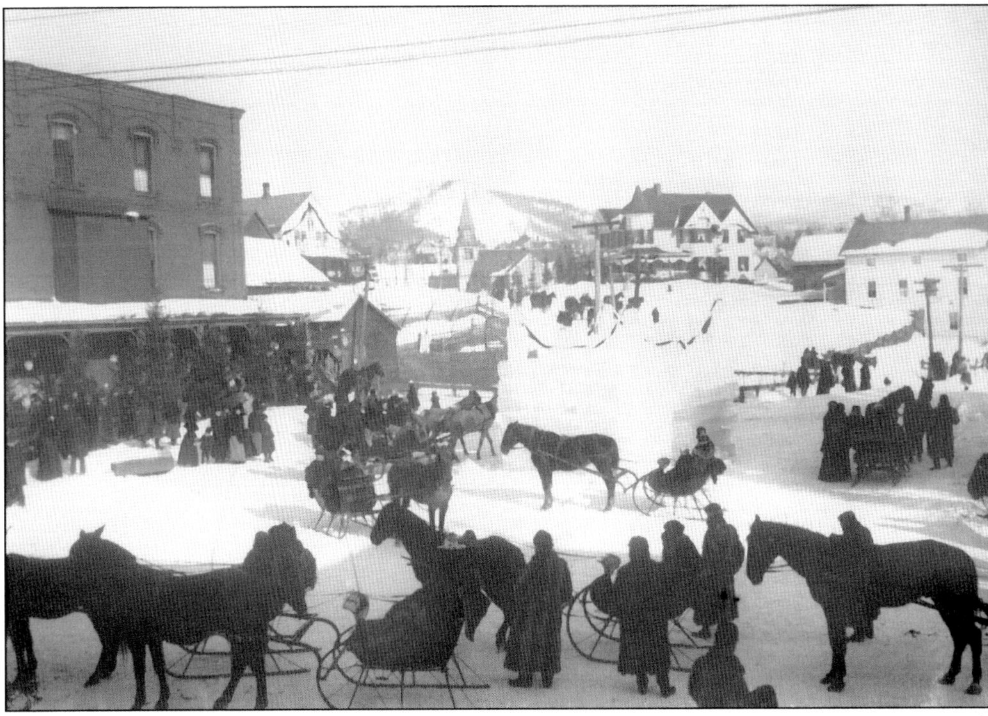

River Street, in the vicinity of Main and St. Bernard's Streets, was once known as Riverside Square. In this 1901 photograph, the square is crowded with sleighs. The brick building on the left is the Spaulding Block, which was erected on the corner of Main and River Streets in the early 1880s; it was the first brick building in town. The Spaulding Block was torn down to make room for a gas station in 1955.

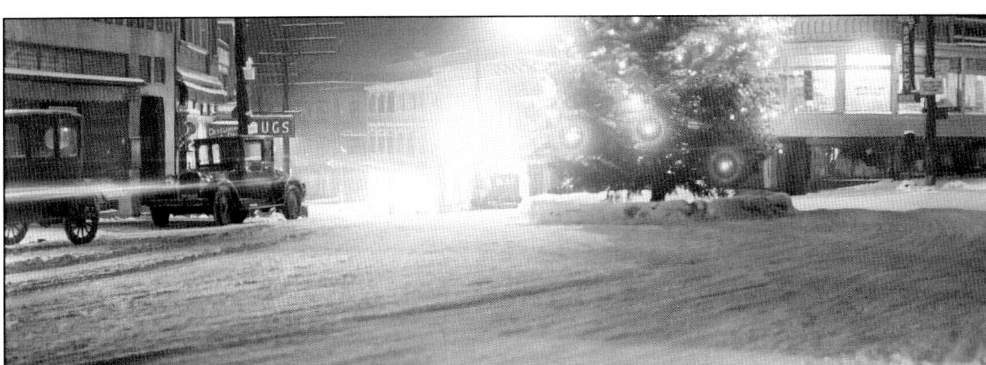

This 1920s photograph features a quiet evening at Christmastime in Berkeley Square.

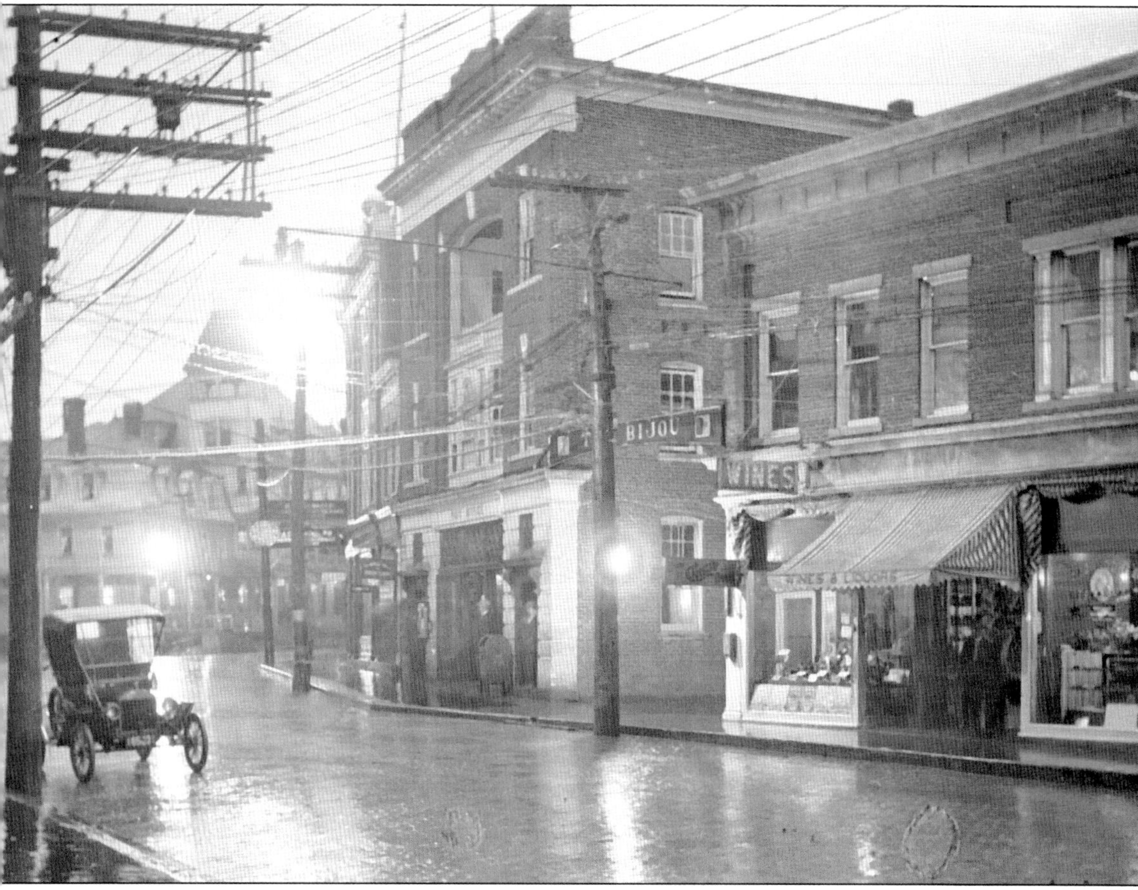

This picture of Main Street, with a view looking toward Berkeley Square, was taken in the late 1910s or early 1920s. Before neon signs were invented, stores that wanted illuminated signs had to have individual lightbulbs outlining the sign's individual letters. An example can be seen on the wine sign on the liquor store across the street. To the left of that are the sign for the Bijou Theatre and, farther, the old post office location at 74 Main Street.

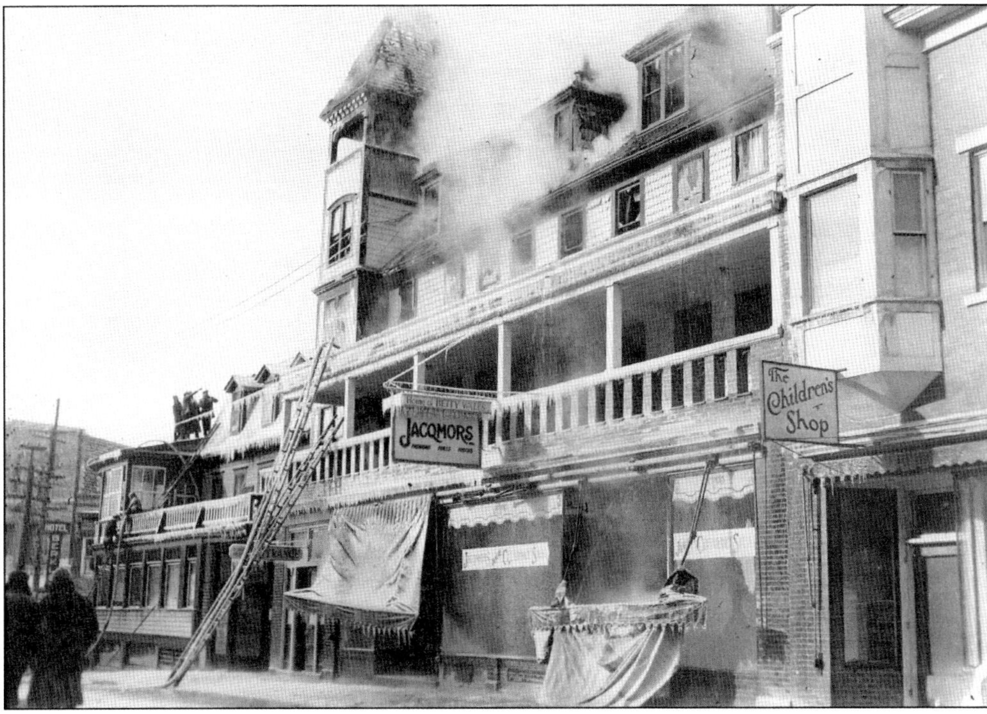

The fire that destroyed the Berkeley in 1981 was not the first. The first occurred on New Year's Day in 1925.

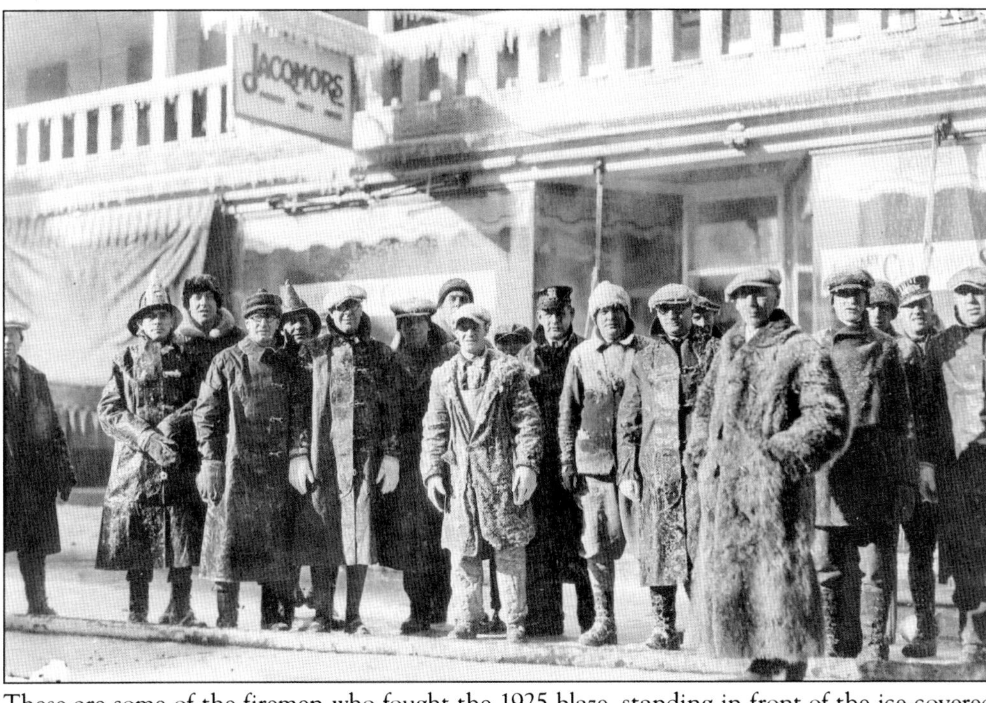

These are some of the firemen who fought the 1925 blaze, standing in front of the ice-covered remains after the battle. Enough of the building was saved that the top floor was torn off, and a new roof was put on while the bottom three floors continued to be used for many years.

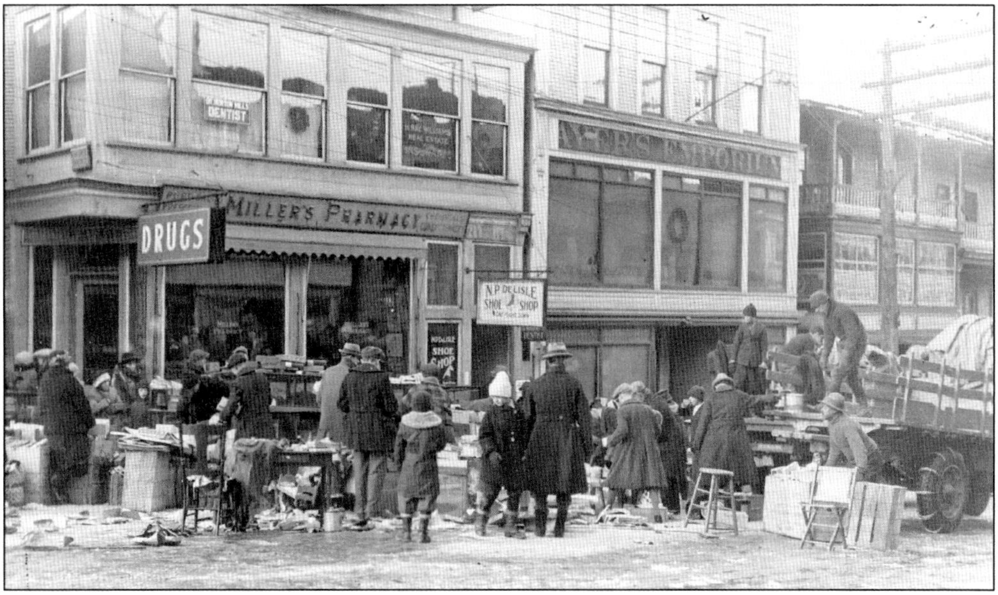

These village residents are out on Broadway and Main Street, going over the remains rescued from the Berkeley fire in 1925.

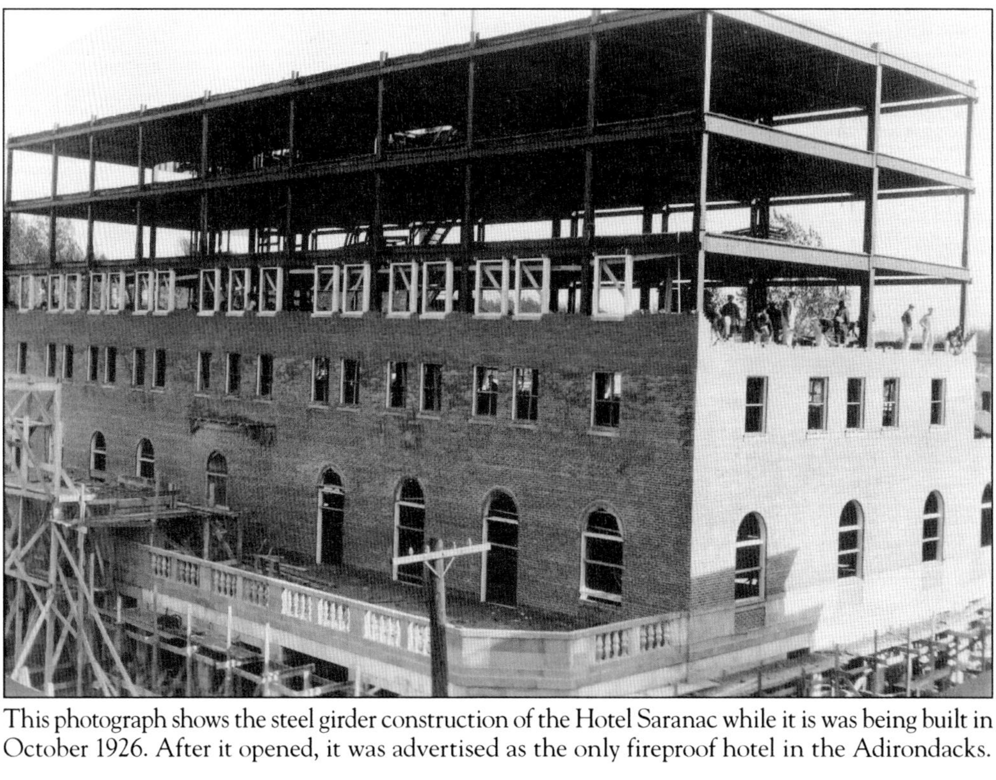

This photograph shows the steel girder construction of the Hotel Saranac while it is was being built in October 1926. After it opened, it was advertised as the only fireproof hotel in the Adirondacks.

The Potter Block was built in the late 1890s at the corner of Broadway and Bloomingdale Avenue, and it contained the Arlington Hotel and other businesses. This view shows how it was remodeled some years later. Across Bloomingdale Avenue was the St. Regis Hotel, and across Broadway was the Alpine Hotel. The Potter Block was torn down in 1978.

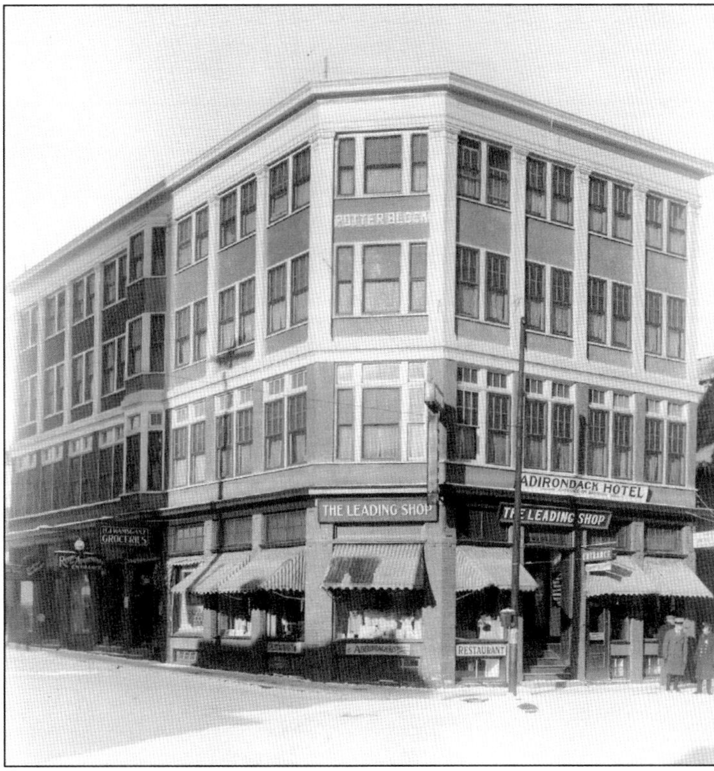

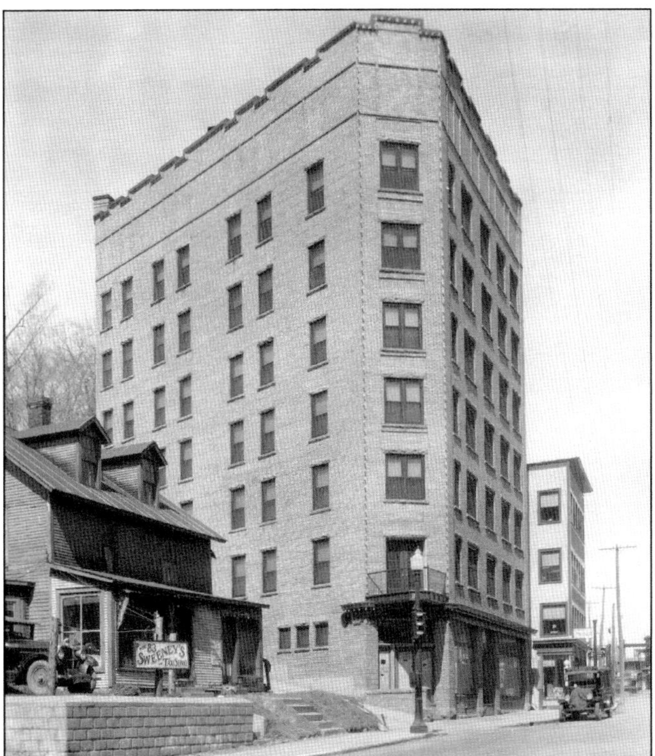

The Hotel Alpine stood at 84 Broadway, now the empty lot next to the Rusty Nail. The glittering mural is on what's left of the Alpine's back wall. The Alpine was demolished in 1977, but this photograph was taken shortly after its construction in 1926.

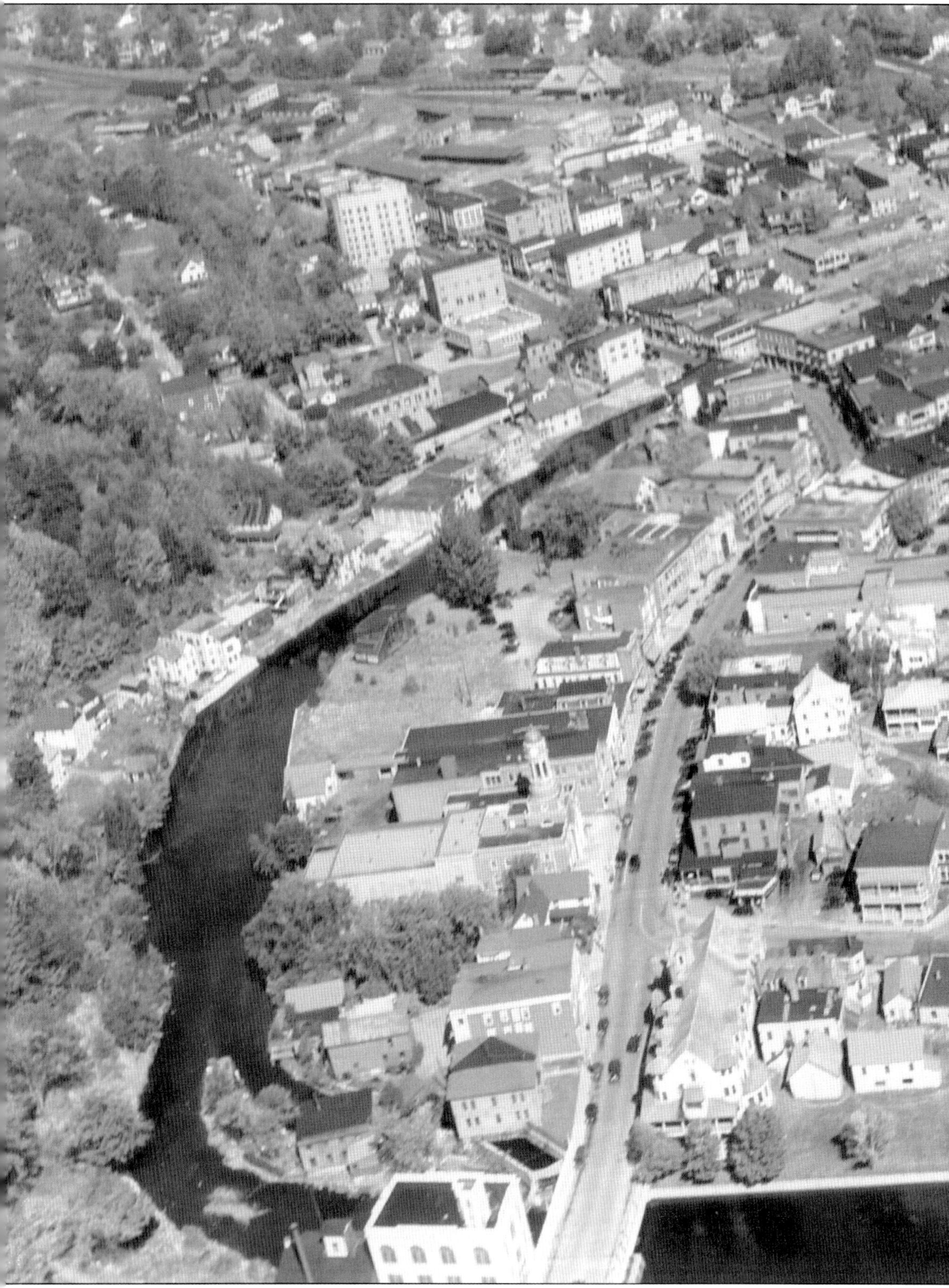

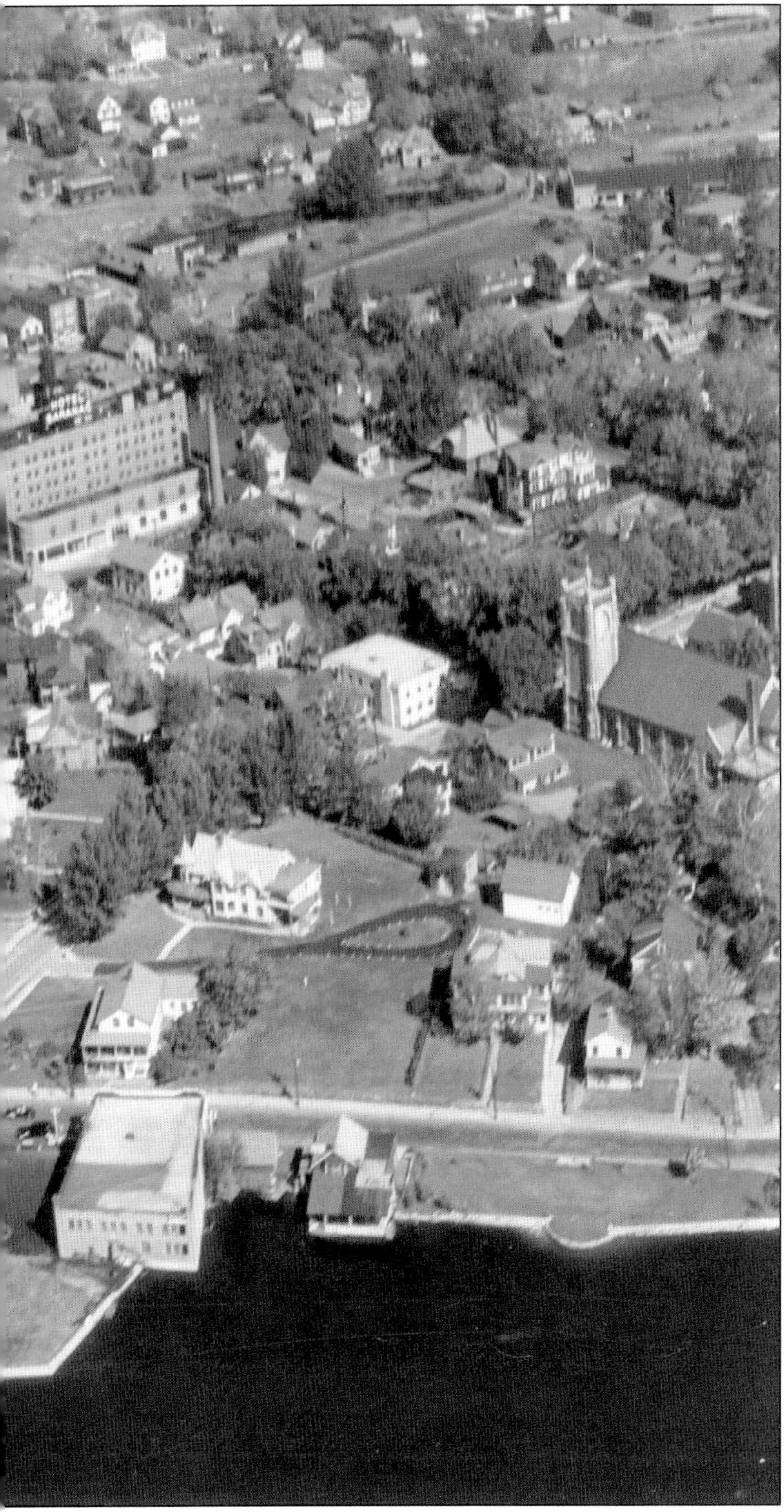

This early-1930s aerial photograph of the central part of the village shows how it has changed over the years. The Riverside Inn, torn down in 1934, and several other buildings still occupy the site of today's Riverside Park. Across River Street, the Spaulding Block is still in place, but today there is a gas station there. Among many other differences one could look for, there is also no LaPan Highway at the end of River Street.

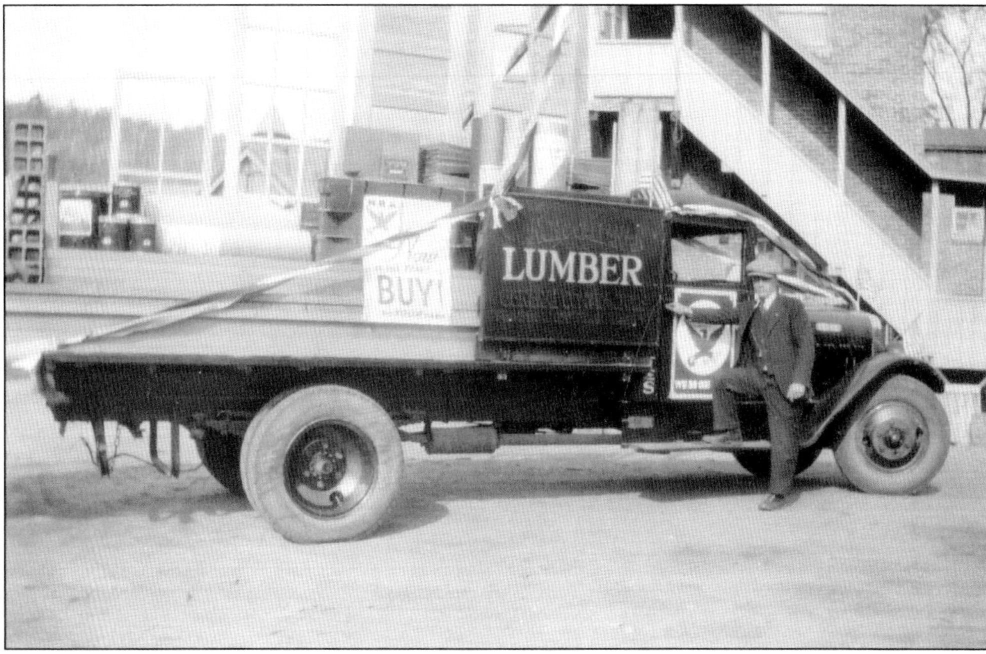

When the National Recovery Administration (NRA) was established by Franklin Roosevelt's New Deal in 1933, parades were held across America to gather support for this Depression-fighting measure. Branch and Callanan displayed the Blue Eagle, symbol of the NRA, on their truck for the local parade. Looking through the windows on the truck, one can see the steeple of the train depot in the distance.

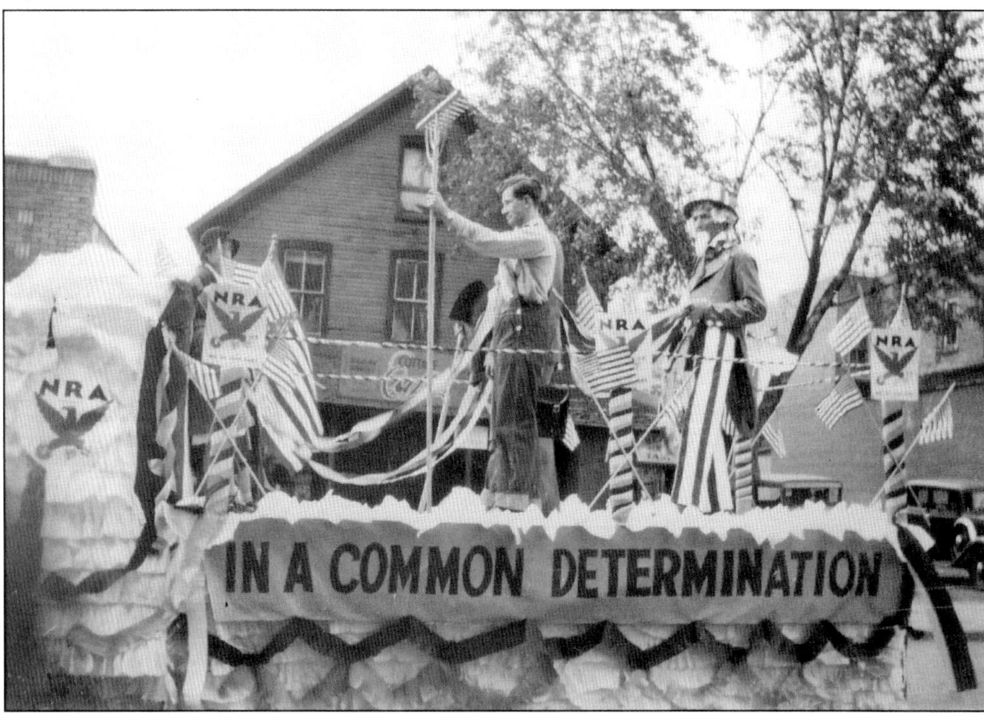

Uncle Sam rides this float in the 1933 National Recovery Administration parade.

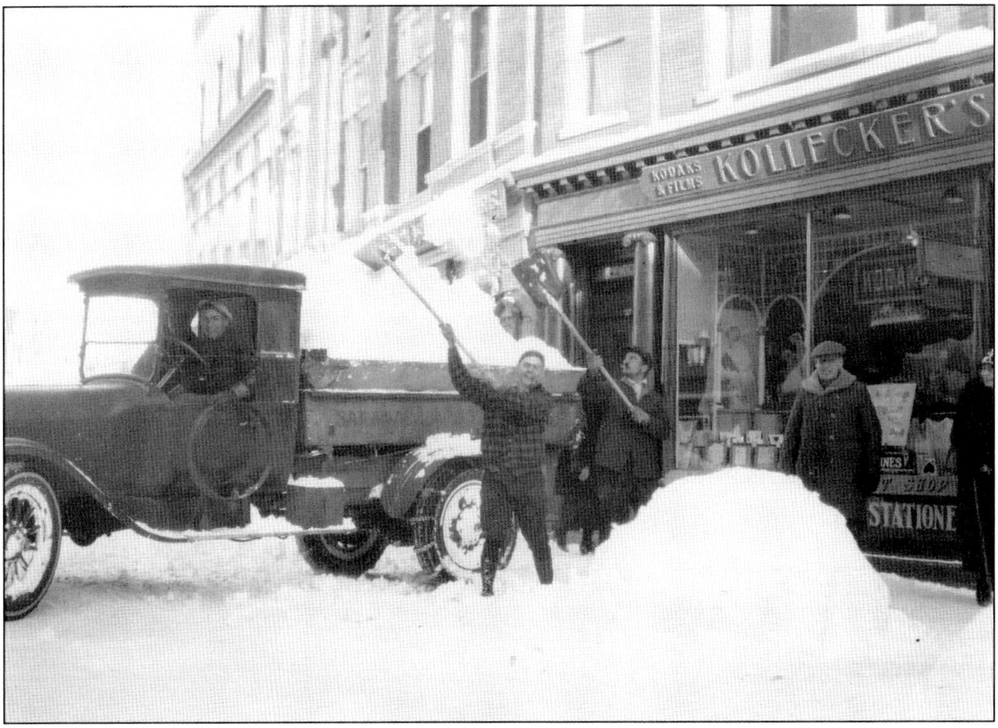

These men are shoveling snow in front of Kollecker's Kodak and Gift Shop on Main Street around 1930.

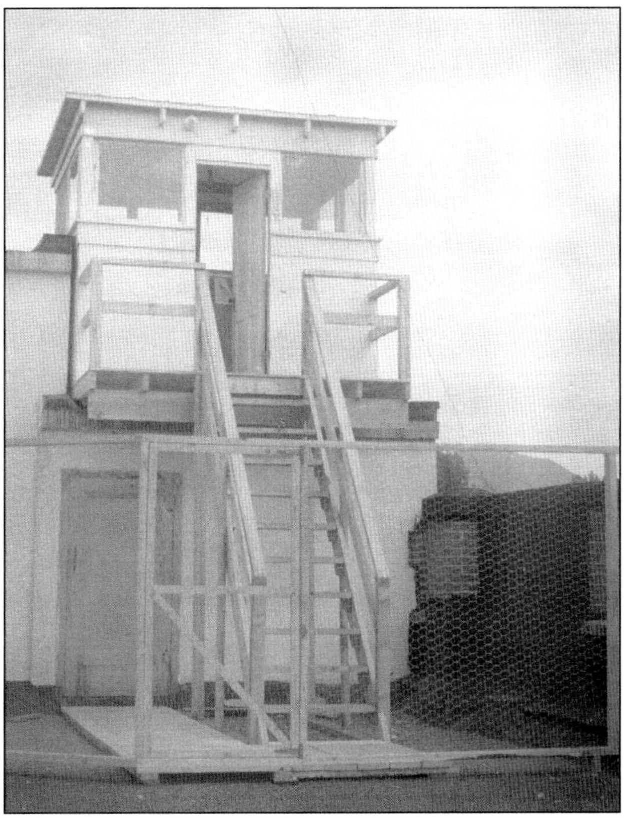

This structure was built on the roof of the Hotel Saranac shortly after the bombing of Pearl Harbor started the American involvement in World War II on December 7, 1941. It was used as an observation tower to scan the skies for enemy bombers when America was unsure if another attack would come from our new enemies. Native and longtime resident Natalie Leduc remembers bringing dinner to her father when it was his turn to man this tower.

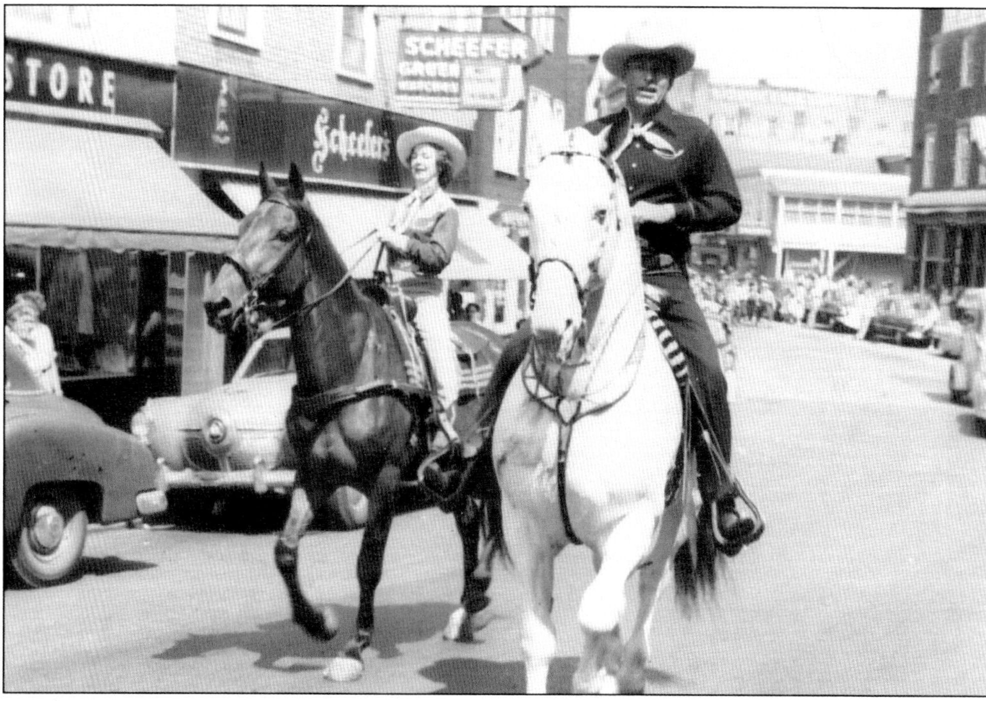

In July 1953, the big event was the Adirondack Championship Rodeo. In addition to bull riding, bronco busting, and dancing horses, one of the biggest attractions was movie star Buster Crabbe, shown here with Maggie Duffy. Crabbe won an Olympic gold medal for swimming in 1932 and starred in over 100 movies including recurring roles as Tarzan, Flash Gordon, and Buck Rogers. Crabbe also owned a camp on Rainbow Lake.

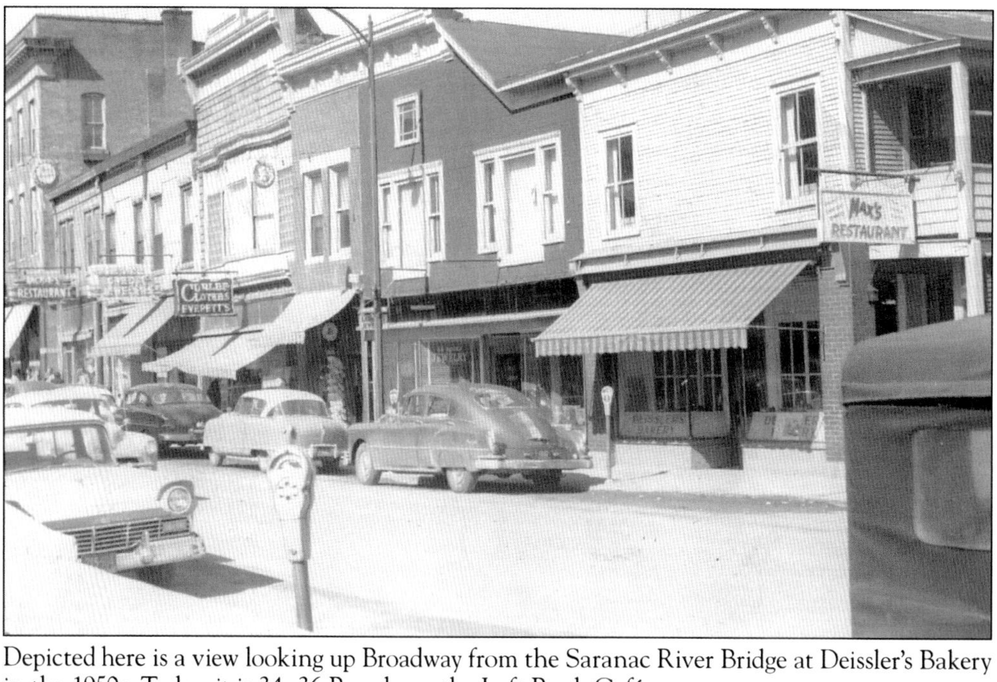

Depicted here is a view looking up Broadway from the Saranac River Bridge at Deissler's Bakery in the 1950s. Today, it is 34–36 Broadway, the Left Bank Café.

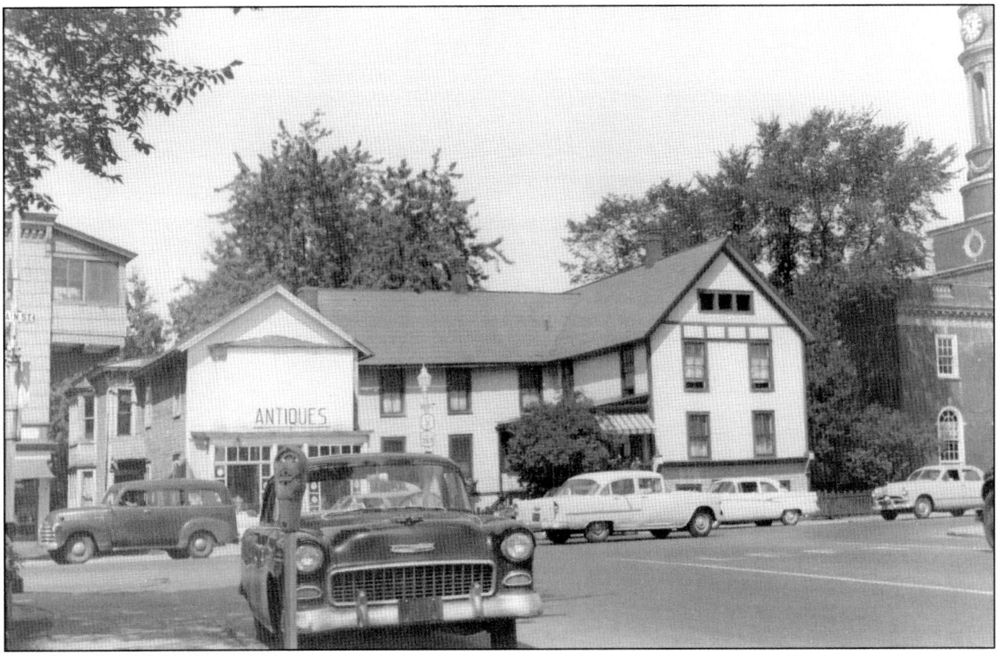

This 1950s photograph is the view from the corner of River and Main Streets. River Street used to end in a T-shaped intersection at Main Street. Before the construction of the LaPan Highway, there were several buildings between the town hall and the Currier Block, the current location of Little Italy. These buildings were torn down in 1958 to make way for the highway.

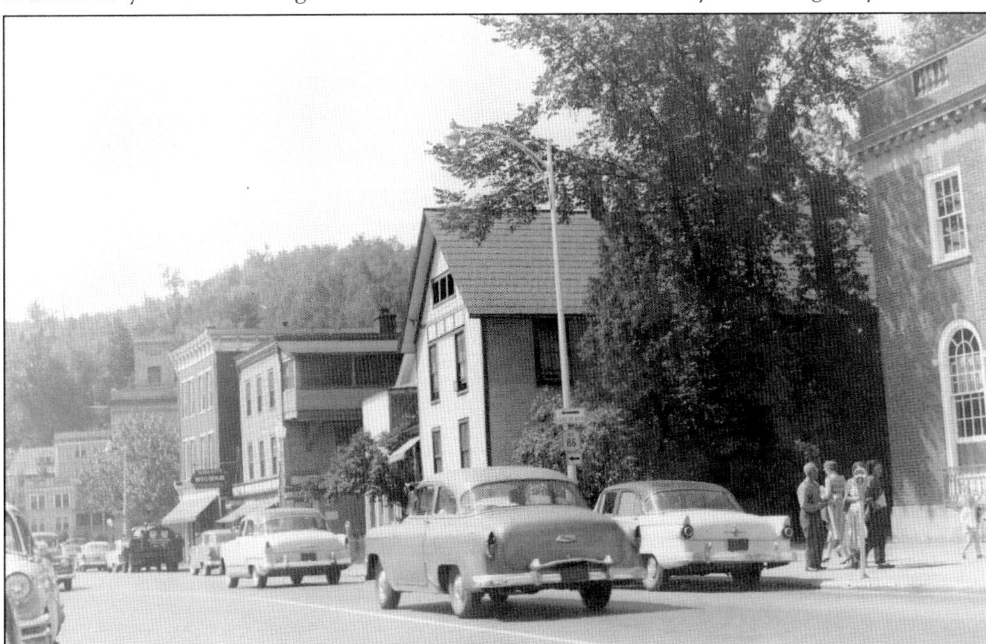

This view looks down the row of the now missing Main Street buildings from the street in front of the town hall; the corner of the town hall, however, is visible in the right side of the picture. The Seaver Miller Cottage, Hoffman's Sporting Goods, and The Wigwam – Souvenirs, Yarn, and Gifts Store were among the occupants of the sites torn down for the LaPan Highway.

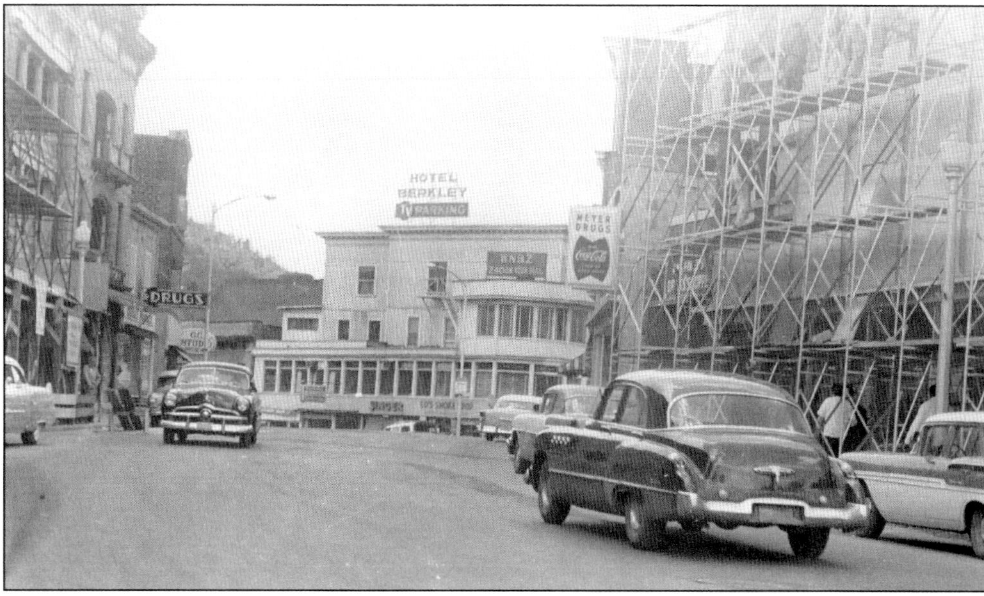

In this photograph of Main Street, looking toward the Berkeley, scaffolding covers the fronts of both Newberry's, on the right side of the street, and the Adirondack National Bank building, on the left. Local historian Phil Gallos gives the date of the destruction of the bank facade as 1962. The cars pictured in this street scene would agree with that date.

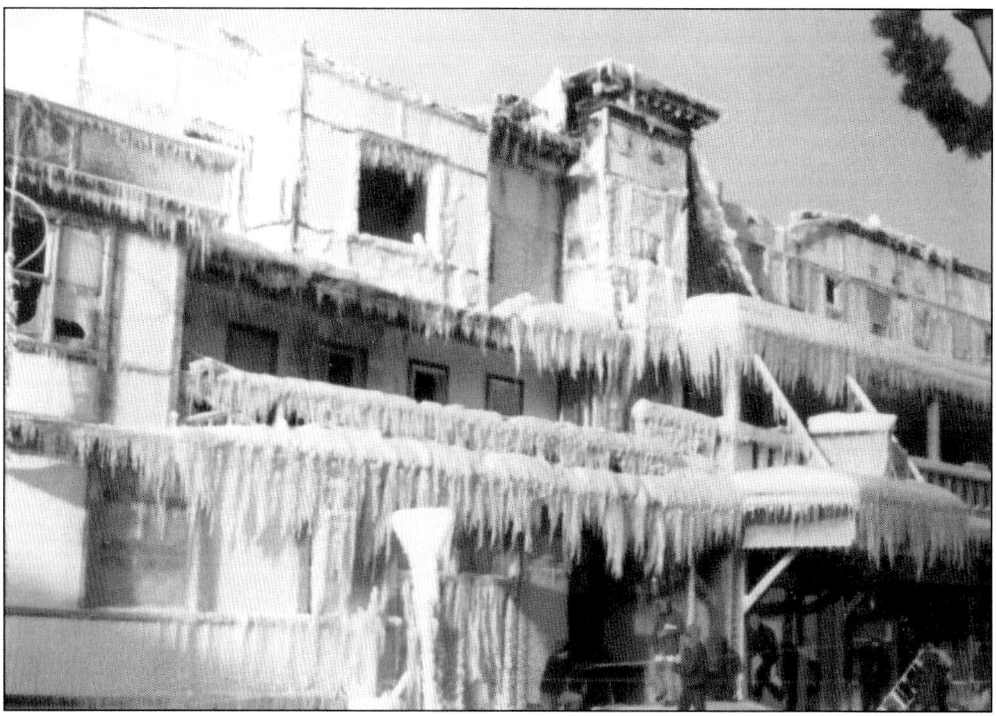

The Berkeley looked like this the morning after a fire destroyed it on January 10, 1981. The night the Berkeley burned, the temperature outside was 30 degrees below zero. It was so cold the fire department lost two lengths of four-inch hose because they split in the extreme temperatures. It was the end of this village landmark, but the Berkeley Green commemorates its location.

Four

AROUND THE VILLAGE

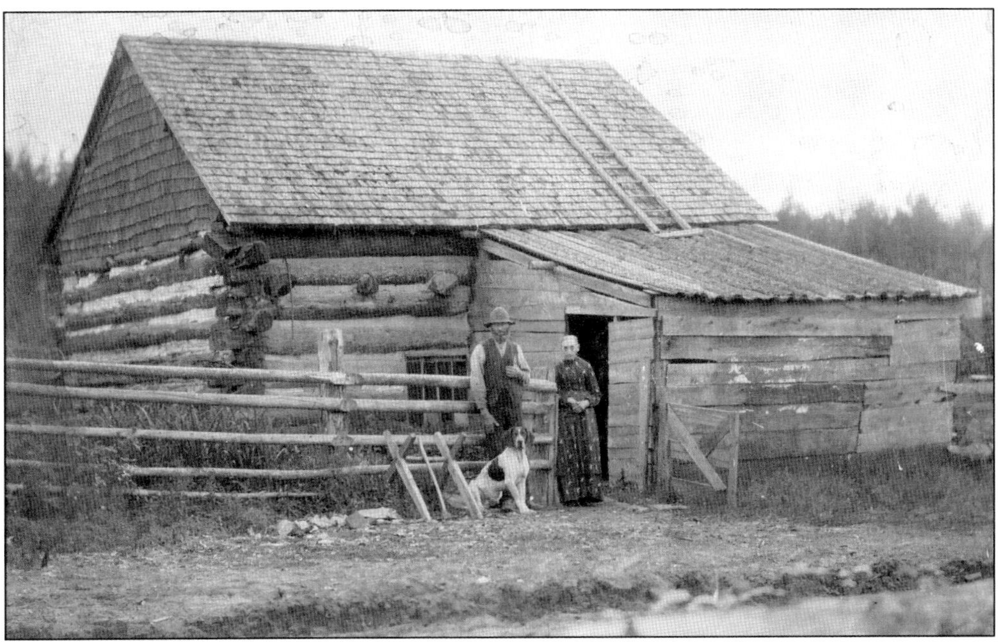

Author Alfred Donaldson says that Jacob Moody was the first settler in what is now the Village of Saranac Lake when Moody arrived in 1819. The unidentified pioneers in this picture are not the Moodys, but readers can get an idea of what life was like for these early settlers from this couple's log home.

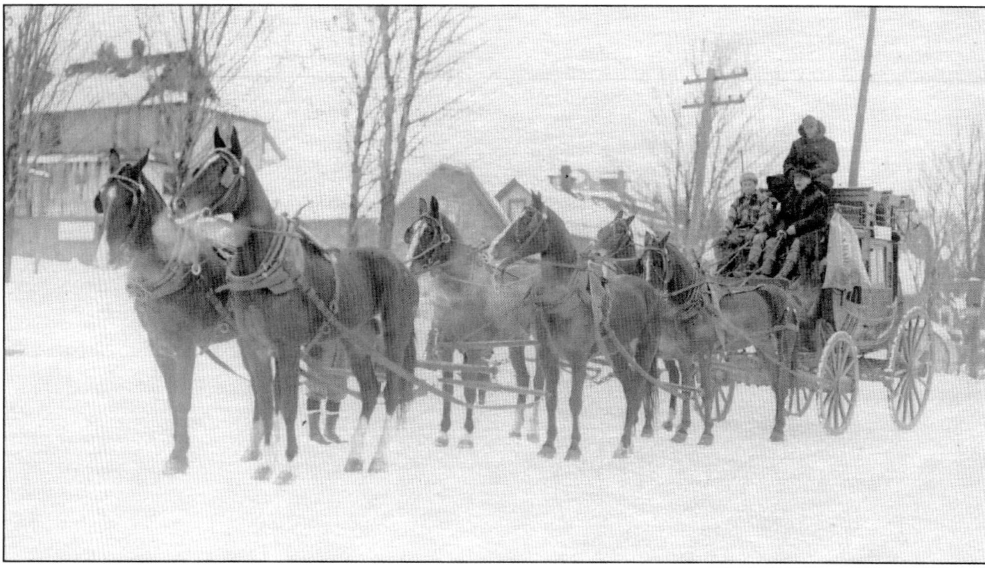

When people wanted to travel from one town or hotel to another in the 19th century, the stagecoach was the only way to go. In this winter scene, the US Mail pouch is visible on the side of the coach—another important duty of stagecoaches.

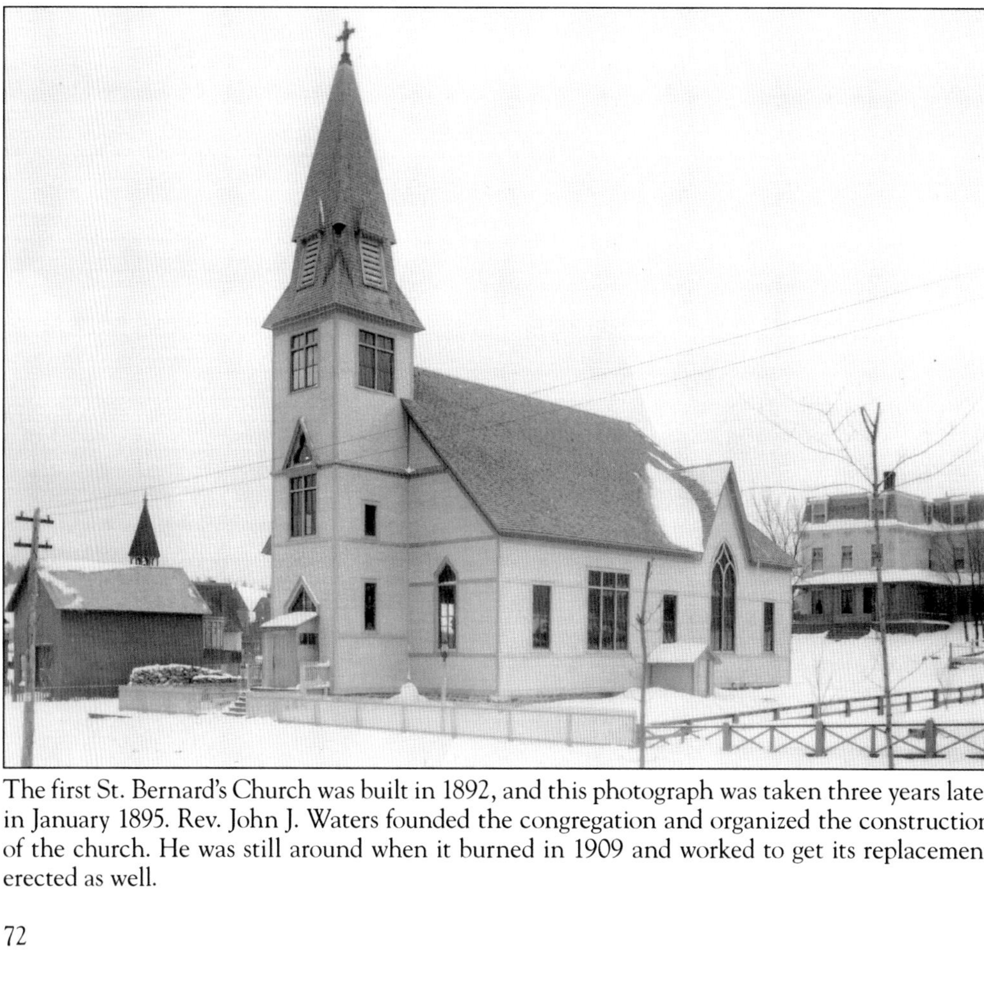

The first St. Bernard's Church was built in 1892, and this photograph was taken three years later in January 1895. Rev. John J. Waters founded the congregation and organized the construction of the church. He was still around when it burned in 1909 and worked to get its replacement erected as well.

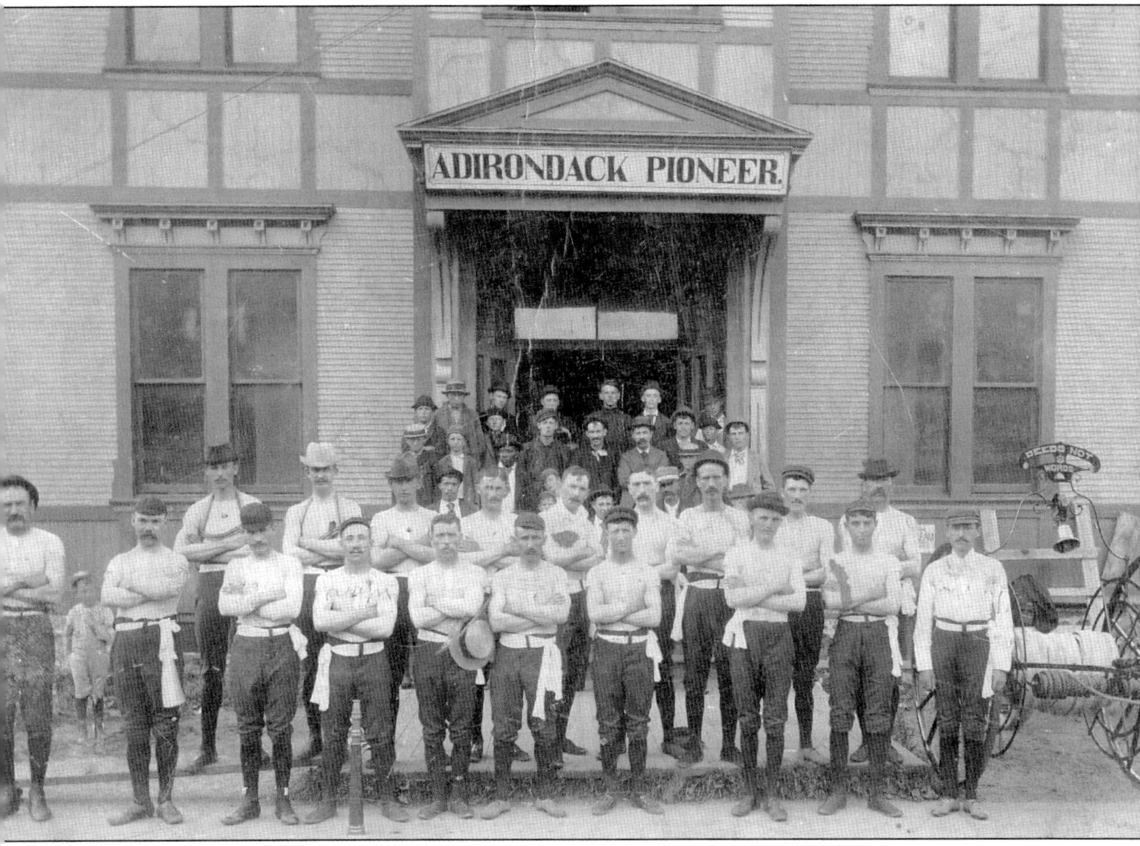

The Miller Hose Company is standing in front of the old town hall in the 1890s. The sign over the entrance reads "Adirondack Pioneer," because the building also housed the early newspaper named the *Pioneer* beginning in 1892. Later, the *Enterprise* was housed in the building. From left to right, the firemen are (first row) unidentified, Mack Pasho, Bert Munn, John Marquary, unidentified, Napoleon Bailey, two unidentified, Felix Delisle and Fred Lamy; (second row) two unidentified, Frank Sheldon, three unidentified, Joe St. Peter, Will Demerse and ? LeBrake. The sign on the hose cart to their right reads "Deeds Not Words."

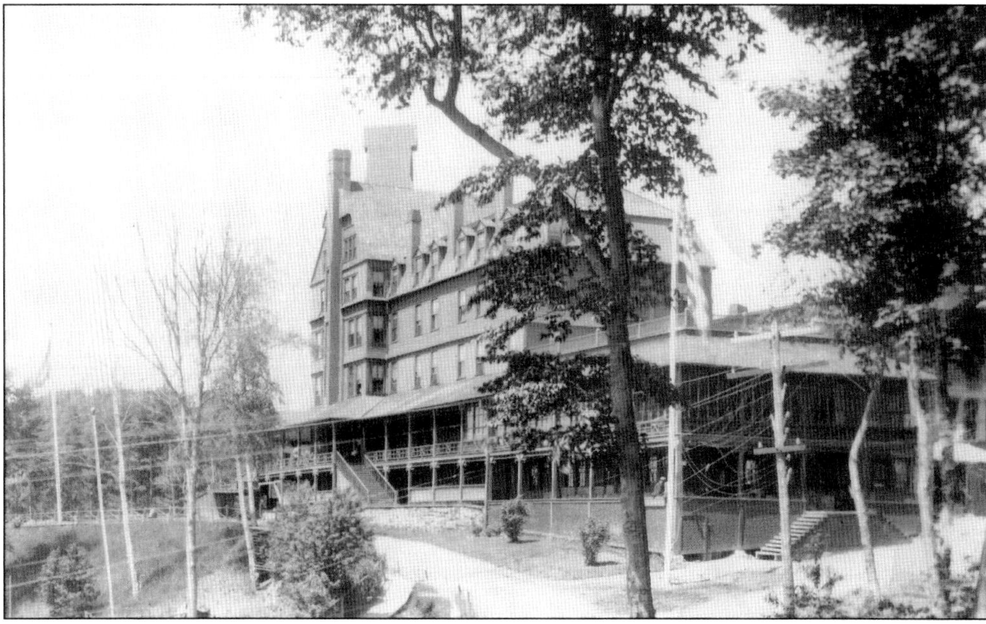

The Hotel Ampersand was built in 1888 and sat on a small rise overlooking Ampersand Bay of Lower Saranac Lake. The 1894 edition of *Wallace's Guide to the Adirondacks* says "the hotel is supplied with all the appliances of the modern resort . . . an elevator, electric bells, steam heat, gas illumination, general and private bathrooms, a barbershop . . . telephone, telegraph and a Post Office."

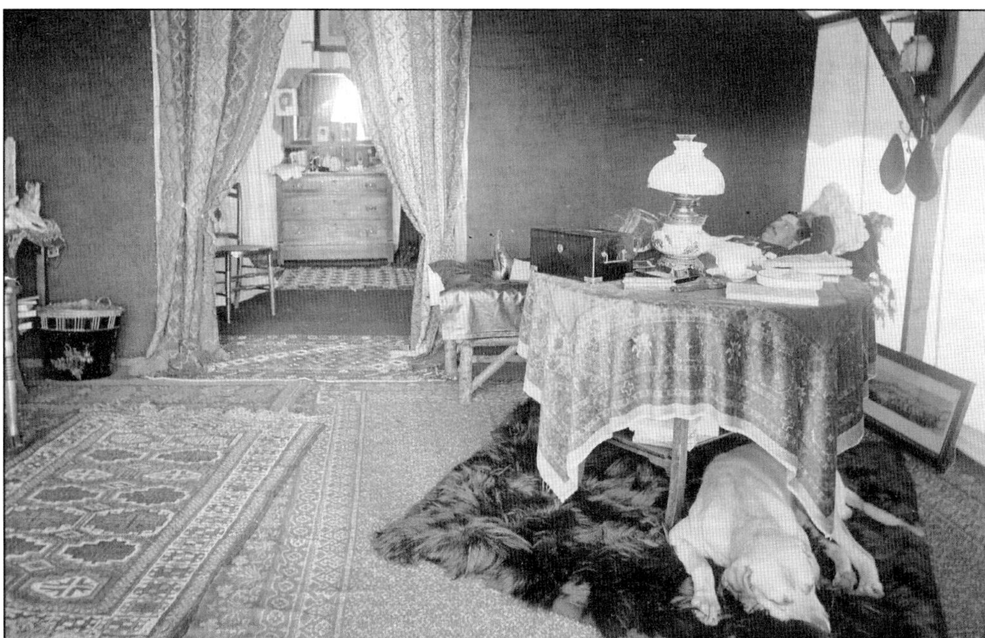

At the height of the summer season, it was not uncommon for the better hotels to be so full that they had to set up tents for some of their guests. As is evident from this interior view, even the guests staying in the tents were not exactly roughing it. Both dog and man seem to be very comfortable in this tent on the grounds of the Hotel Ampersand.

Jabez D. Alexander of Vermontville built the Algonquin Hotel in 1884 on Lower Saranac Lake. After changing hands several times, it was converted to a sanitarium briefly in 1913. The building was torn down from 1958 to 1959 and today the site is home to the Trudeau Institute.

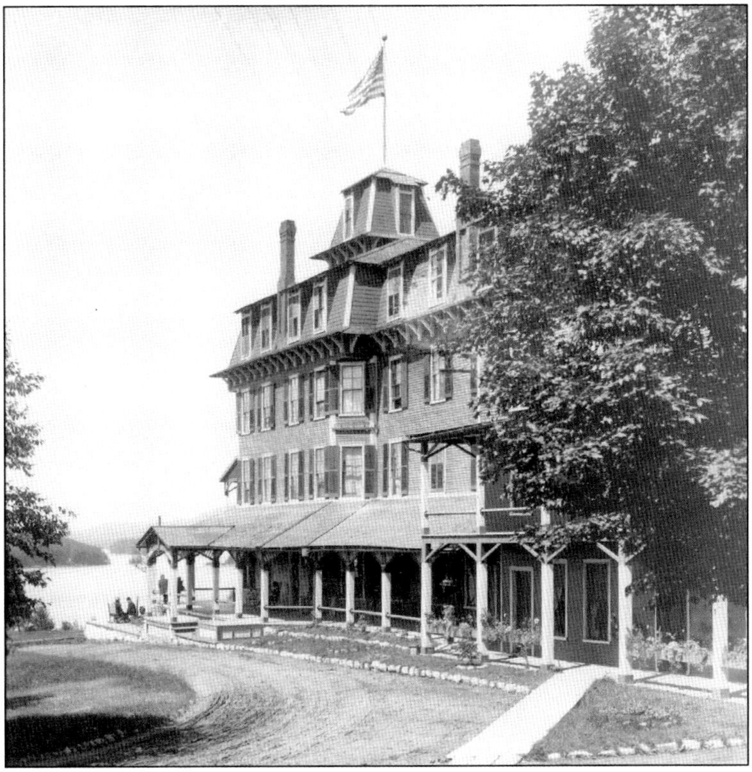

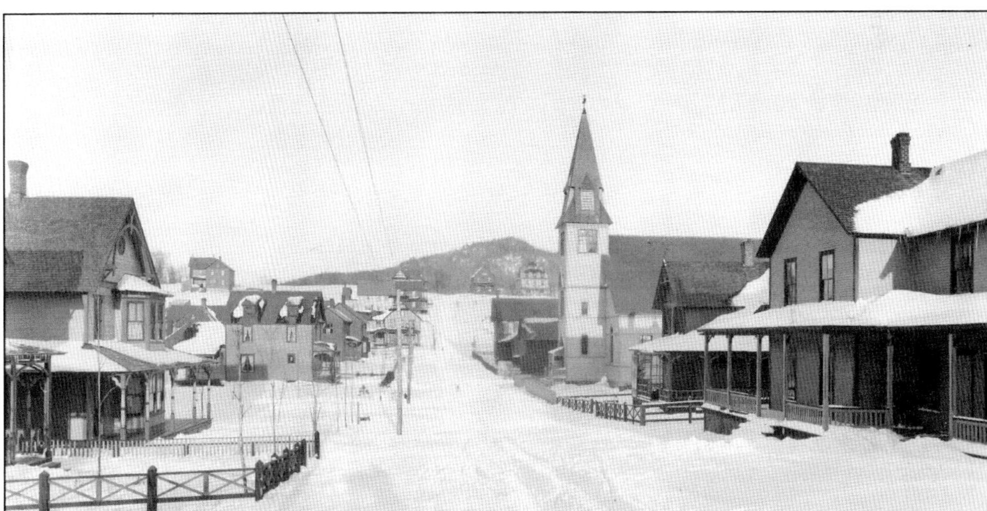

This was the view up St. Bernard's Street toward Helen Hill in 1894. St. Bernard's Church is on the right, with almost no houses on Helen Hill. Similar to other pictures taken before 1900 around the village, there are also almost no trees.

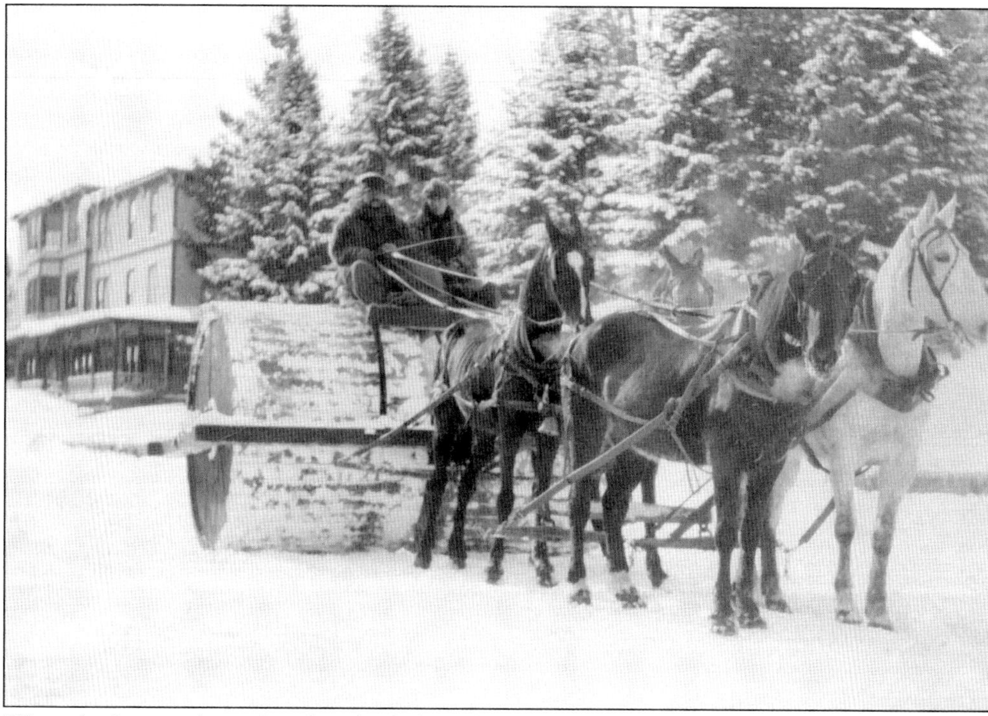

When sleighs were the preferred method of travel in the winter, the village used snow rollers—like the one shown—to compact the snow in the streets to make it easier for the sleighs to get around.

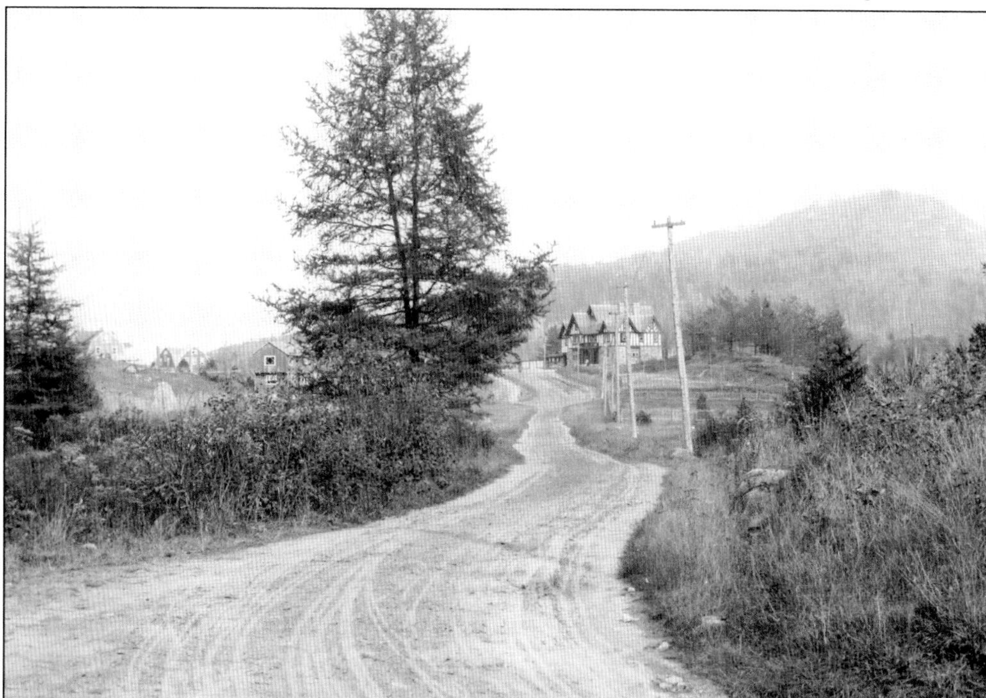

Park Avenue is shown here when it was a dirt street in 1900. The home on the right belonged to J. Nichols, and the address was listed as 300 Park.

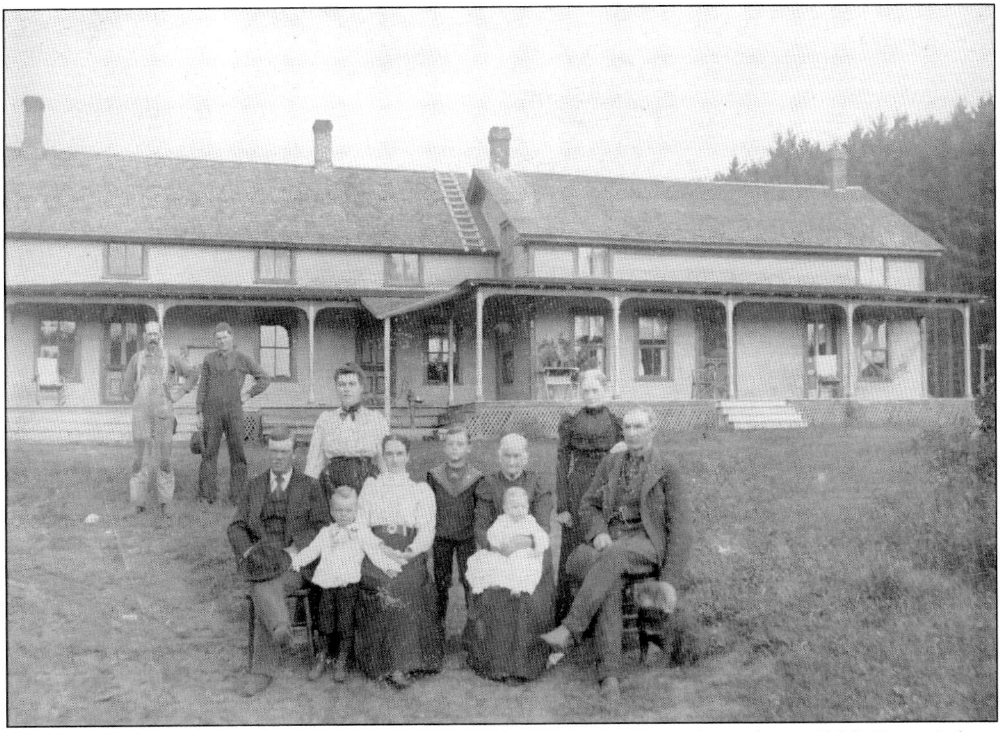

The Moody homestead was built in 1875, and this portrait was taken about 1900. From left to right are (first row) B.O. Moody, Clarence Moody, Etta Anson Moody, "Mother" with baby Oscar, and B.R. Moody; (second row) Daisy Moody Sheldon, Harold Sheldon, and Mrs. B.R. Moody. The two men in back are identified only as hired hands. Alfred Donaldson lists this address as 154 River Street in 1921.

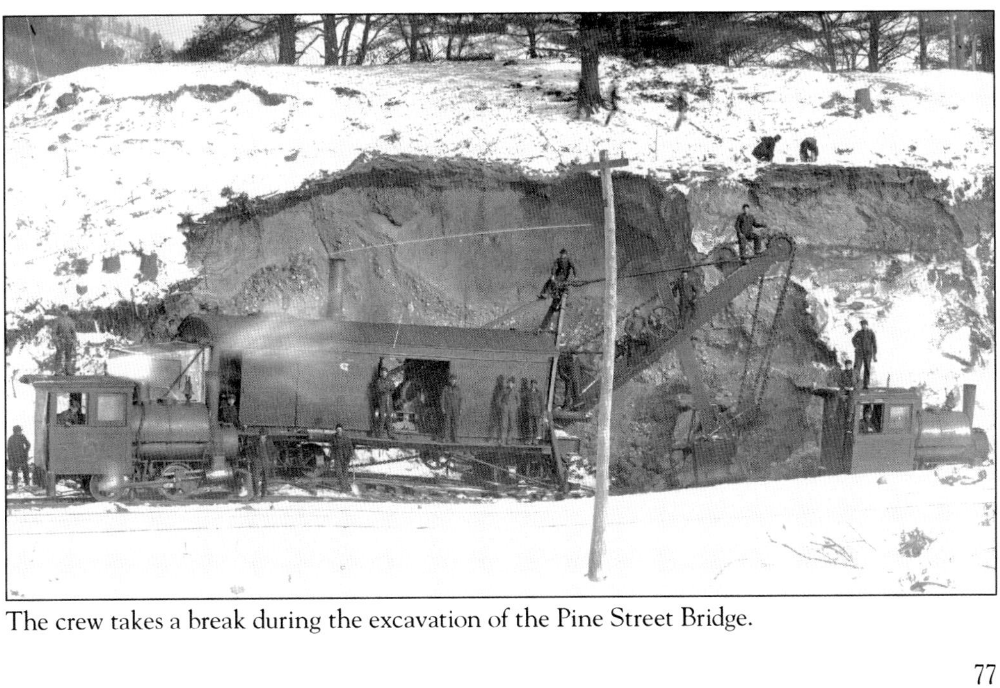

The crew takes a break during the excavation of the Pine Street Bridge.

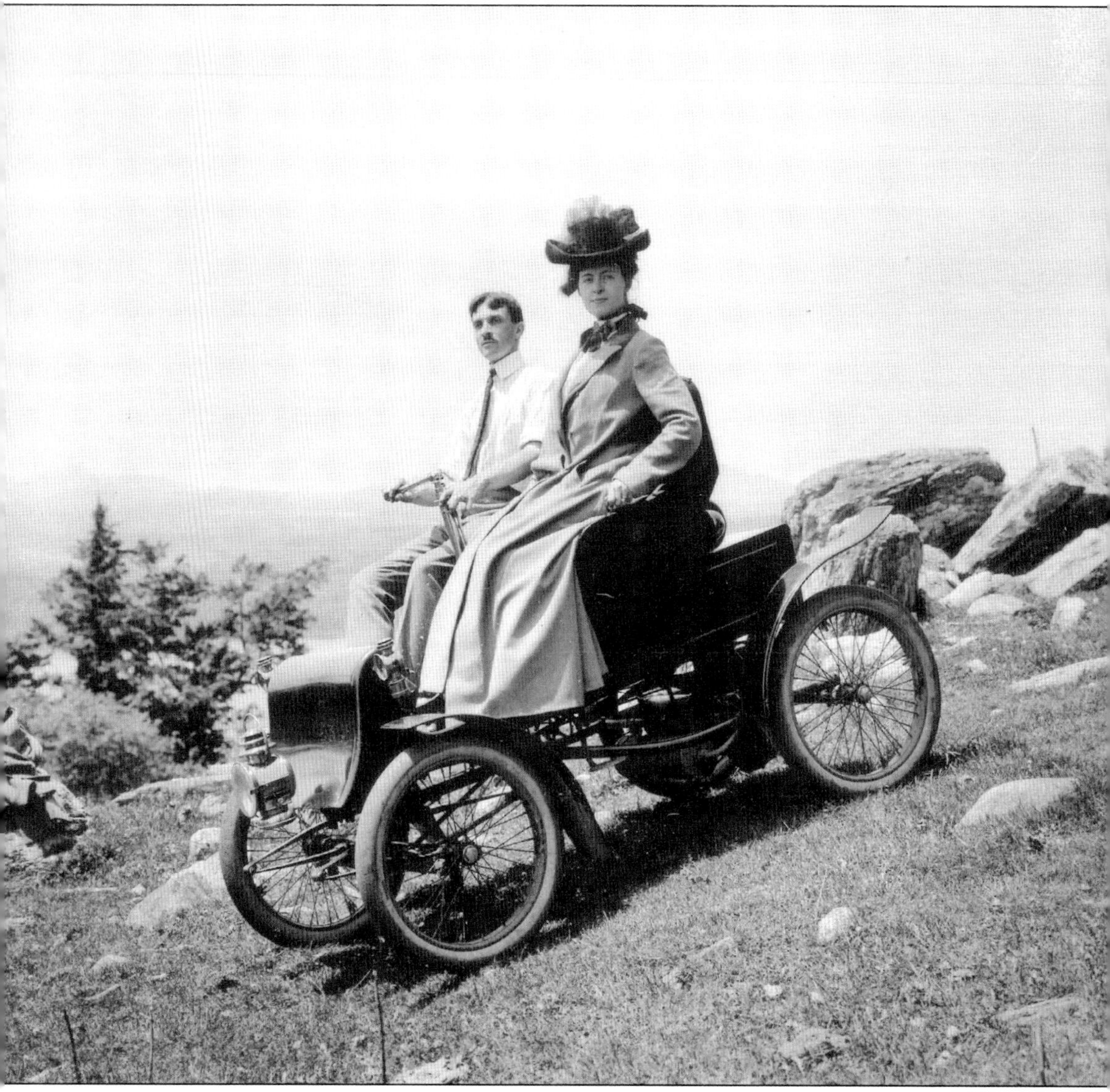

Mr. and Mrs. Herbert Sackett are out for a ride in their horseless carriage. In *A Past to Remember, A Future to Mold: The Growing Years*, Mary "Bunnie" Catillaz and Mildred Keough write that the first automobile arrived in Saranac Lake when the Sacketts visited the Ampersand Hotel while on their honeymoon in July 1902. "Terror spread through the village as this car puffed and pounded through the streets, causing many runaway horses." Fortunately, there were no injuries.

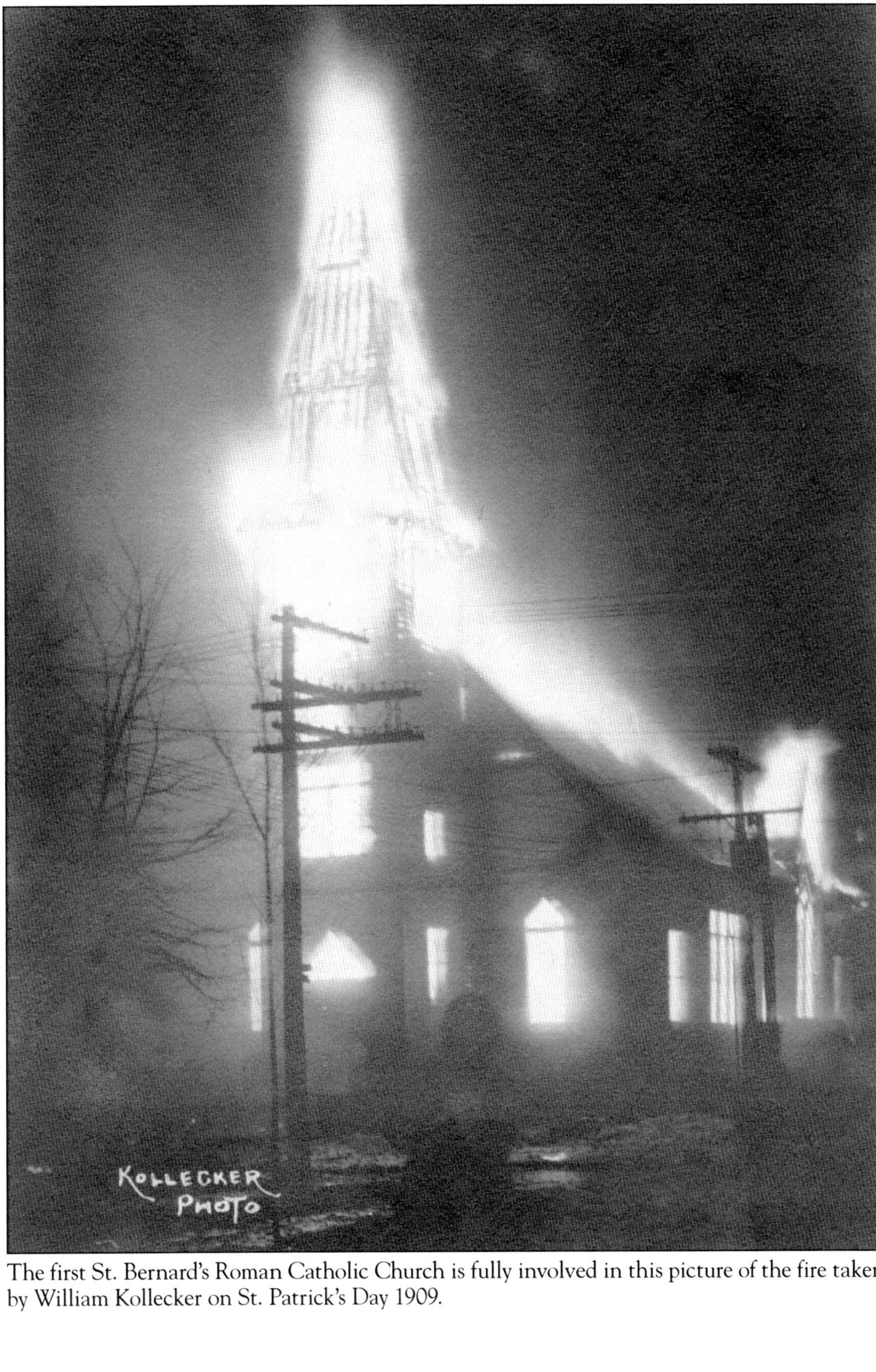

The first St. Bernard's Roman Catholic Church is fully involved in this picture of the fire taken by William Kollecker on St. Patrick's Day 1909.

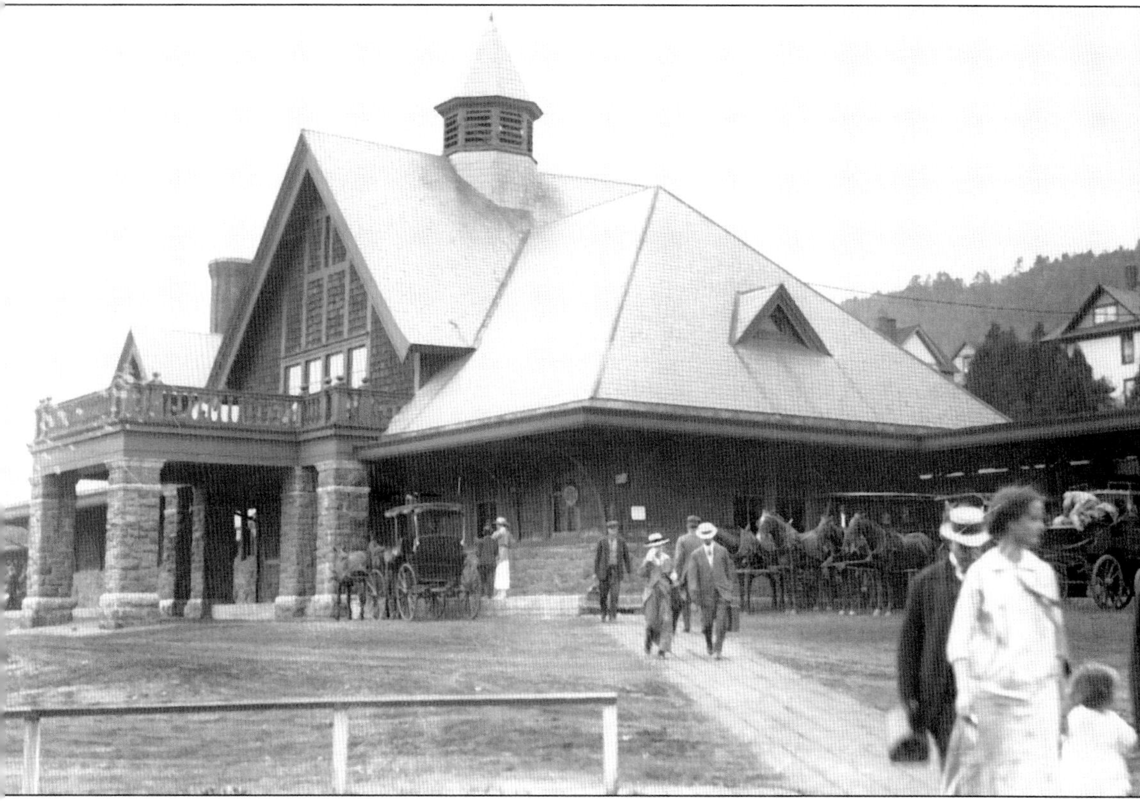

The Delaware & Hudson Railway built Union Depot in 1904. It was the largest station on the line north of Utica, handling up to 18 to 20 trains per day during its busiest years, 1912 to 1940. The last New York Central passenger train left Union Depot on April 24, 1965, and the station was closed. The Union Depot was restored between 1997 and 1998 and is now the home of the Adirondack Scenic Railroad (HSLW).

These people are waiting for the train on the platform of the Saranac Lake Union Depot in the early 1900s.

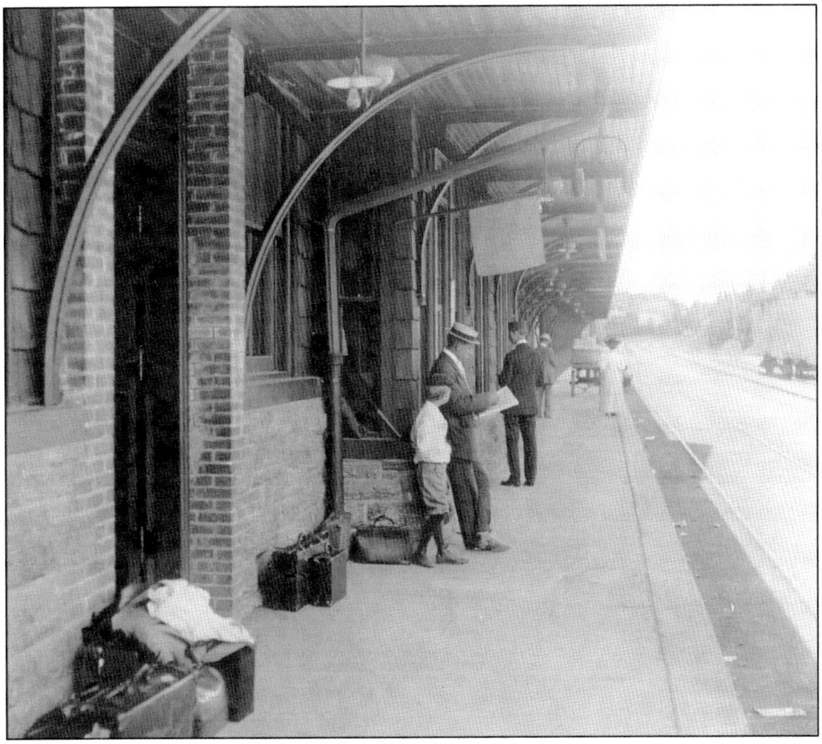

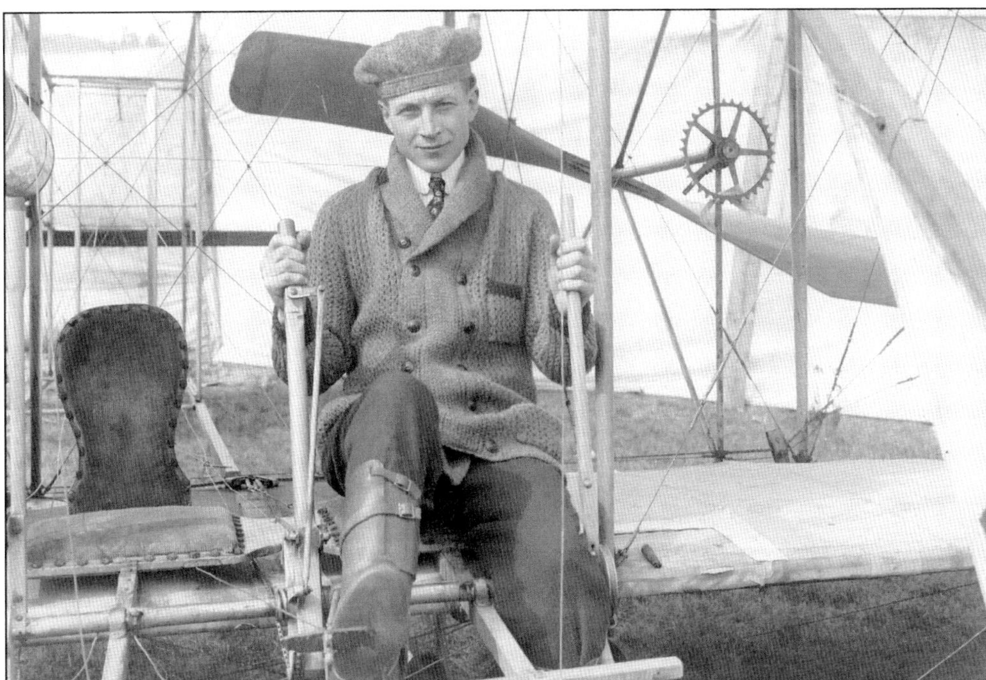

The first airplane ever to visit Saranac Lake landed near the edge of town on Bloomingdale Avenue on October 10, 1912. This is the pilot of that first plane, George A. Gray of Boston, Massachusetts.

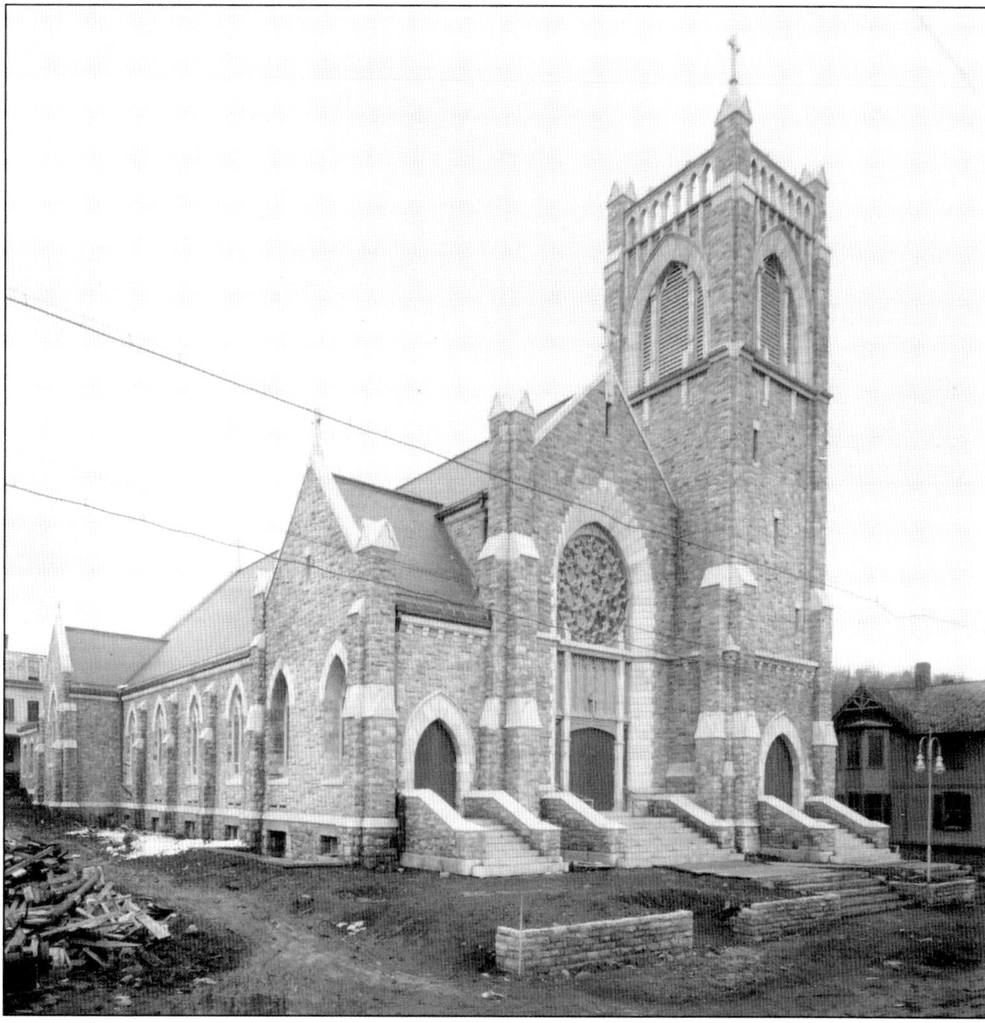

Max H. Westhoff, of the local firm Coulter and Westhoff, designed the second St. Bernard's Church. The cornerstone was laid in 1910, and this picture was taken a year later in 1911 before the construction site was cleaned up after completion. Adirondack Architectural Heritage calls the Vermont marble building a late example of High Victorian Gothic style. This church burned on December 5, 1967.

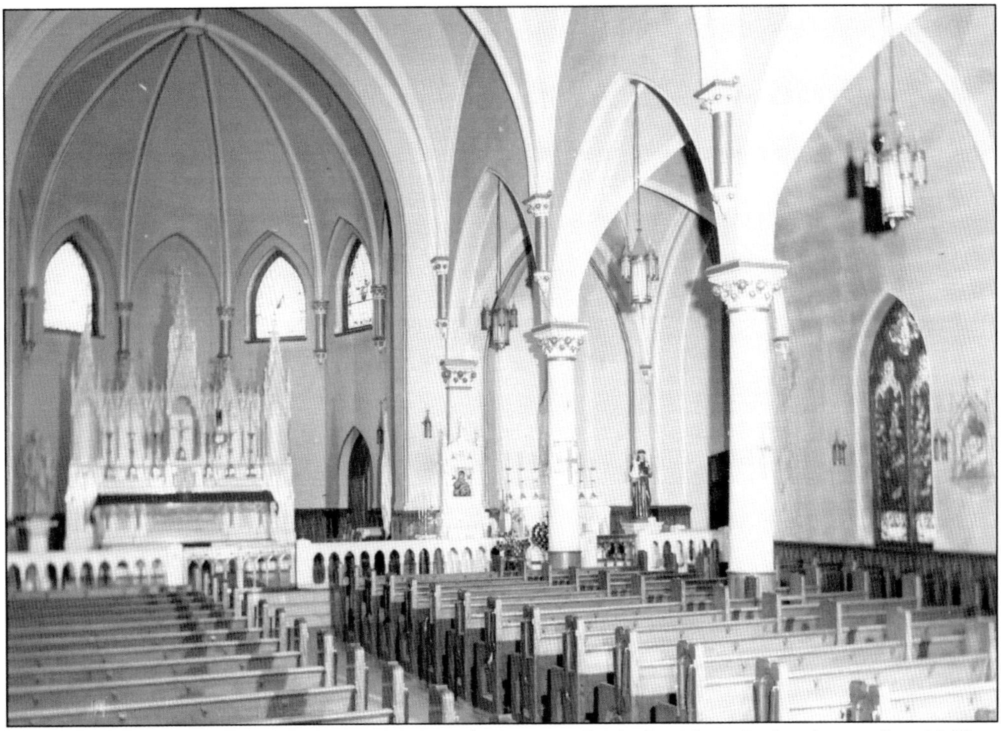

This is the interior of the second St. Bernard's Roman Catholic Church that burned in 1967.

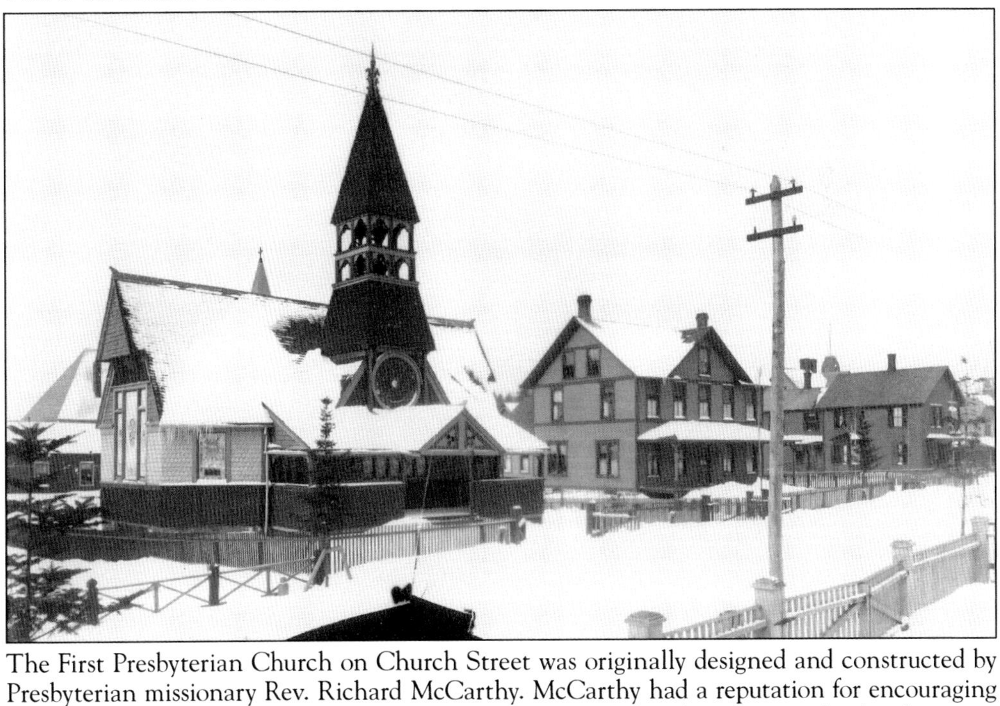

The First Presbyterian Church on Church Street was originally designed and constructed by Presbyterian missionary Rev. Richard McCarthy. McCarthy had a reputation for encouraging congregations in his Adirondack Missionary region to build churches. He is credited with getting new churches built in Childwold, Indian Carry, Lake Clear, and Brandon, among other locations between 1889 and 1905.

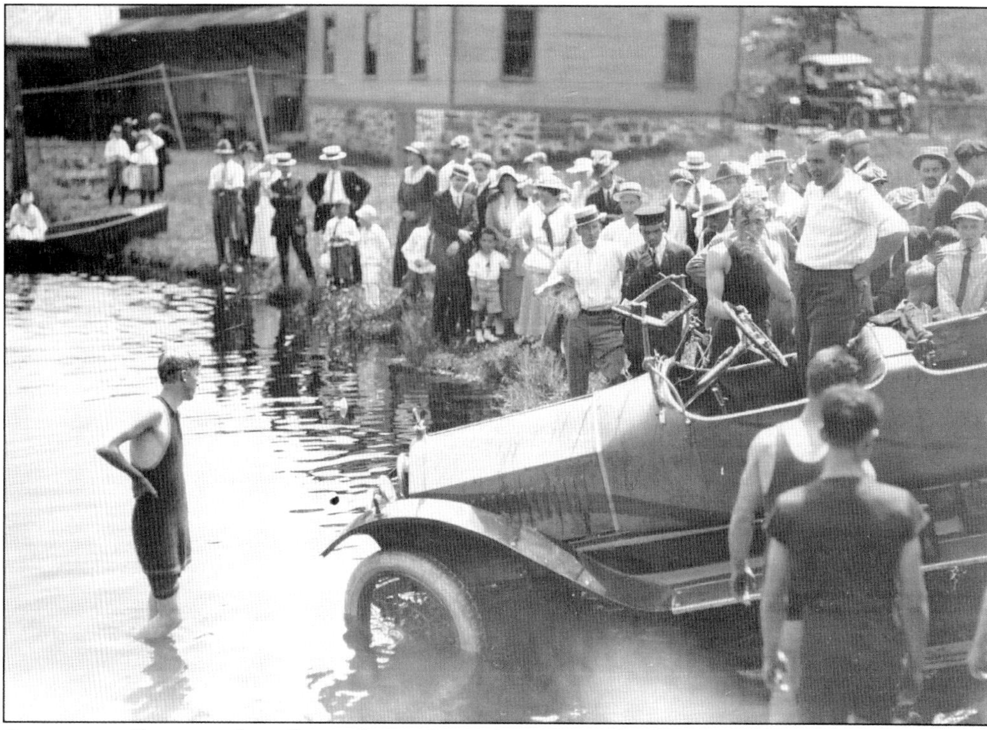

Cars were still new to the village when a driver forgot to set his hand brake and the car rolled all the way down Blood Hill into Lake Flower on a summer afternoon.

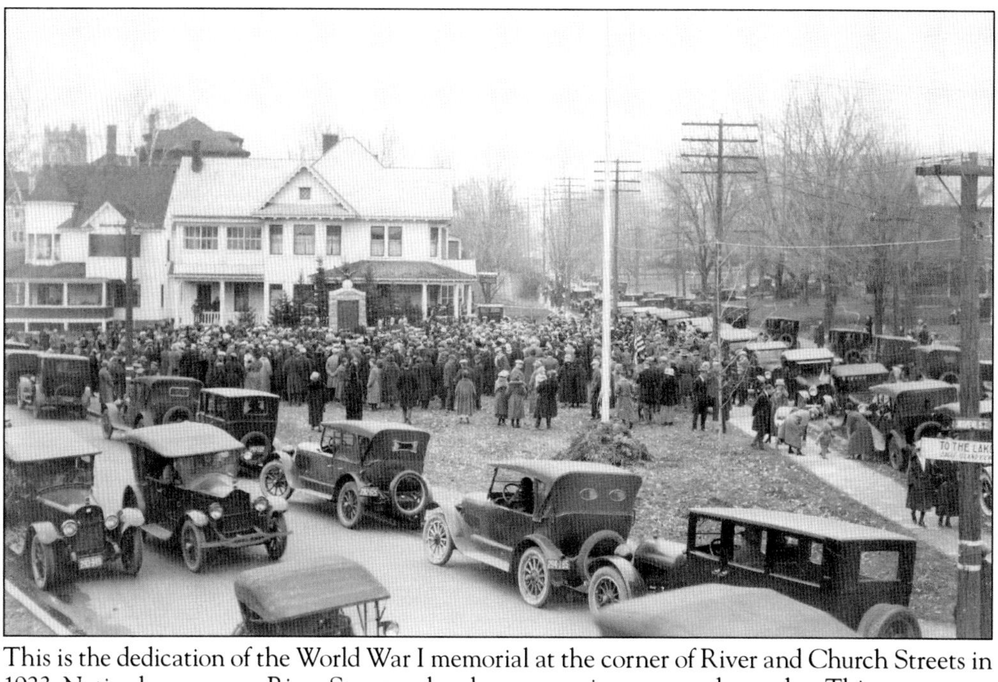

This is the dedication of the World War I memorial at the corner of River and Church Streets in 1923. Notice how narrow River Street—the closer one—is, compared to today. This monument still stands.

Five

Outdoor Recreation

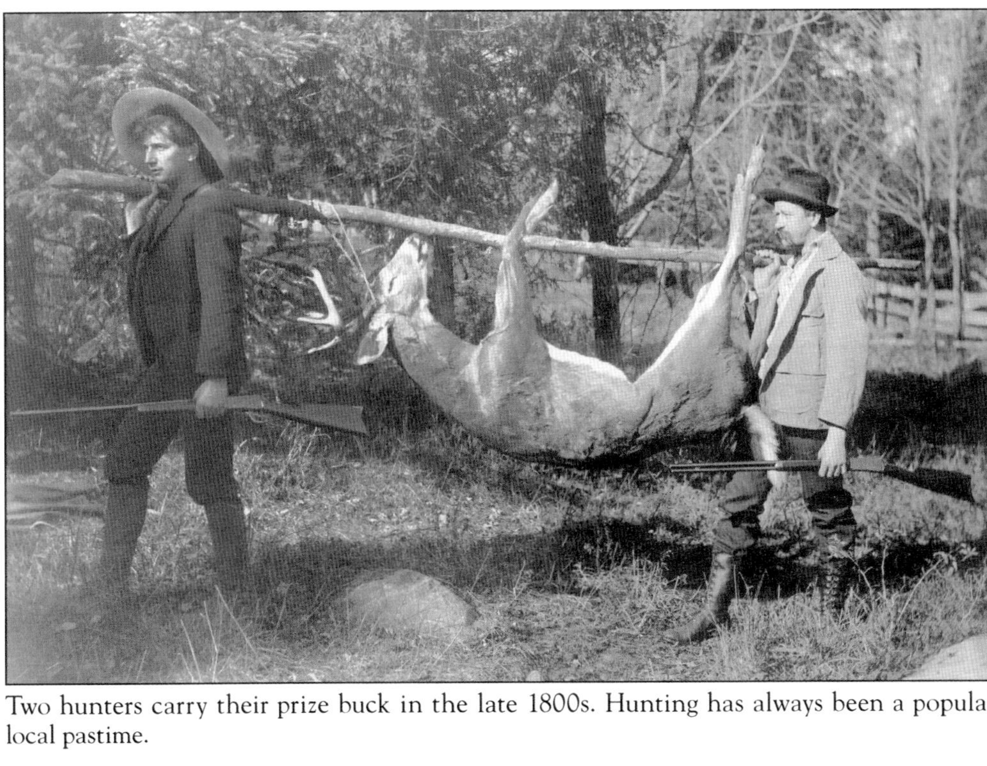

Two hunters carry their prize buck in the late 1800s. Hunting has always been a popular local pastime.

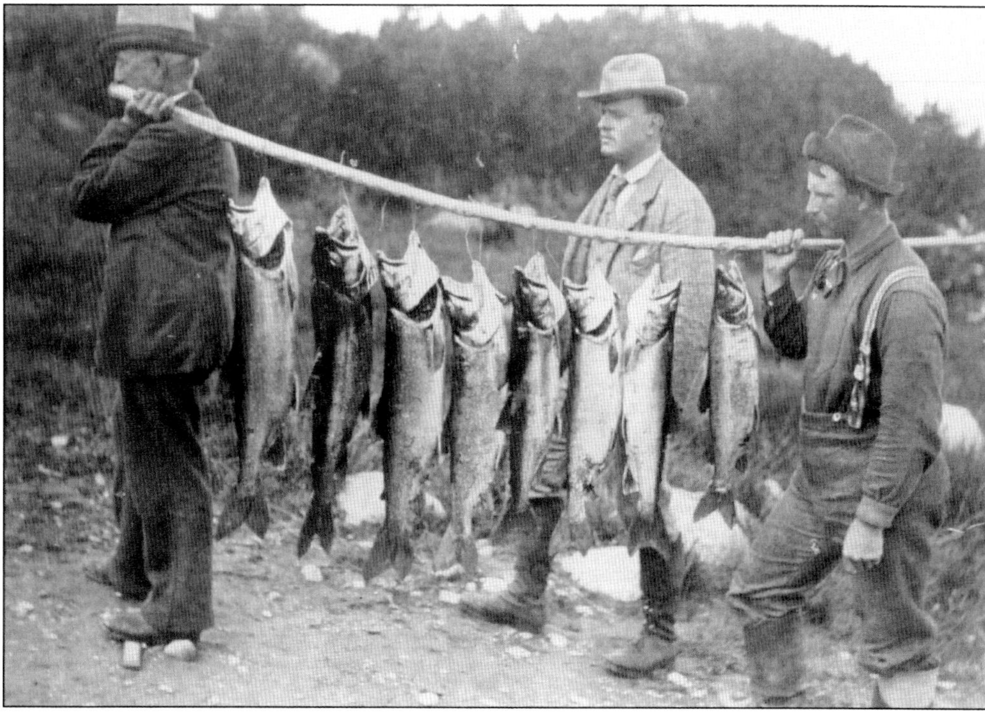

According to the caption on this photograph, these two guides are hauling the day's catch of trout for the sport they were guiding. One can hardly imagine catching one trout this size today.

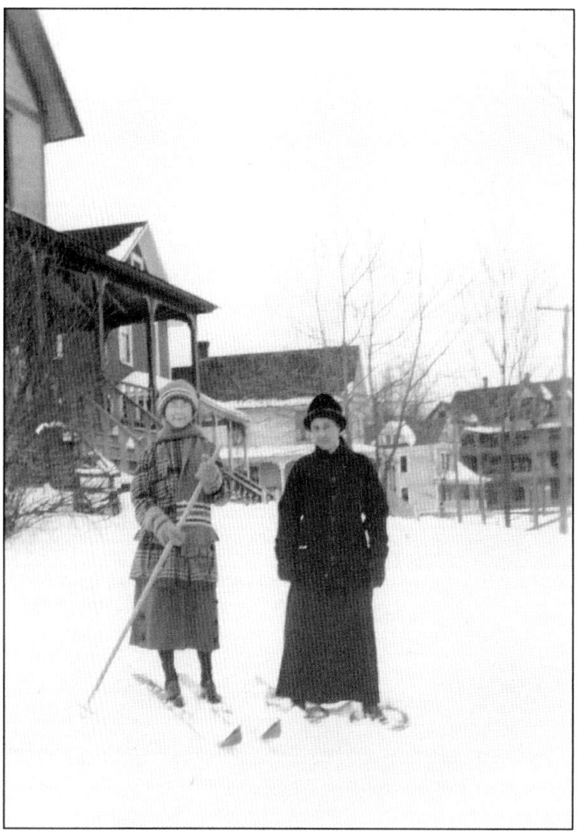

The woman on the left in this 1890s photograph is on skis. She is using one long ski pole instead of two, which was common for the time. The woman on the right is on snowshoes.

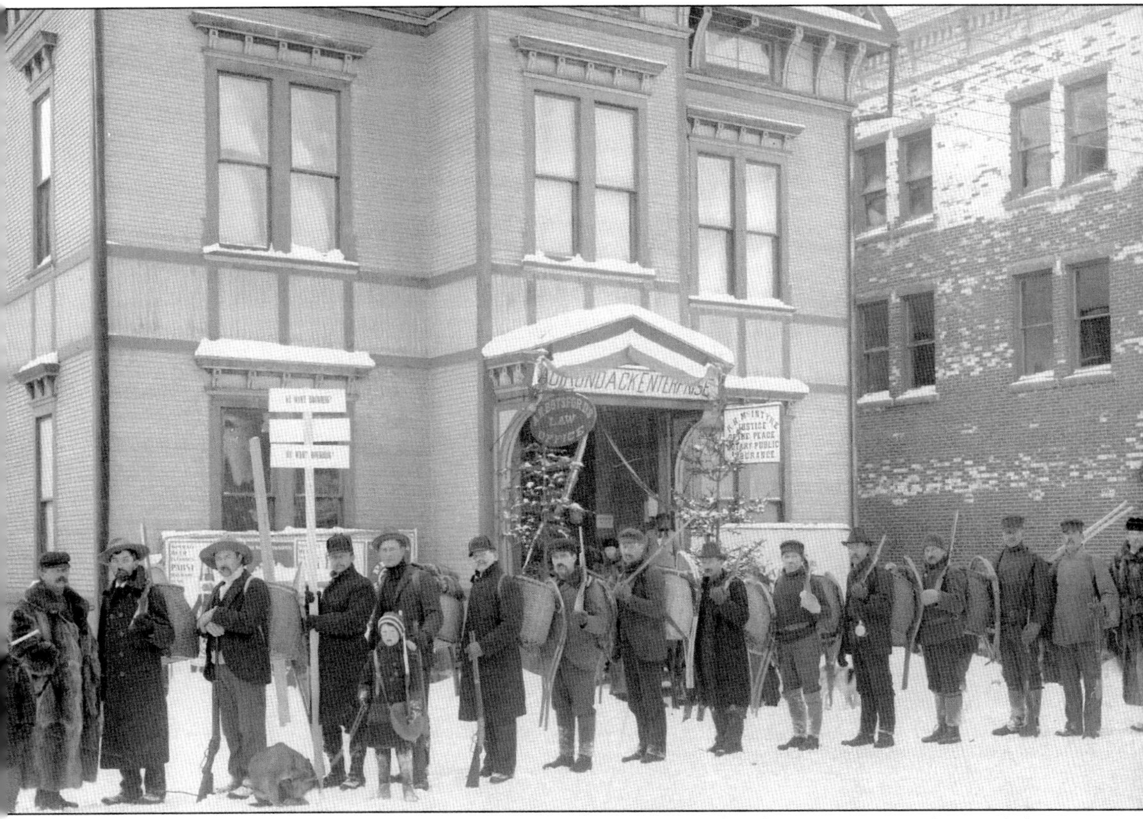

Members of the Adirondack Guides Association are lined up for their portrait in front of the town hall in 1905. The sign that the fourth man from the left is holding reads, "We Want Hounding!" because this hunting practice of driving deer with dogs had been recently outlawed. The *Adirondack Enterprise* sign in the background advertises that the newspaper office was located in the Harrietstown Town Hall at this time.

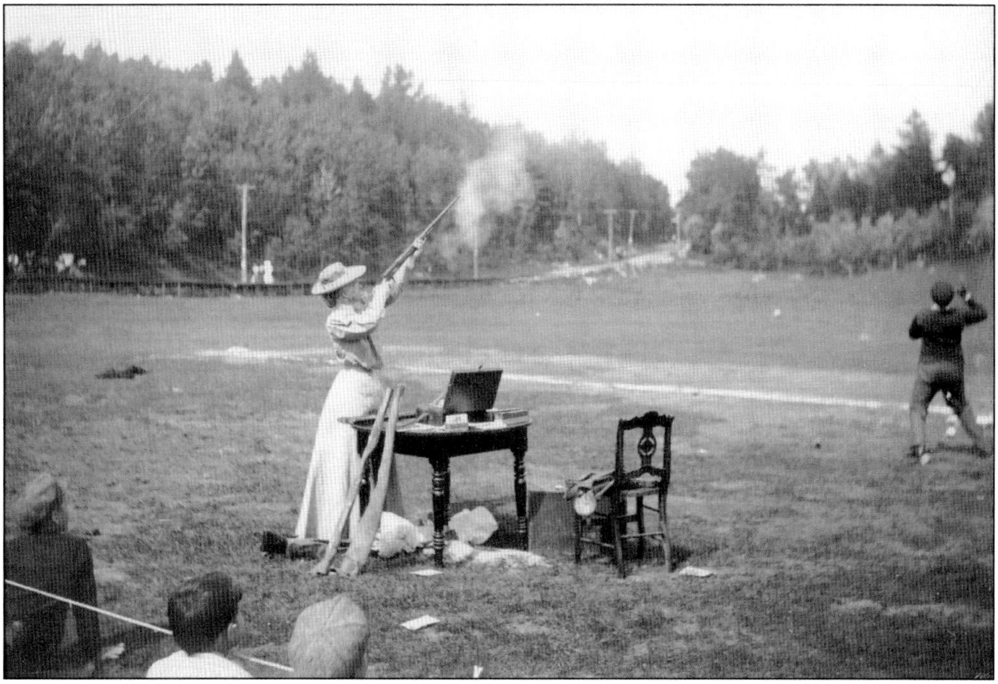

The title of this photograph is *Woman Shooting Trap, Ampersand Avenue*. This appears to be the current location of the soccer and ball field behind the high school also known as Schroeter's Field.

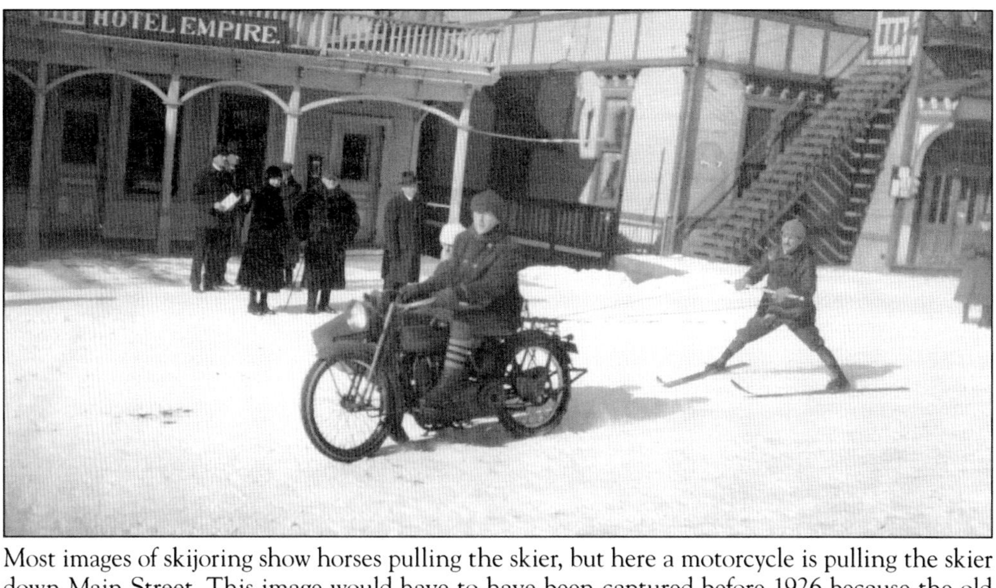

Most images of skijoring show horses pulling the skier, but here a motorcycle is pulling the skier down Main Street. This image would have to have been captured before 1926 because the old town hall in is the background.

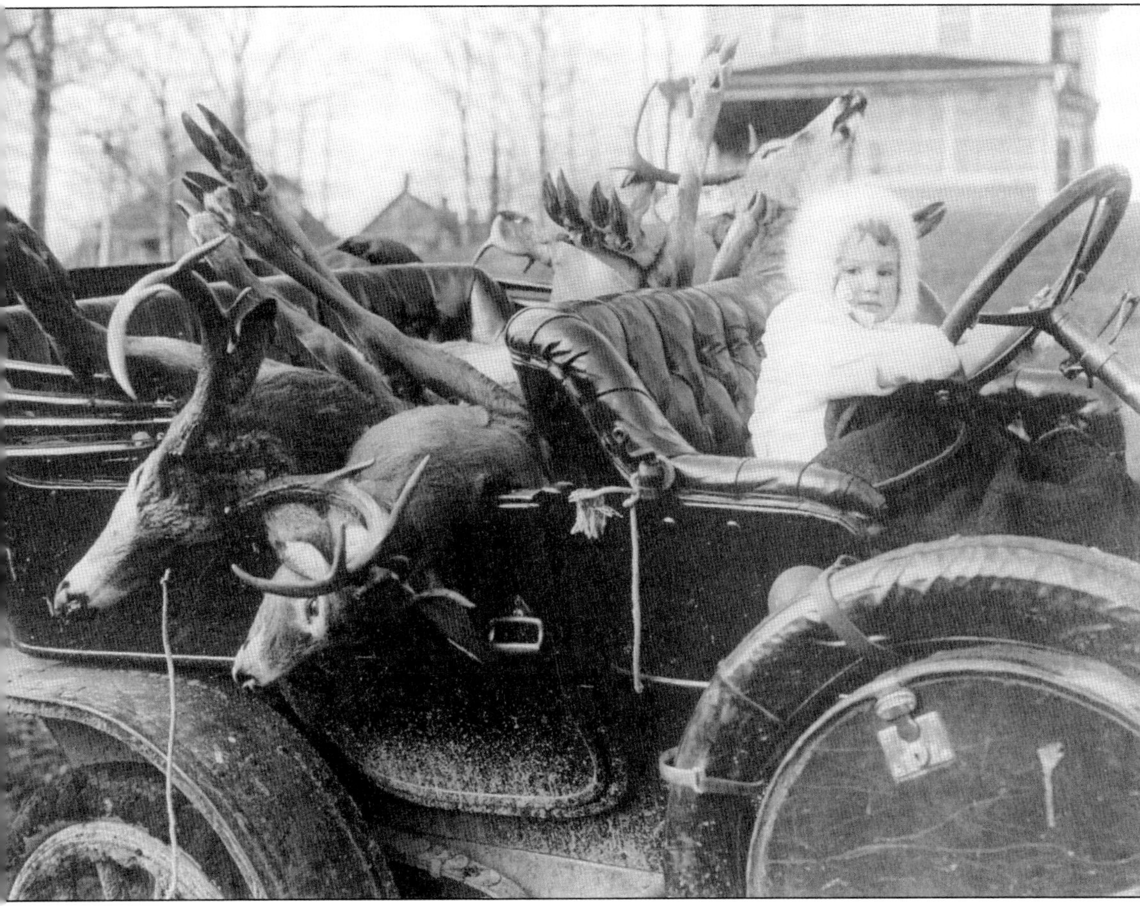

This young hunter had a very good day. There are four bucks arranged in the backseat of this early convertible.

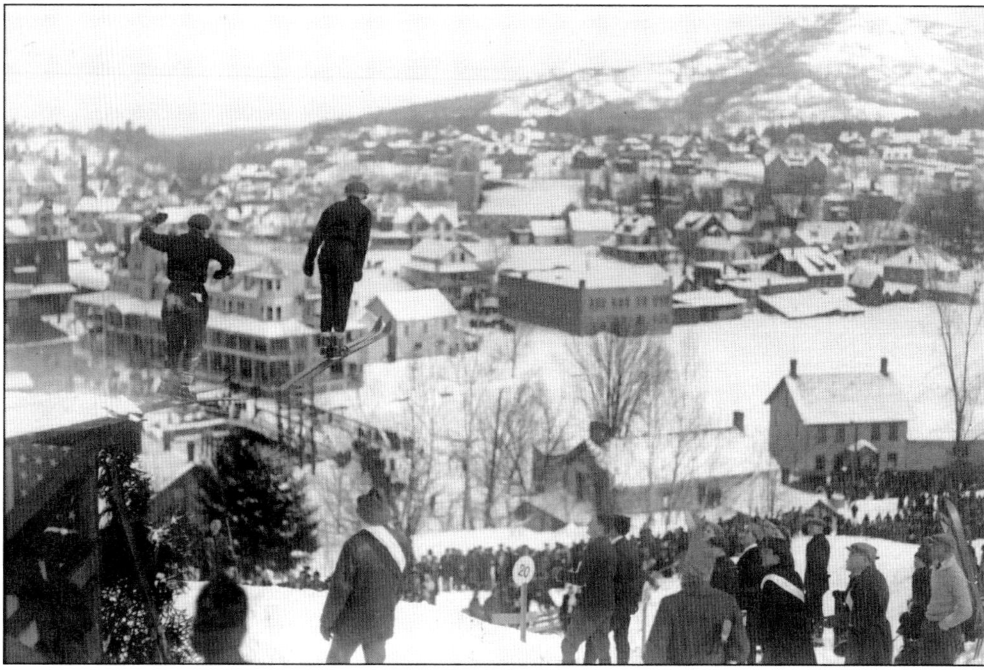

Saranac Lake Ski Club built the jump on Blood's Hill. Two ski jumpers take off at the same time from the Blood Hill slope above Lake Street.

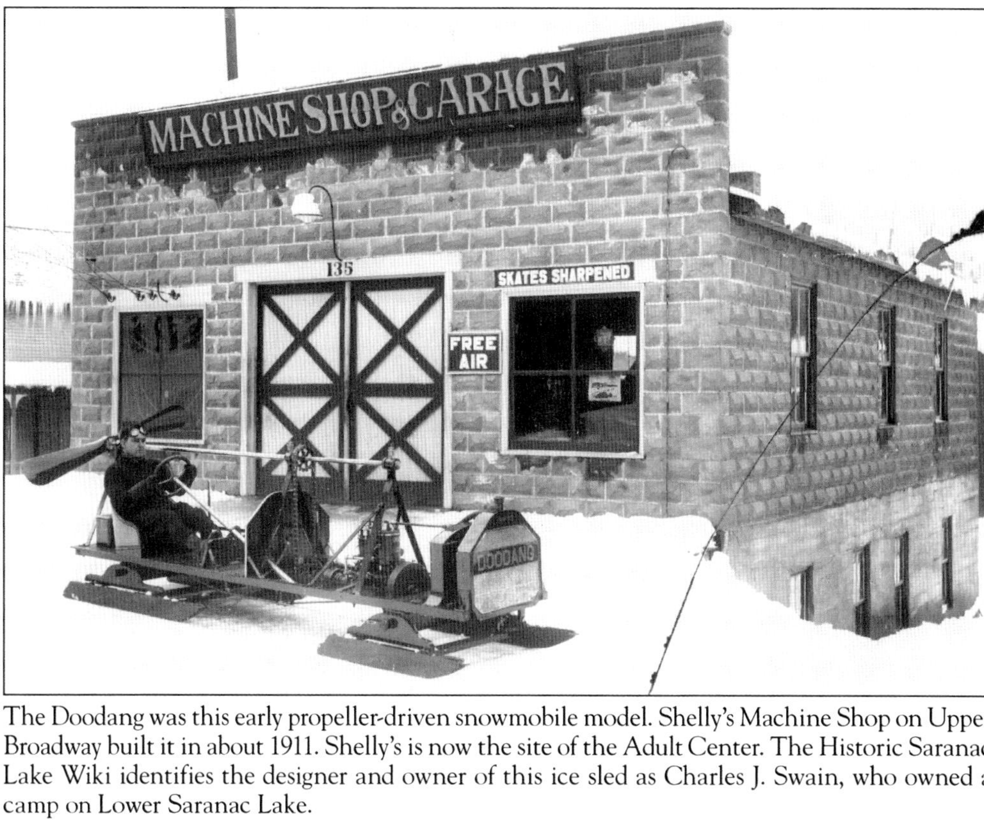

The Doodang was this early propeller-driven snowmobile model. Shelly's Machine Shop on Upper Broadway built it in about 1911. Shelly's is now the site of the Adult Center. The Historic Saranac Lake Wiki identifies the designer and owner of this ice sled as Charles J. Swain, who owned a camp on Lower Saranac Lake.

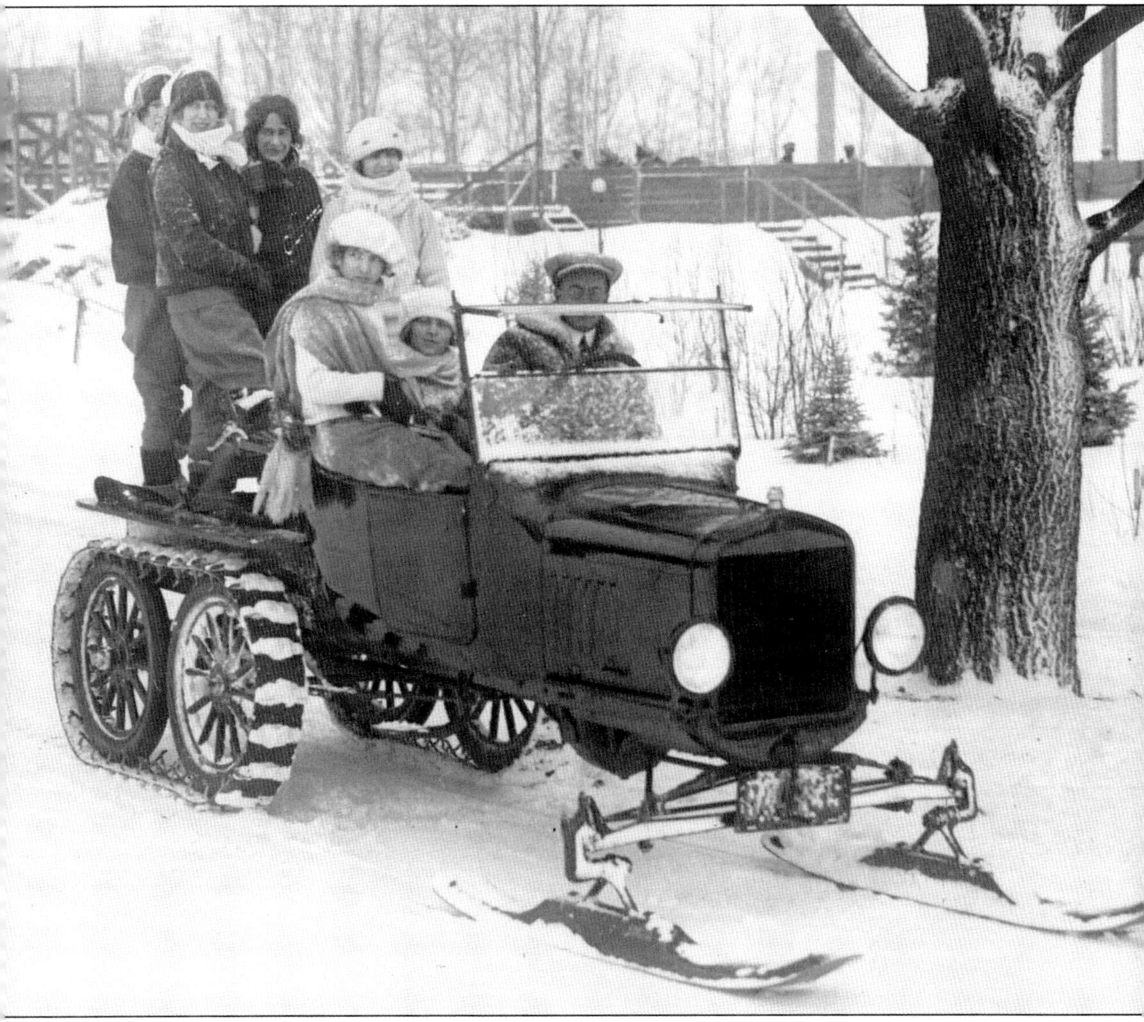

This 1910 snow car is another early attempt at a snowmobile. It came complete with skis instead of front tires.

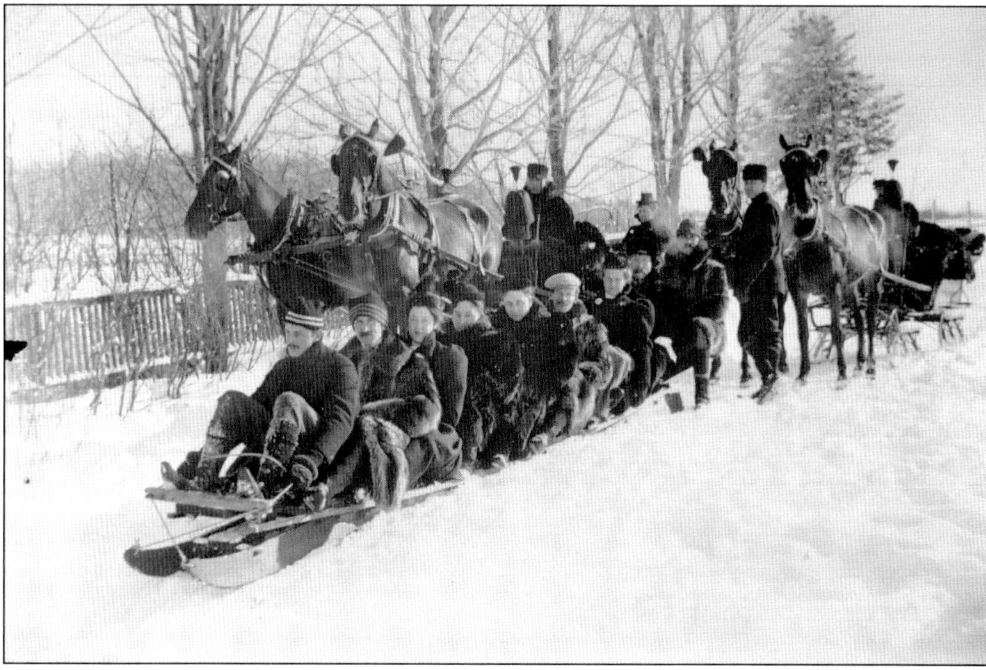

These nine people are posing on an early-20th-century sled. (Courtesy of Paul Smith's College.)

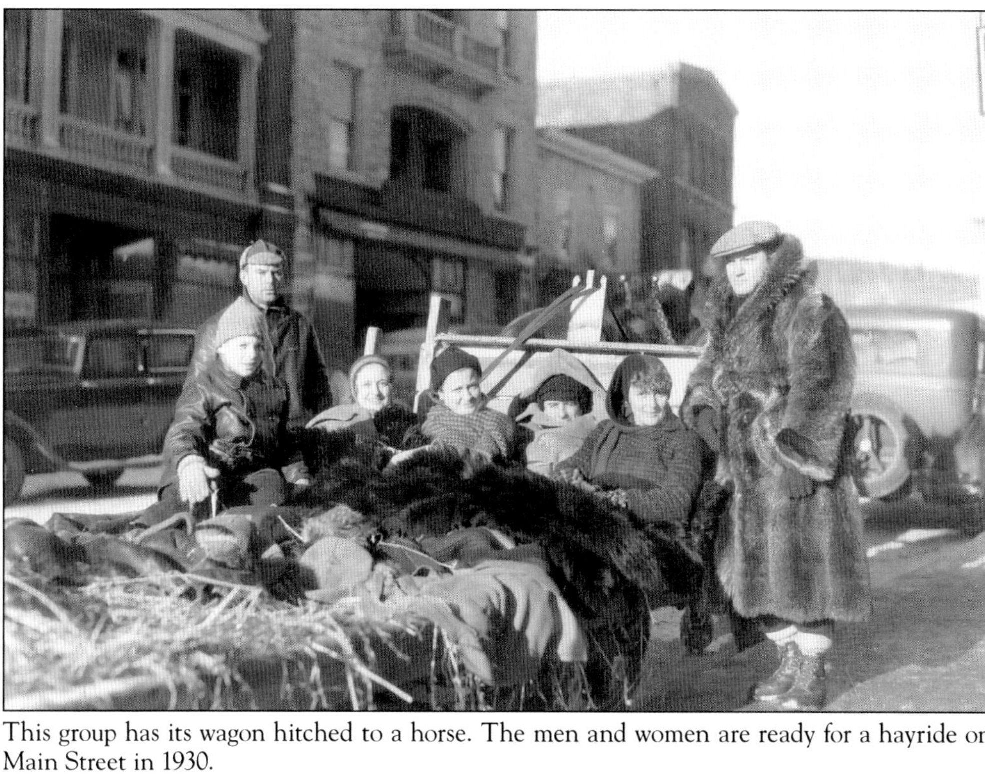

This group has its wagon hitched to a horse. The men and women are ready for a hayride on Main Street in 1930.

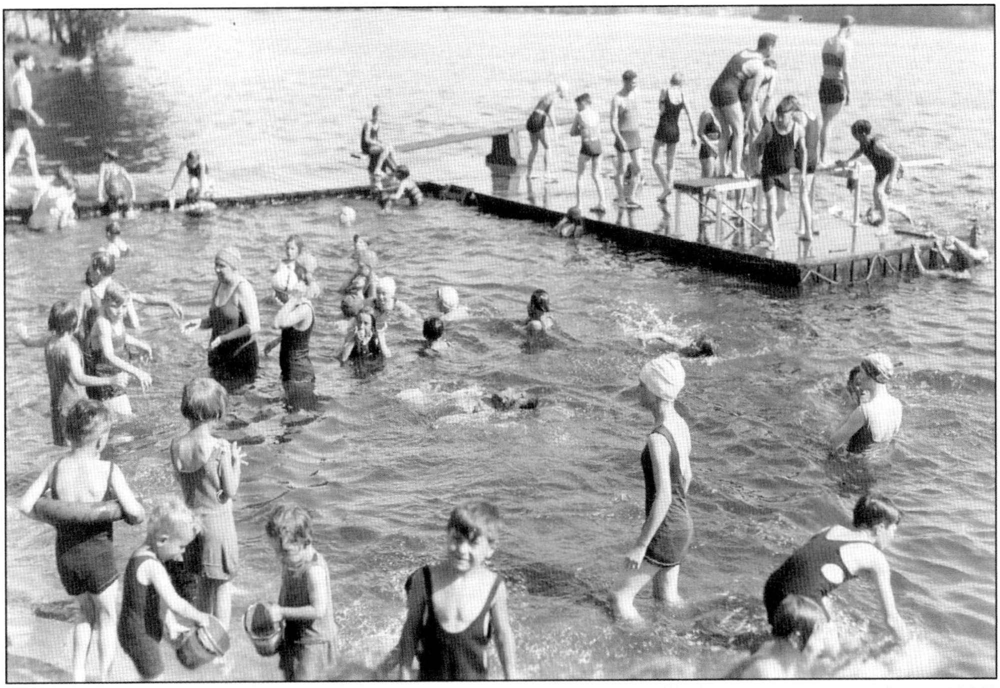

Prescott Park was established on the shores of Lake Flower off of River Street in about 1925. Village Improvement Society founding member Mary R. Prescott donated the land to establish the park and swimming beach (HSLW). This photograph is from about 1930.

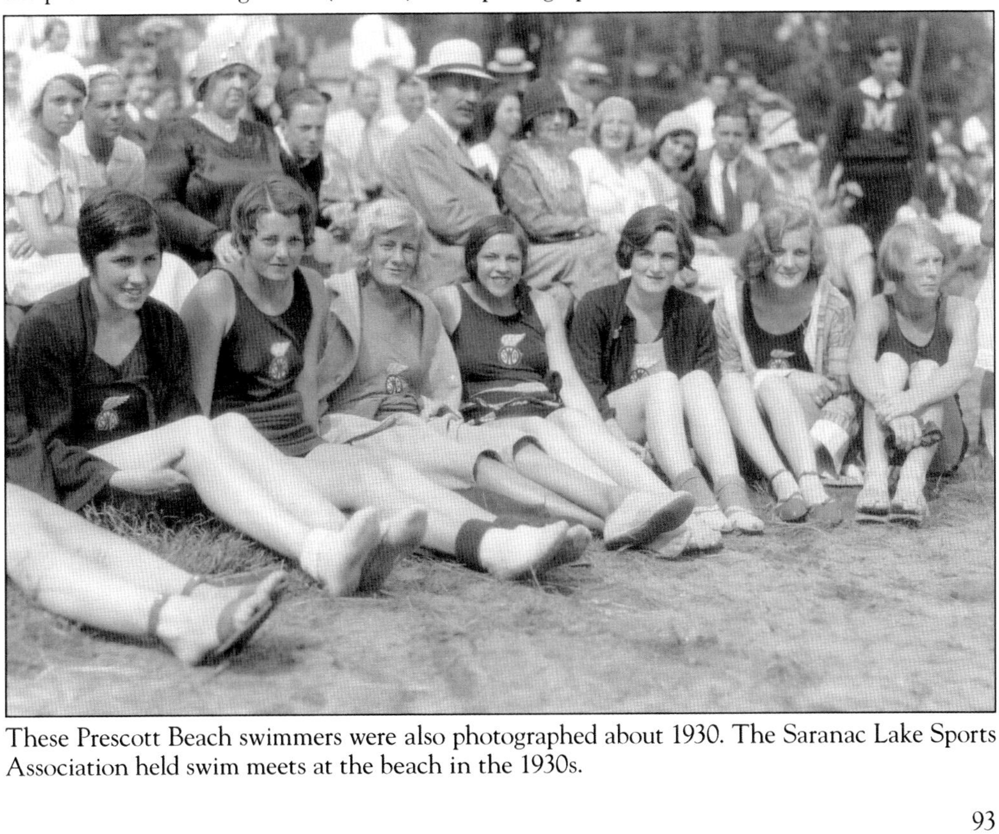

These Prescott Beach swimmers were also photographed about 1930. The Saranac Lake Sports Association held swim meets at the beach in the 1930s.

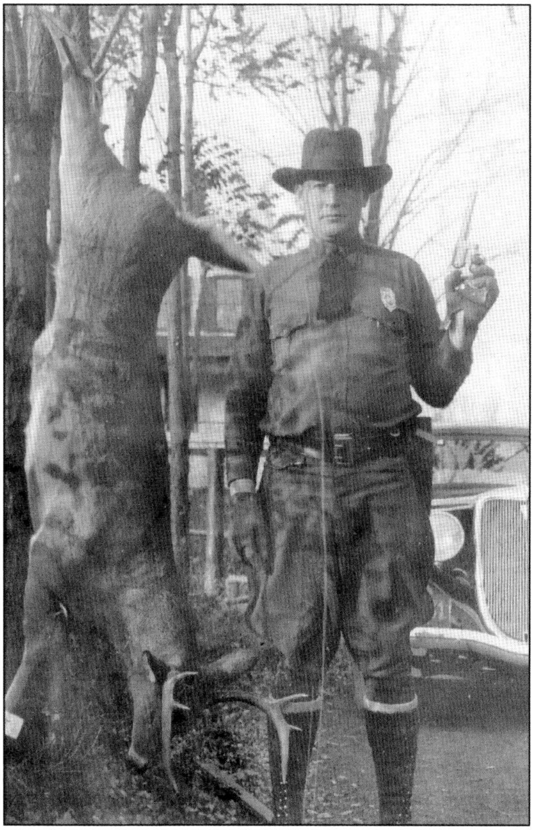

This 1934 image shows an unidentified local game protector with a deer he shot using the pistol he is holding. (Courtesy of Historic Saranac Lake.)

This wolf was caught in the northern Franklin County town of Belmont in February 1934. The game protectors— from left to right, Sheppard, Welch, and Burmaster— are examining it on Main Street. (Courtesy of Historic Saranac Lake.)

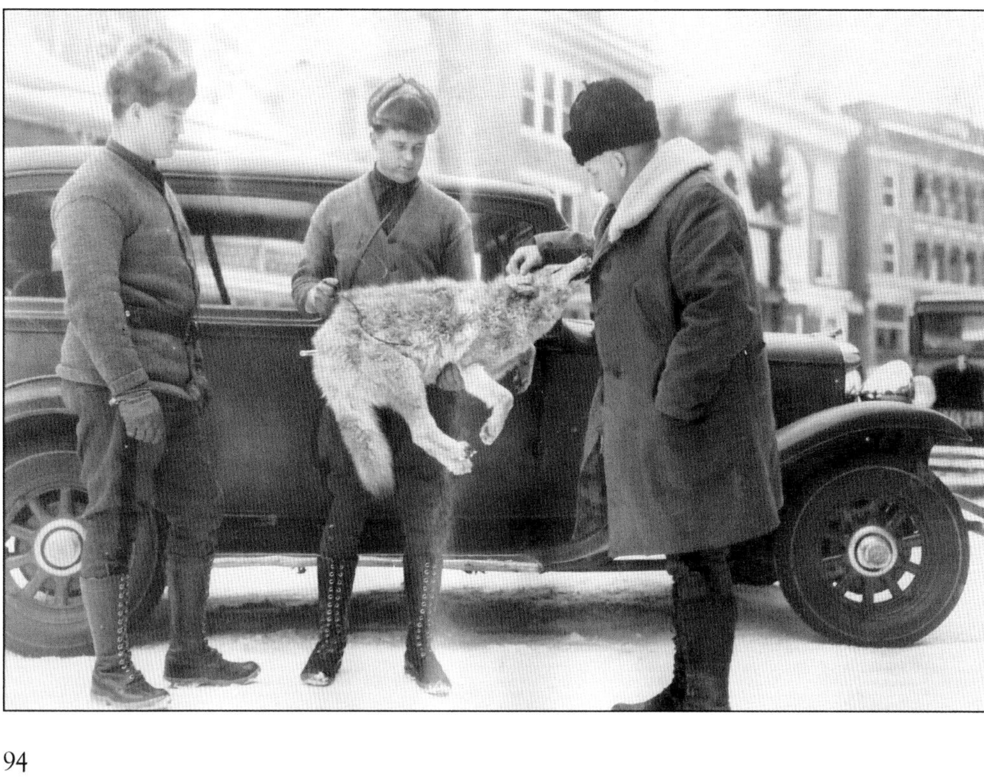

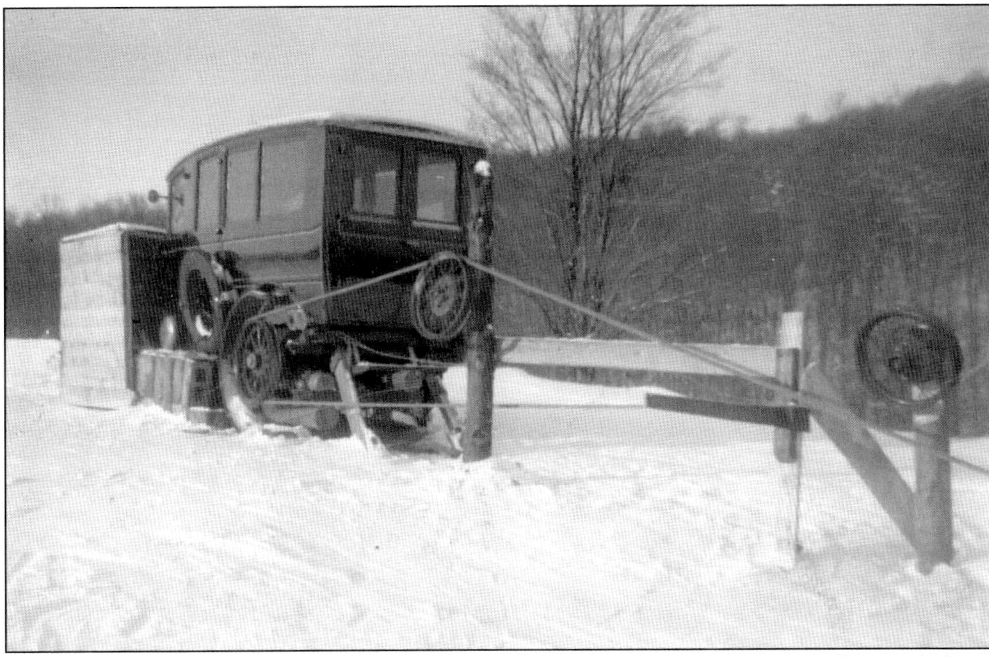

Saranac Lake's first ski tow was located on Better's Hill on Kiwassa Road. A Cunningham ambulance was donated to the Saranac Lake Society in 1921. When the ambulance went out of service, it was sold to Tom Cantwell and Dick Woodruff, and was converted for use as a ski tow. It was sold in 1940 to St. Lawrence University for its ski hill when Cantwell went into the service.

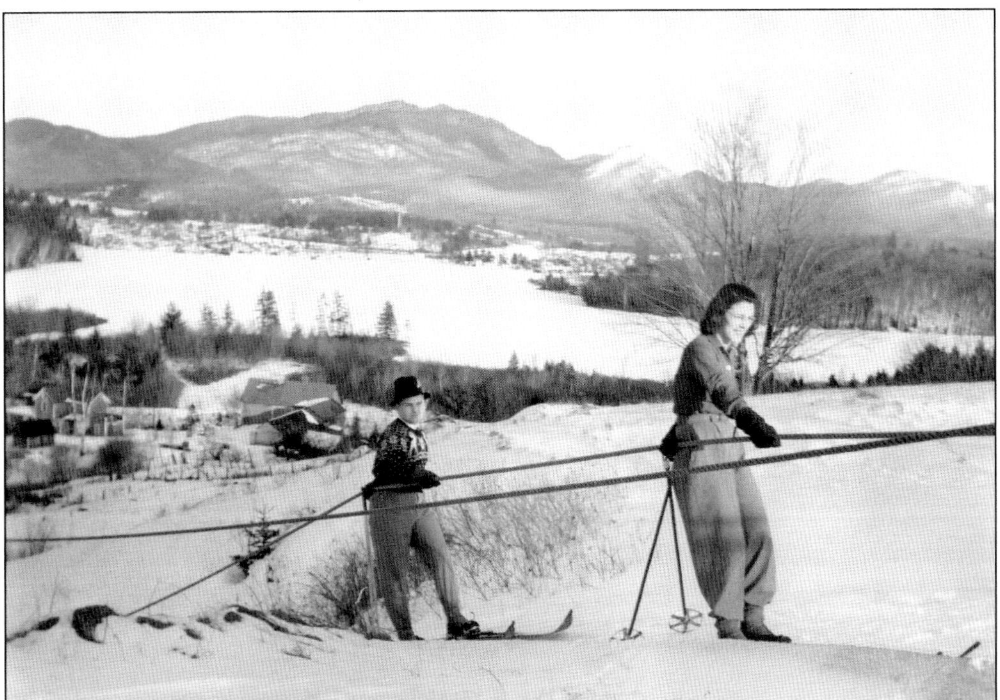

These skiers are using the rope tow on Better's Hill ski hill in about 1940. Maybe the old ambulance is pulling them. On the left is Tom Cantwell, but the woman is unidentified.

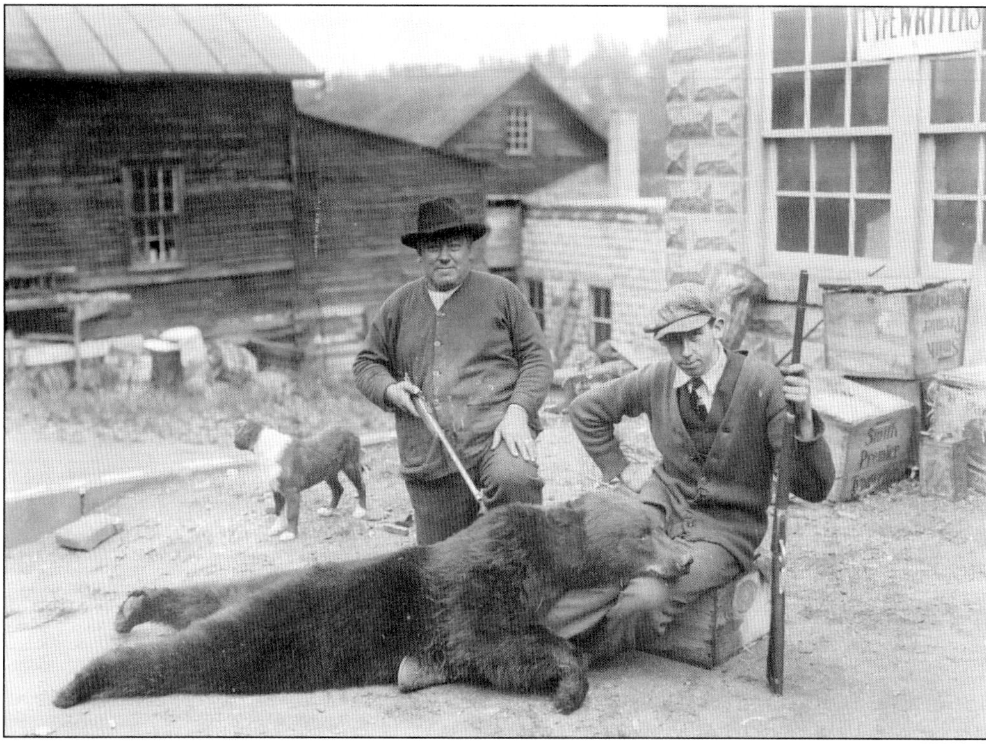

These hunters are proud to get their picture taken with the bear they just bagged.

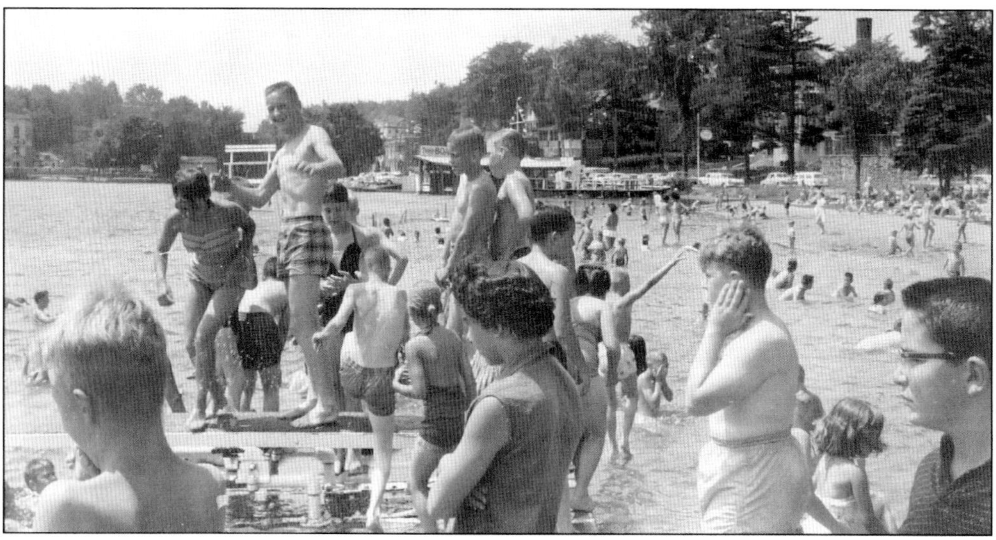

Prescott Beach on Lake Flower continued to be a popular village swimming spot into the early 1960s. The young man standing in the checkered trunks is Henry Homberger, with Thomas Boat Landing in the background. A controversy started over moving the beach to Lake Colby that has not subsided. A study was being made in the summer of 2013 to determine the feasibility of moving the beach back to the Prescott site.

Six

Sports and Teams

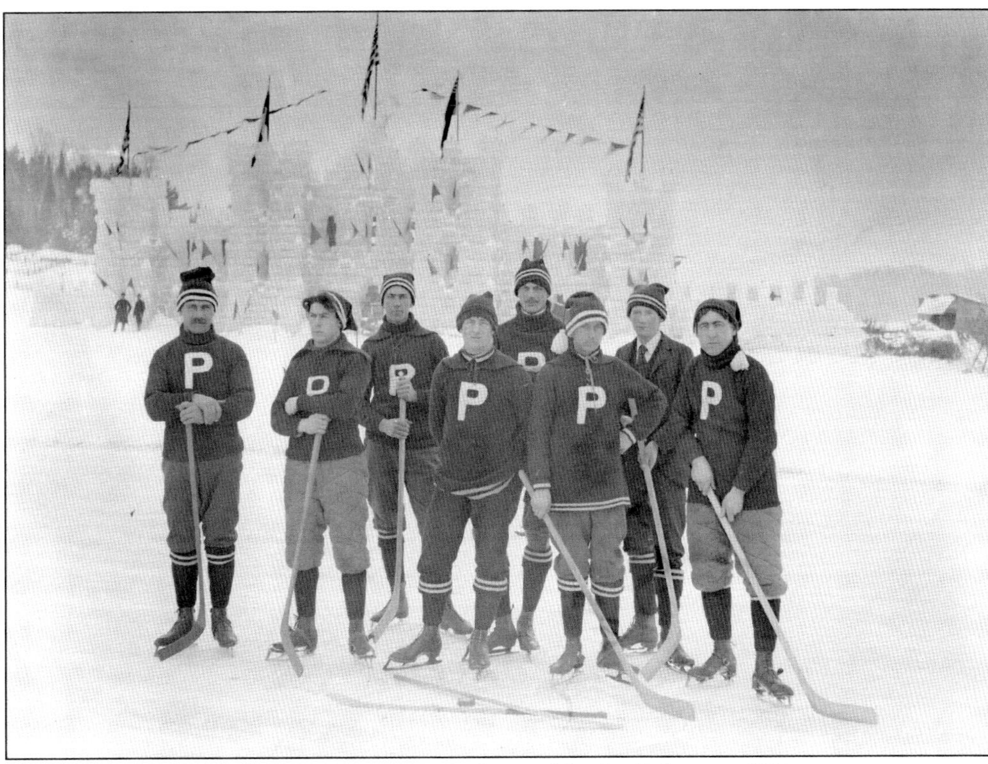

The Pontiac Club Hockey Team is posing in front of the Ice Palace in 1898.

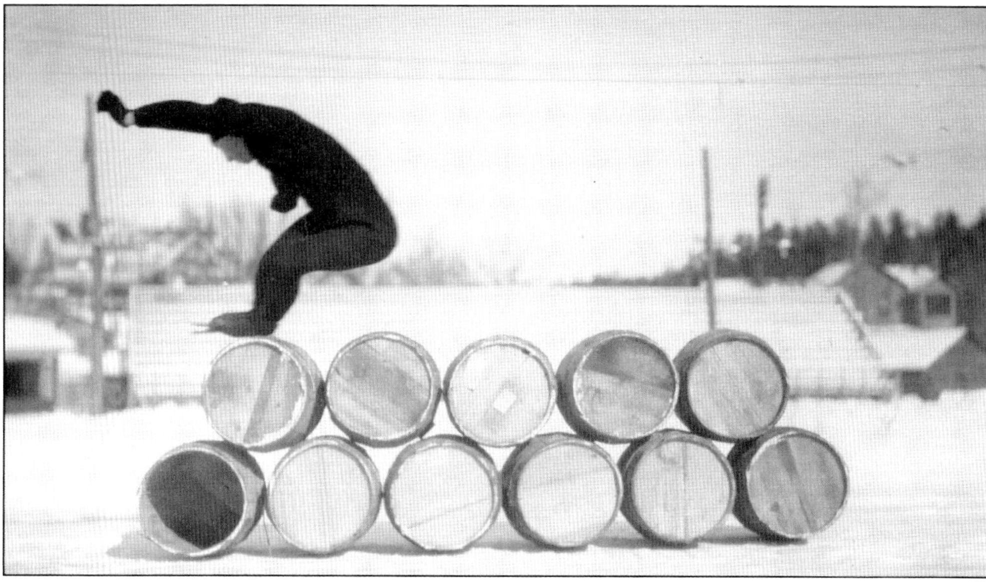

Barrel jumping while on ice skates was a popular national sport in the early 20th century. This jumper is going for a double-decker jump at the Pontiac Rink on Lake Flower in 1915.

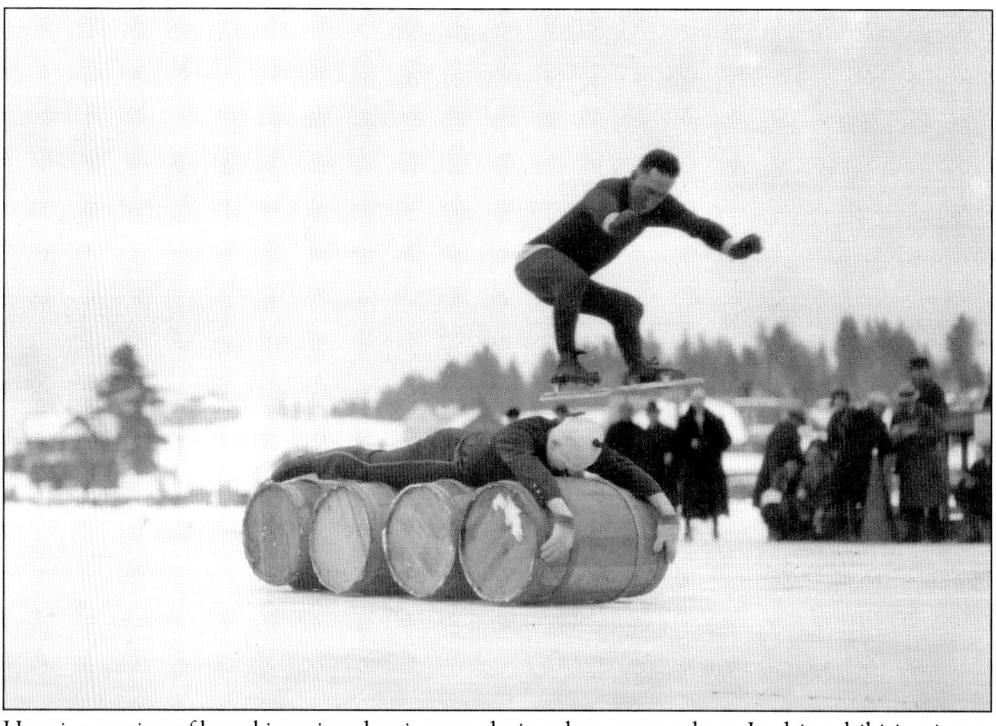

Here is a version of barrel jumping that is more daring than some others. In this exhibition jump, there is a young woman lying on top of the barrels.

Saranac Lake native Edmund Lamy, on the right, was one of America's best speed skaters in the 1910s. He was named a member of the National Speed Skating Museum and Hall of Fame in 1961. He is posing with his brother Ernest, also an excellent skater.

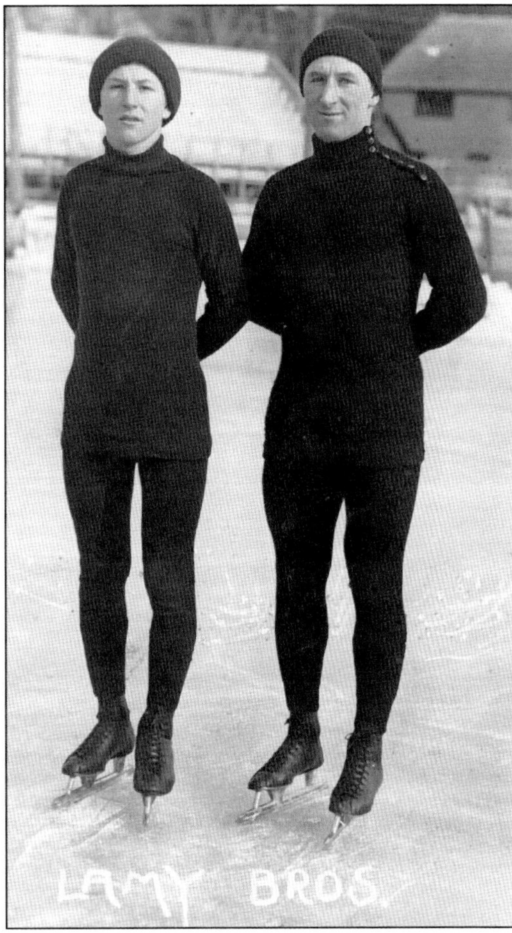

Ed Lamy also became America's premier barrel jumper. He set the first known barrel jumping record at 27 feet and eight inches at Saranac Lake. Here he is jumping in 1923.

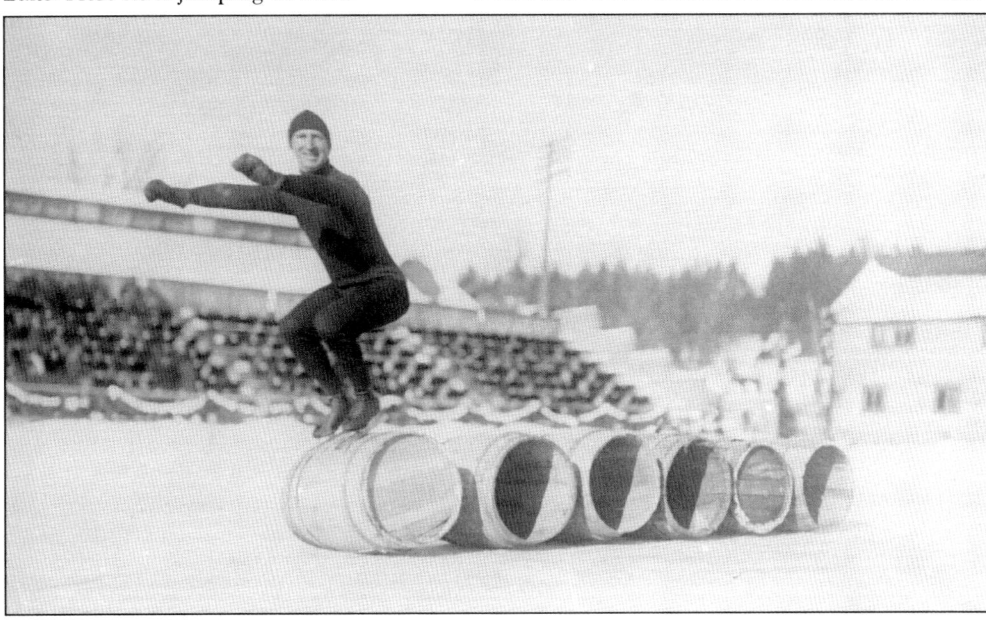

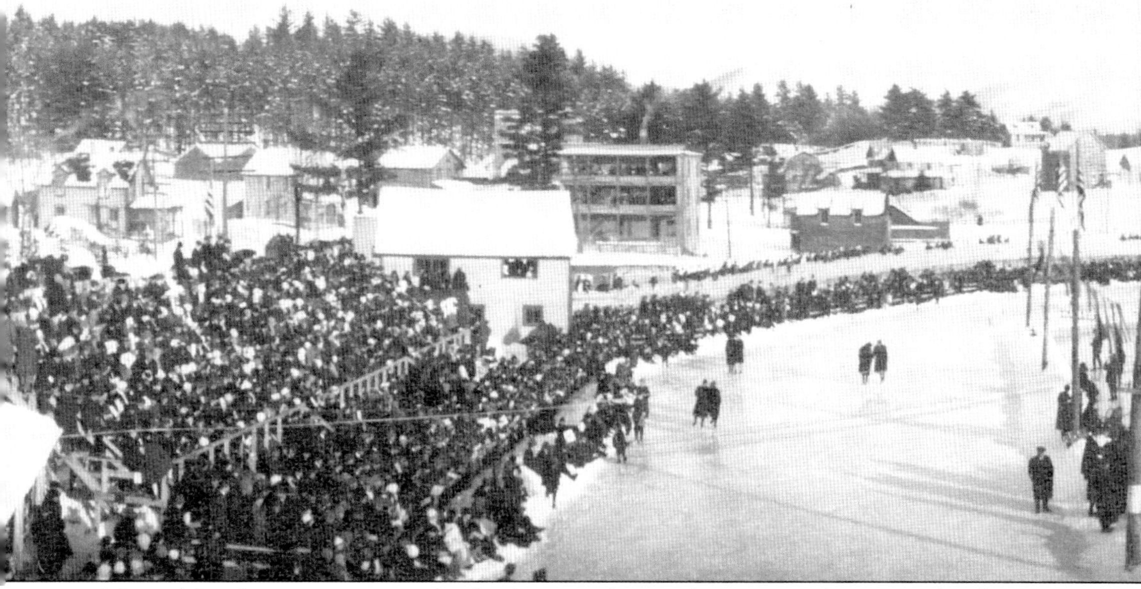

Most of the skating pictures in this book were taken at the Pontiac Skating Rink. The Pontiac hosted regional and national skating races and shows as well as hockey games. It was located on

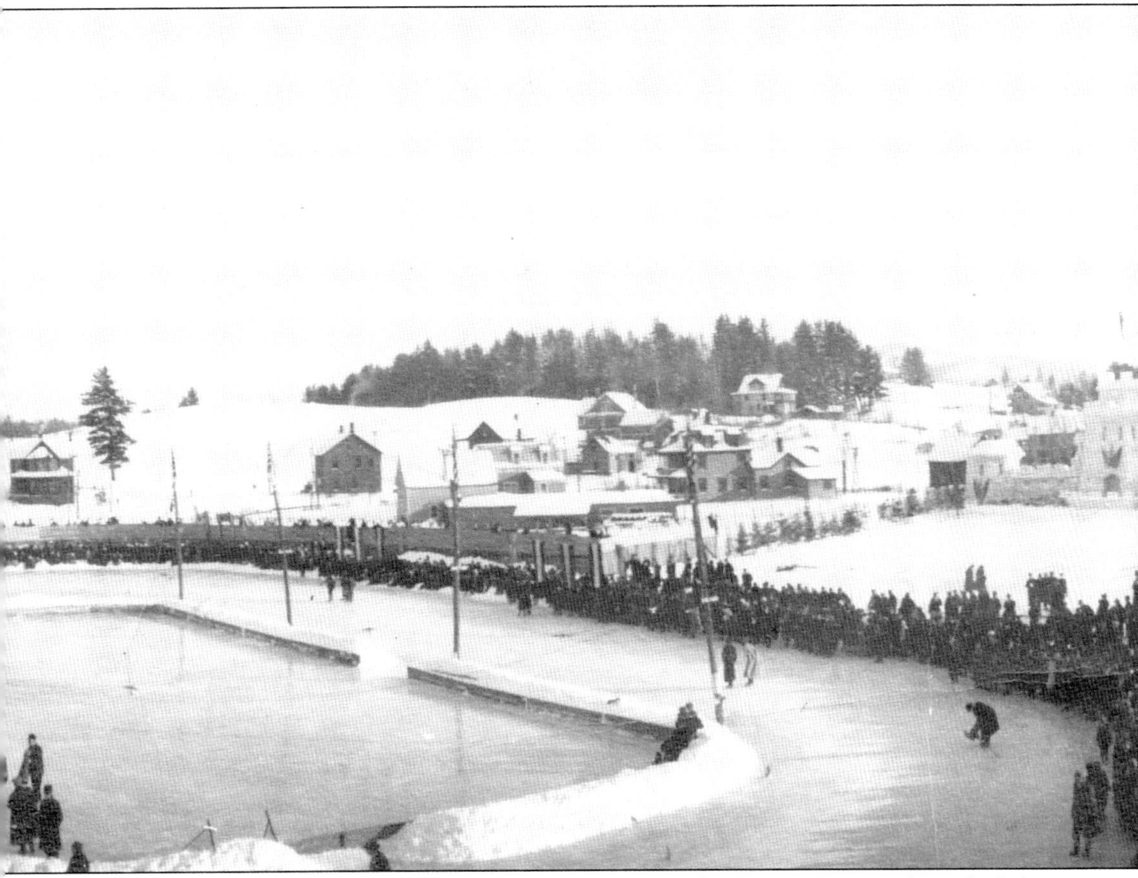

Lake Flower near the intersection of River Street and Lake Flower Avenue. People packed the stands in the early 20th century to watch these events.

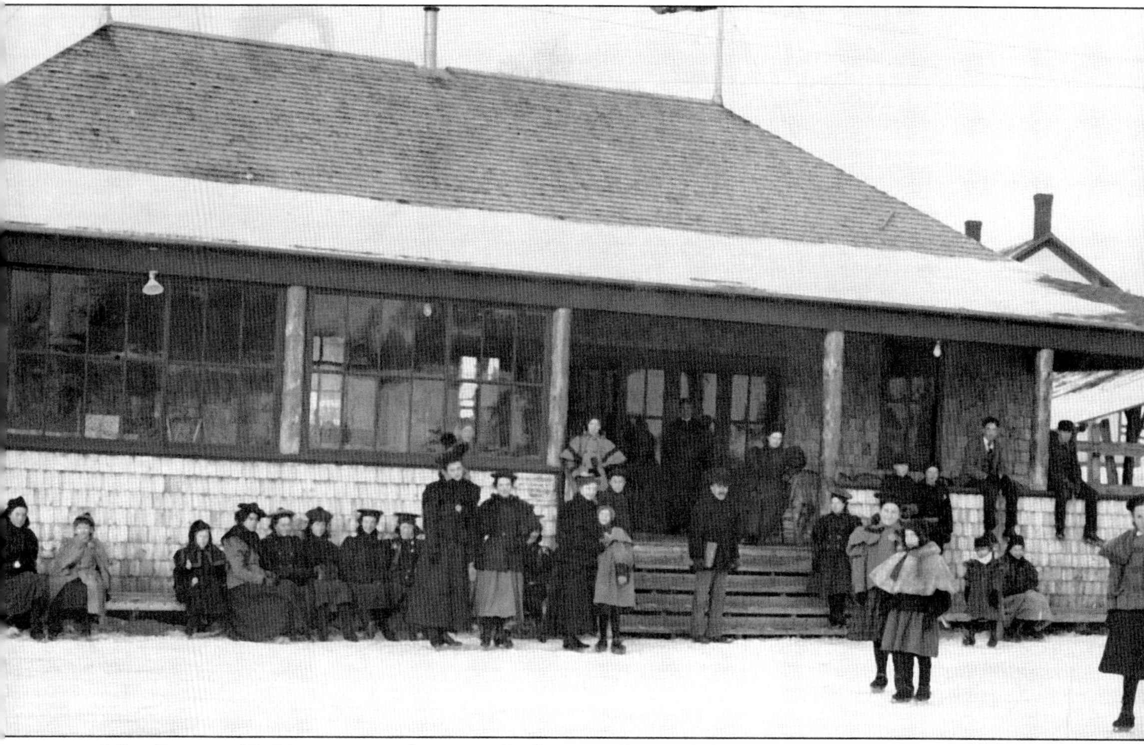

The Pontiac Clubhouse was photographed in 1905. In a February 2013 piece in the *Adirondack Daily Enterprise*, historian Mary Hotaling states that the River Street Clubhouse was on the Lake Flower shore at Pontiac Bay. The site is where the Ice Palace is now constructed every year for Winter Carnival.

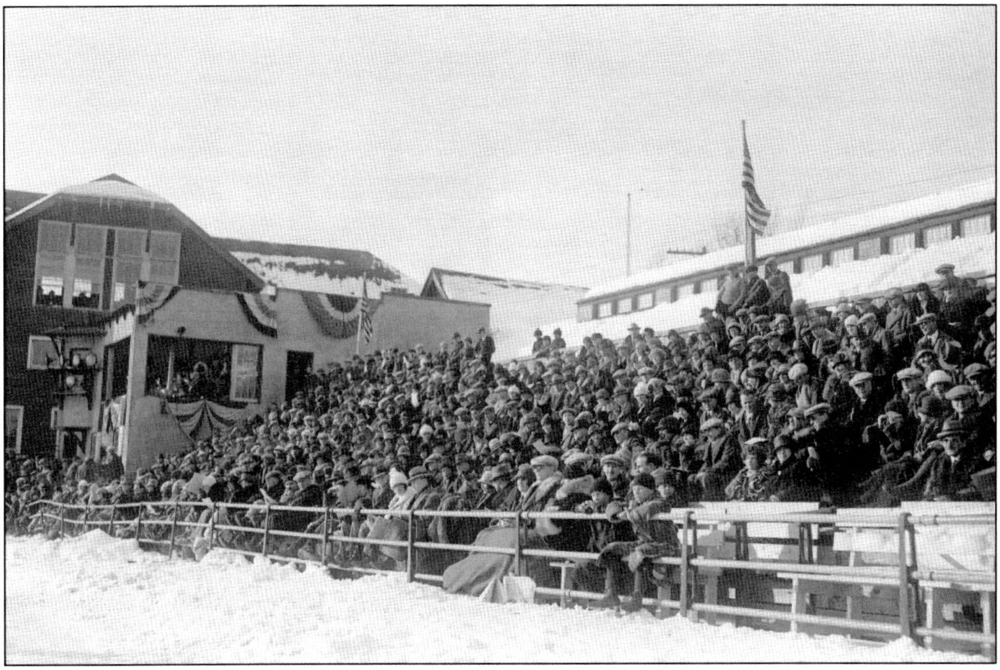

Fans pack the seats at the Pontiac Rink for a day of races in 1925.

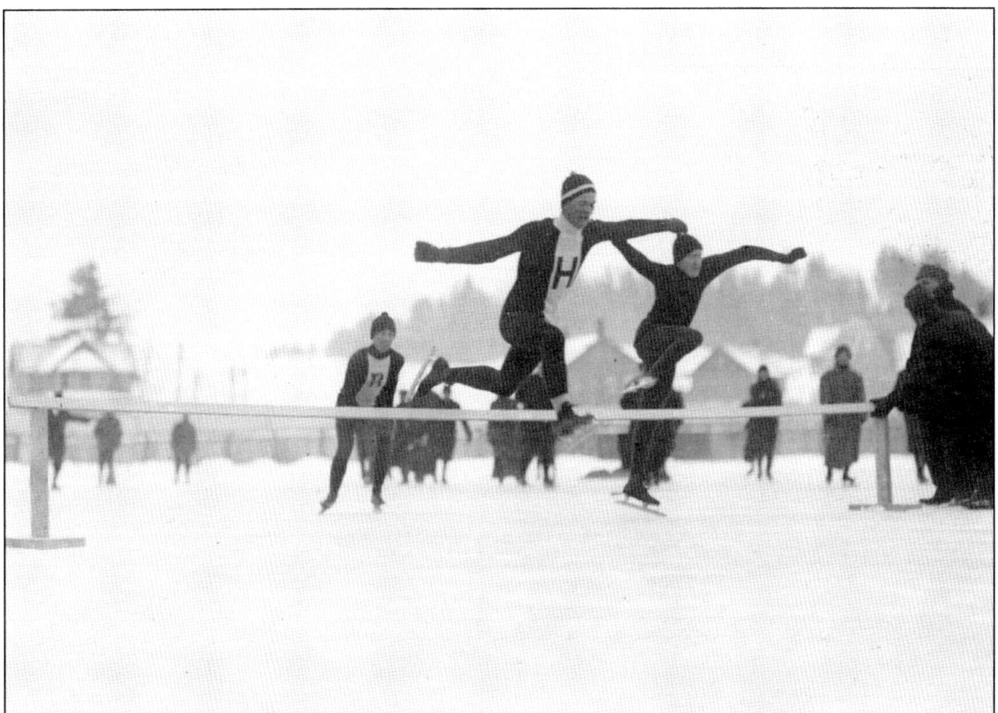

The dangerous event of jumping hurdles in ice-skating races has gone out of style, but it was very popular in 1917.

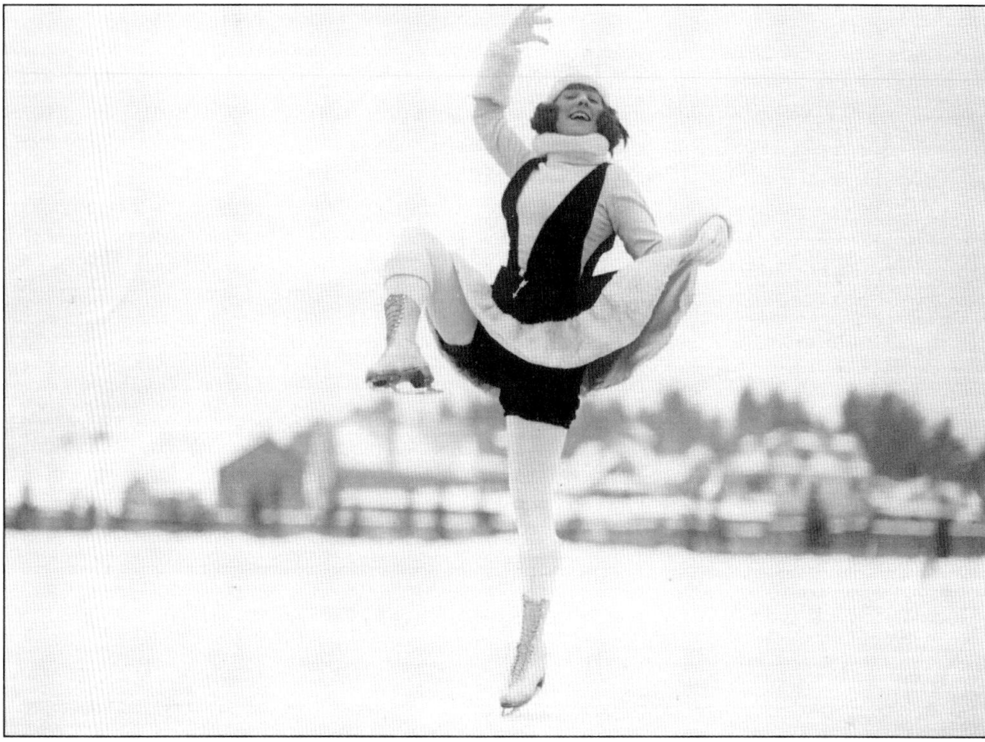

In addition to racing and jumping, the Pontiac Rink also hosted figure skating events. This skater is practicing before her event in 1927.

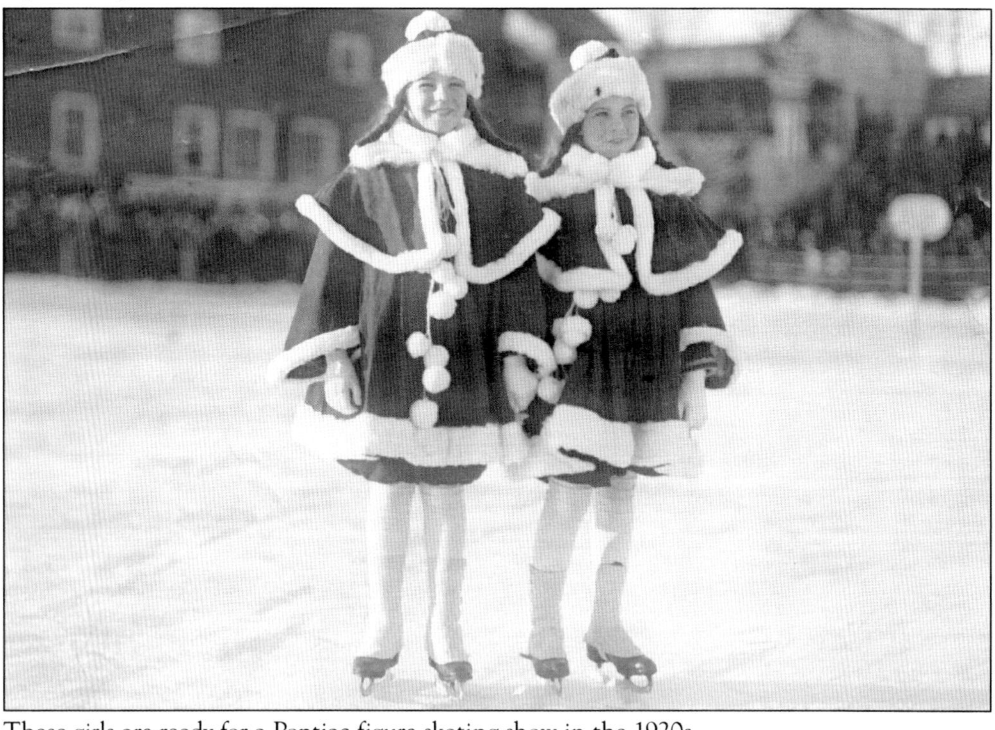

These girls are ready for a Pontiac figure skating show in the 1920s.

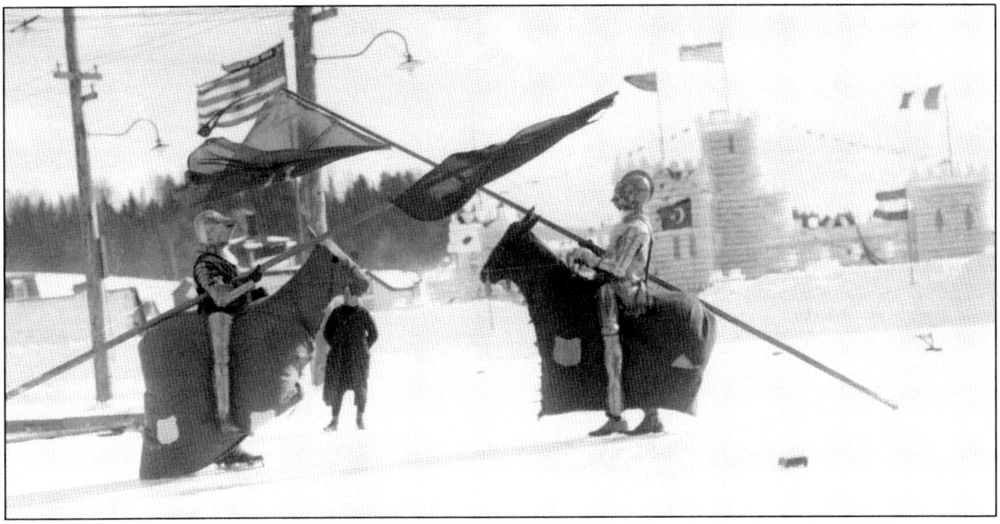

These skating knights are also putting on their show at the Pontiac Rink in the 1920s.

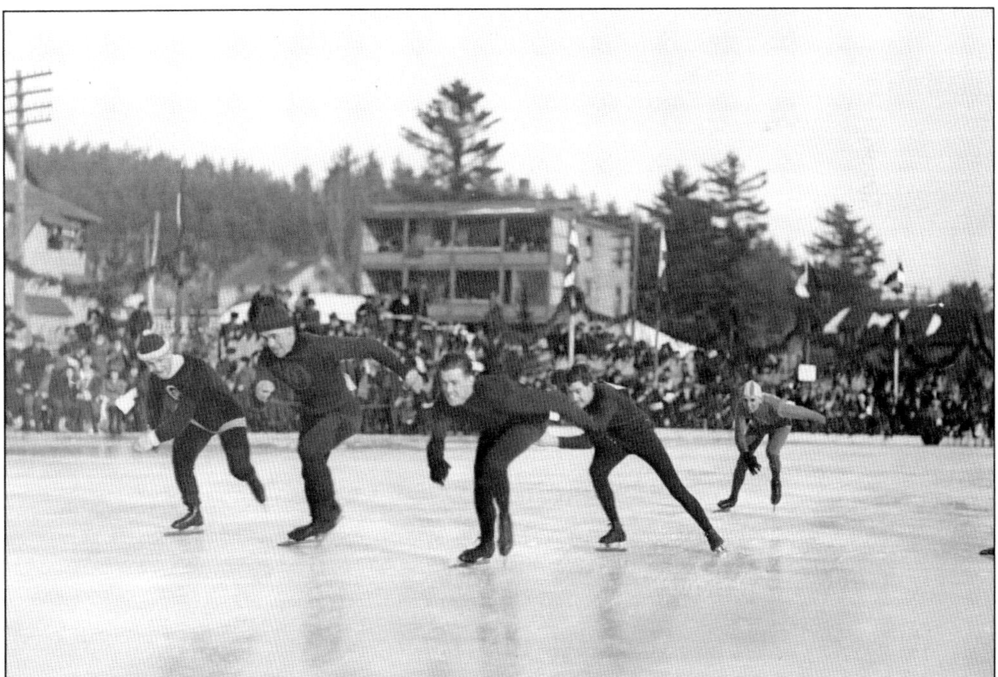

The Pontiac Rink is packed for this speed skating race in 1920. People are even watching from the houses in the distance.

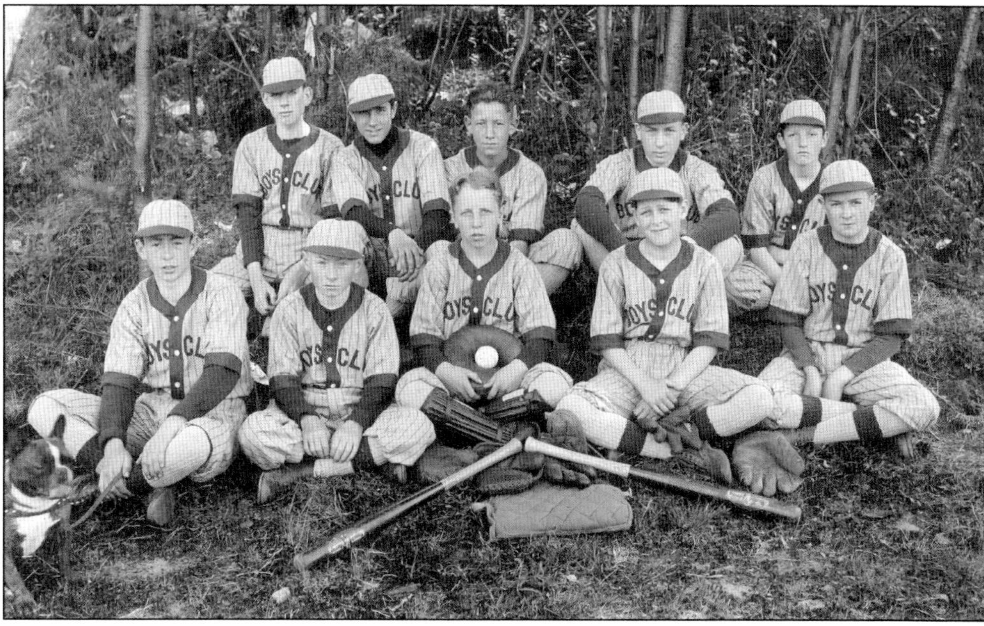

This is the 1919 Saranac Lake Boys Club Baseball team. In a September 5, 1995, article in the *Enterprise*, John Duquette notes, "The Boys Club here opened in 1914 thanks to Mr. Walter H. Cluett who donated the building to youths of the village." The club building was located at 109 River Street. That is now the site of the State Boat Launch on Lake Flower.

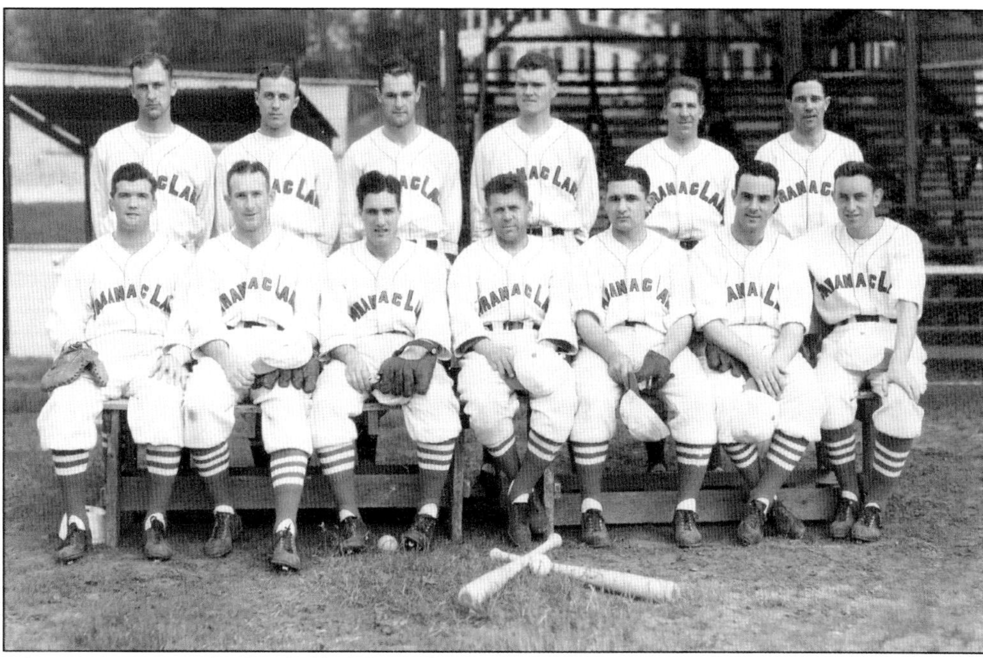

Like most towns in the first half of the 20th century, Saranac Lake had baseball teams for players of all ages. This men's team is from the 1940s. From left to right are (first row) Charlie Kittredge, Red Durand, Johnny Auysian, Doc Gautreau, Hugo Blandori, Bill Hafer, and Frank Goode; (second row) Lefty Febure, Charles Mayuski, George Hines, Mike Klarnick, Clark Abbott, and Neil Mahoney.

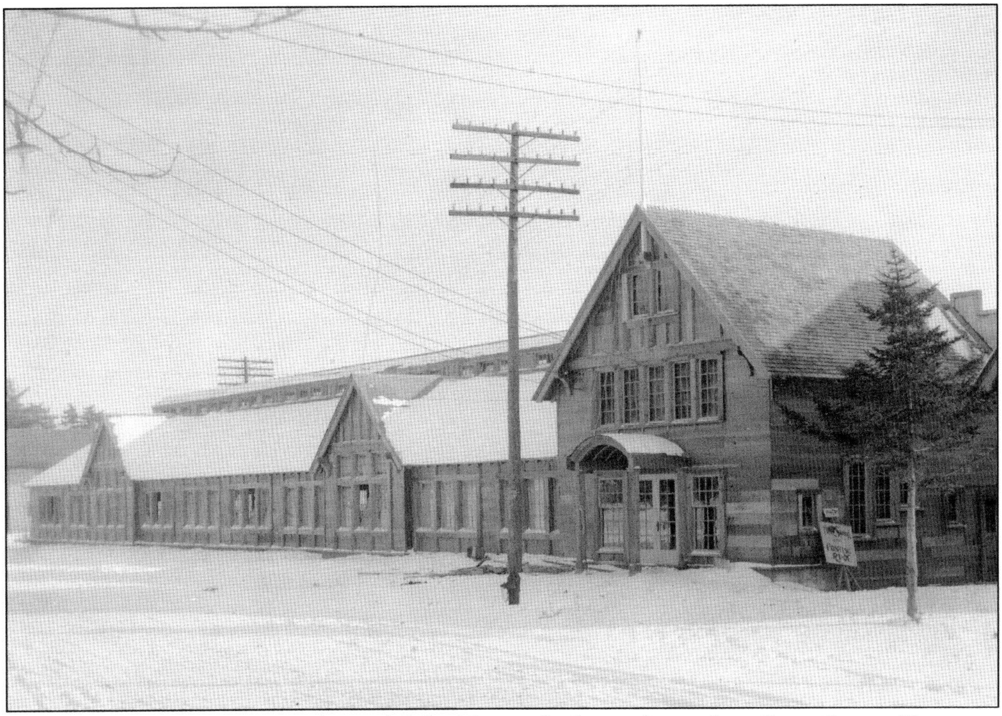

This is the Saranac Lake Curling Club building, which was located on River Street. Historian Mary Hotaling has written that it was built for the village in 1918 by Walter Cluett. In 1931, a new rink was constructed and this building became Al Short's Garage and until it was torn down.

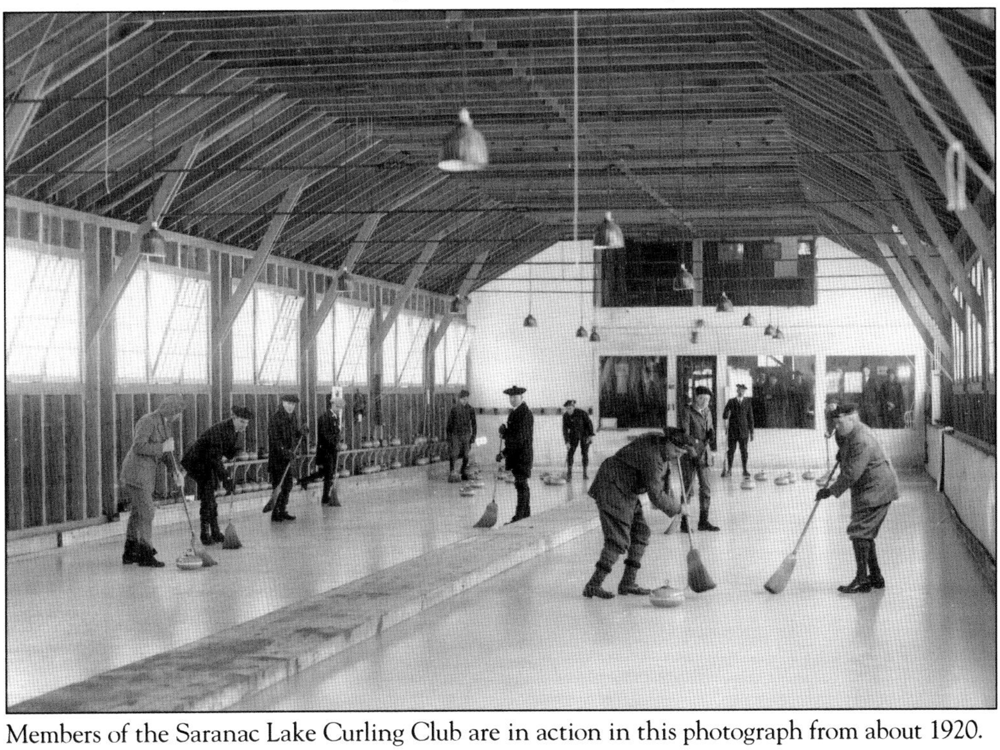

Members of the Saranac Lake Curling Club are in action in this photograph from about 1920.

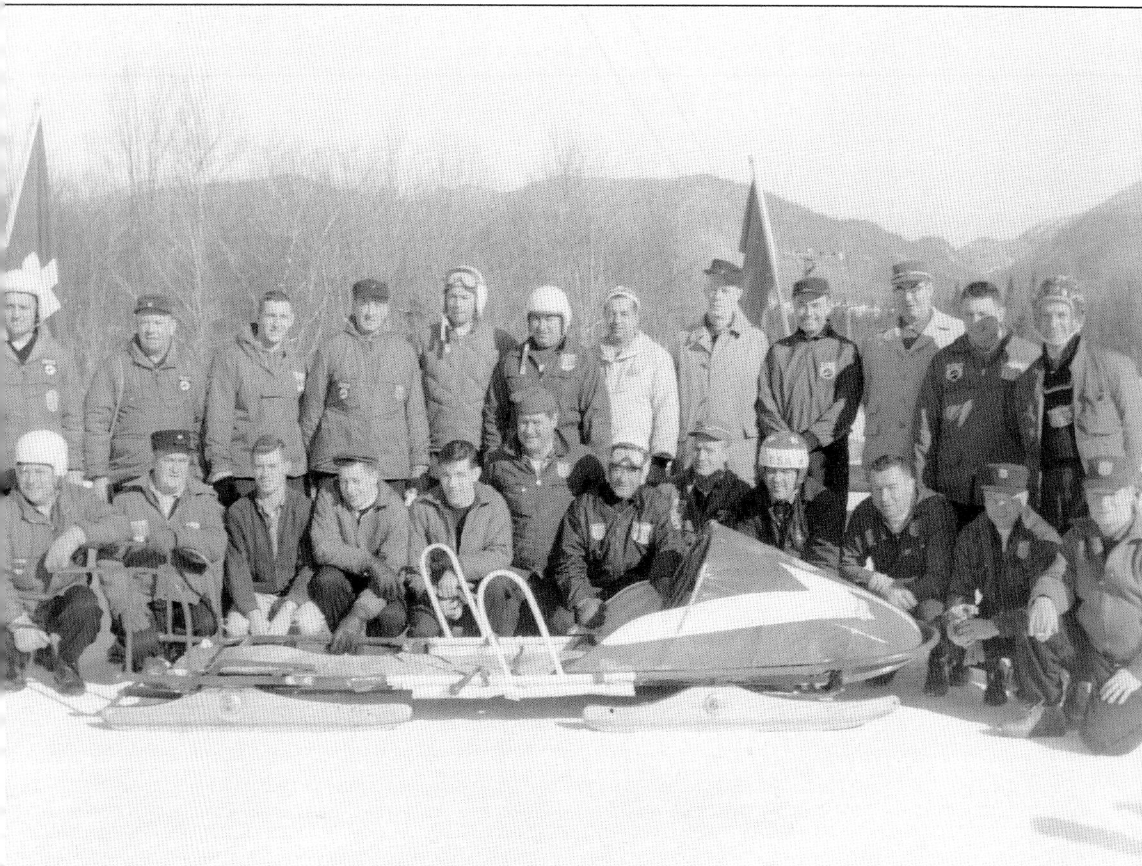

This is the Saranac Lake Bobsled Club in 1960. Only a few of the men are identified in the picture. They are (first row) Jim Lamy (sixth from left), Monk Flagg (seventh from left), Larry McKillip (10th from left), and Ducker Dupree (far right); (second row) Tuffy Latour (second from left), Louis Miron (fourth from left), Jerry Morgan (fifth from left), and Dew Drop Morgan (far right).

Seven

School Days

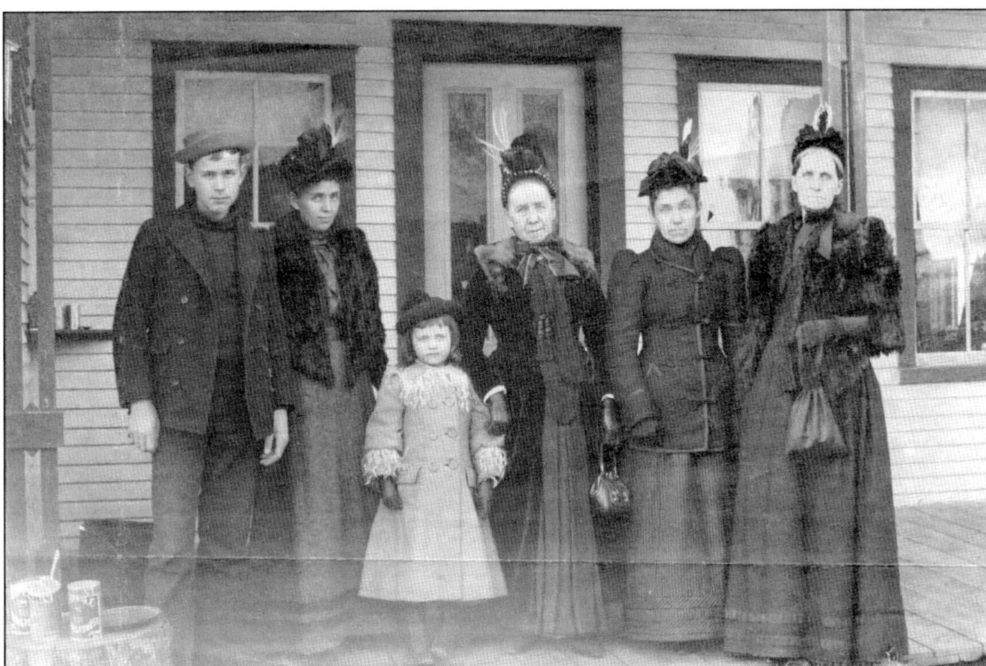

Francis Slater (left) is listed on this photograph as the first graduate of Saranac Lake High School. He is here with, from left to right, his mother, Emma Slater; sister, Isabel; aunt, Minerva Washer; Phoebe Gray; and Emily Washer.

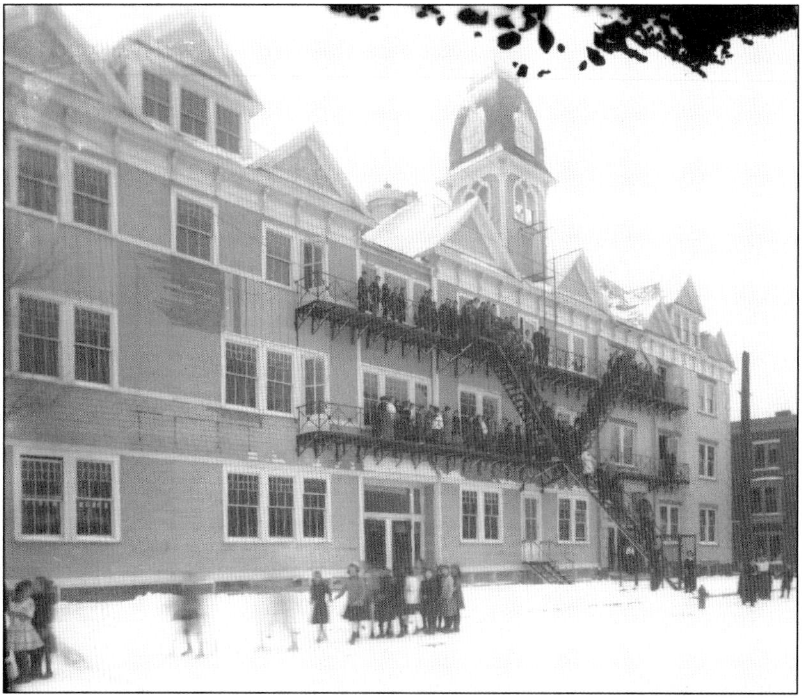

This is a winter fire drill at the Saranac Lake High School on Main Street. This school was built in 1890 and was replaced by the Petrova Avenue School in 1925. The site is now occupied by the Hotel Saranac.

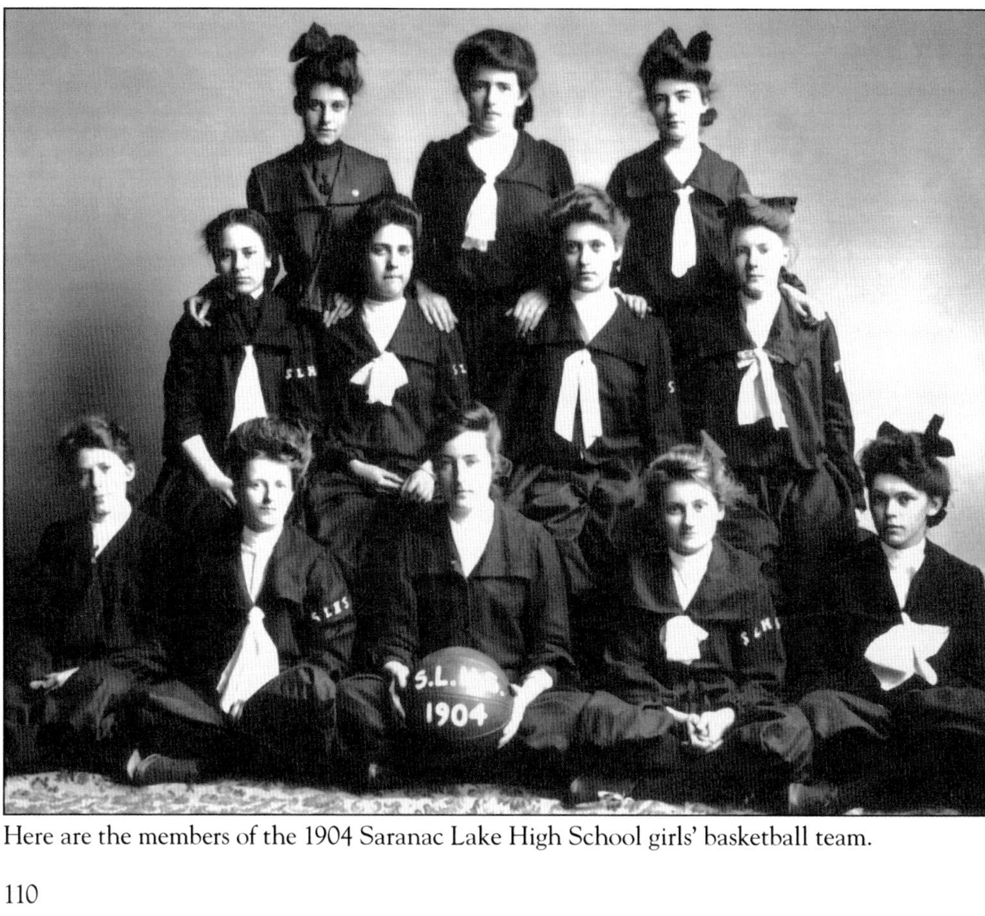

Here are the members of the 1904 Saranac Lake High School girls' basketball team.

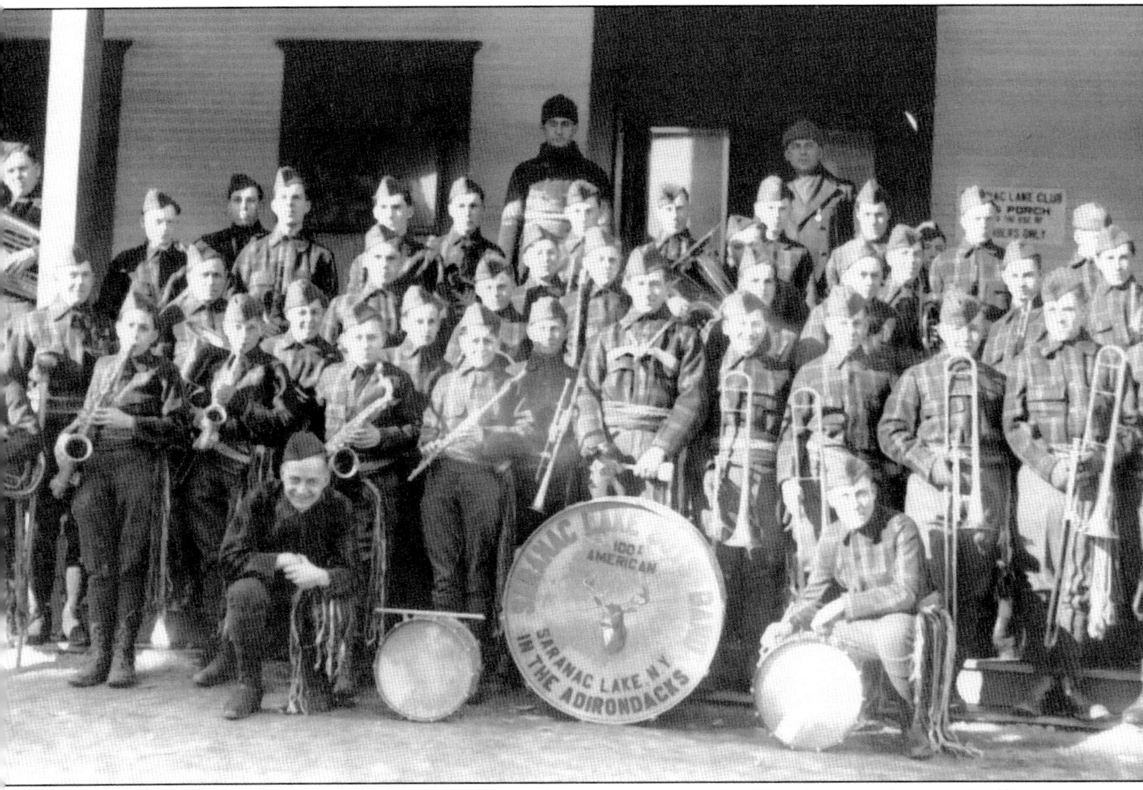

The Saranac Lake Boys Band was an independent group organized by theatrical agent William Morris. In 1929, the organization was taken over by the Saranac Lake High School (HSLW). This picture is from 1920. Identified in the first row are Richard Lytle (fifth from left), holding the flute, and Douglas Bombard (eighth from left), second trombone. (Courtesy of Natalie Bombard Leduc.)

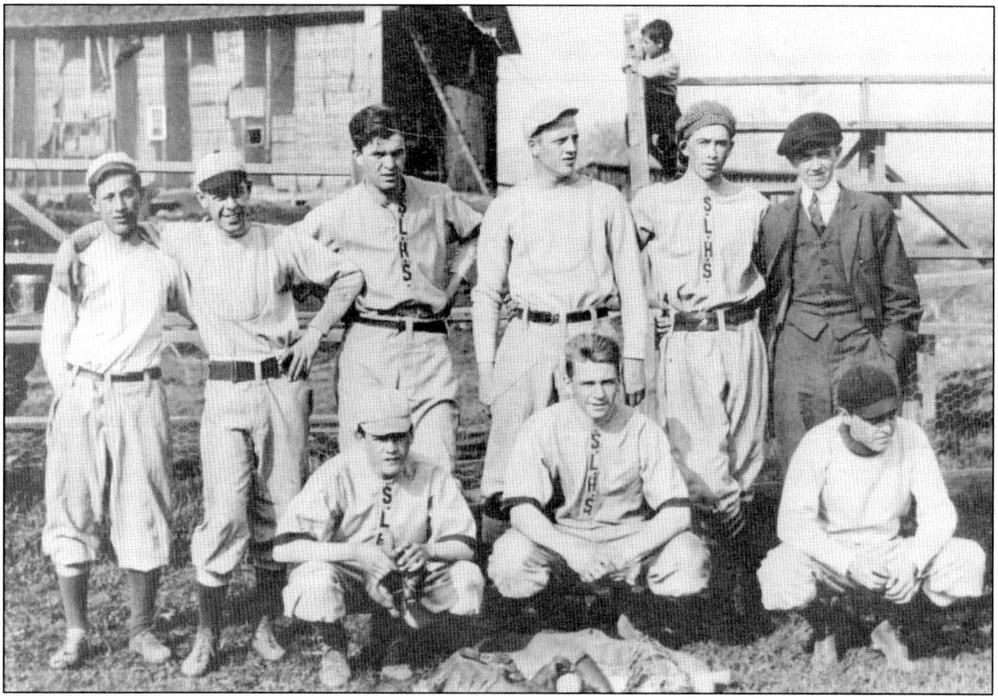

This is the 1912 high school baseball team. From left to right are (first row) ? Gay, ? Neubauer, and ? Jordan; (second row) Leon Kingman, Lyall DelaMater, Ned Patnode, J. Walker, ? Cahoun, and Leo Quirk.

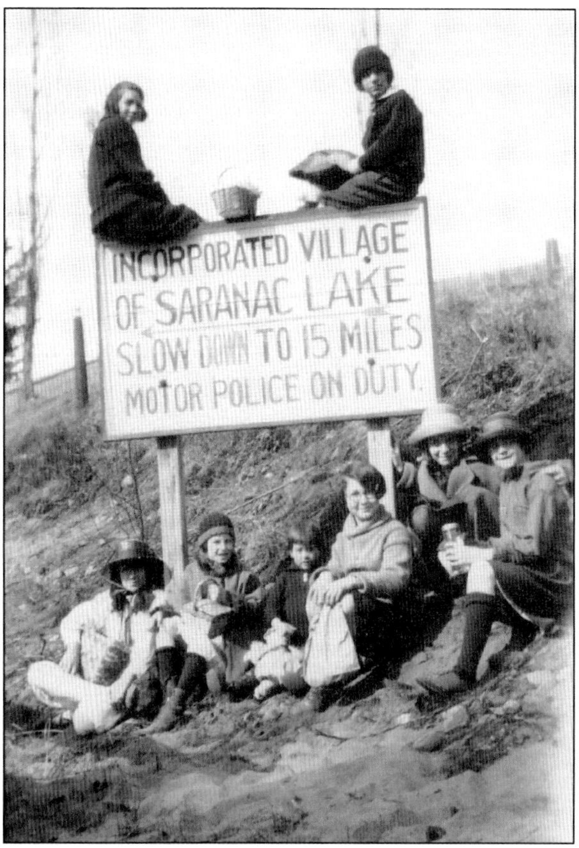

These River Street School students stopped to get their picture taken at the entrance sign to the village while on a school outing in the early days of automobiles.

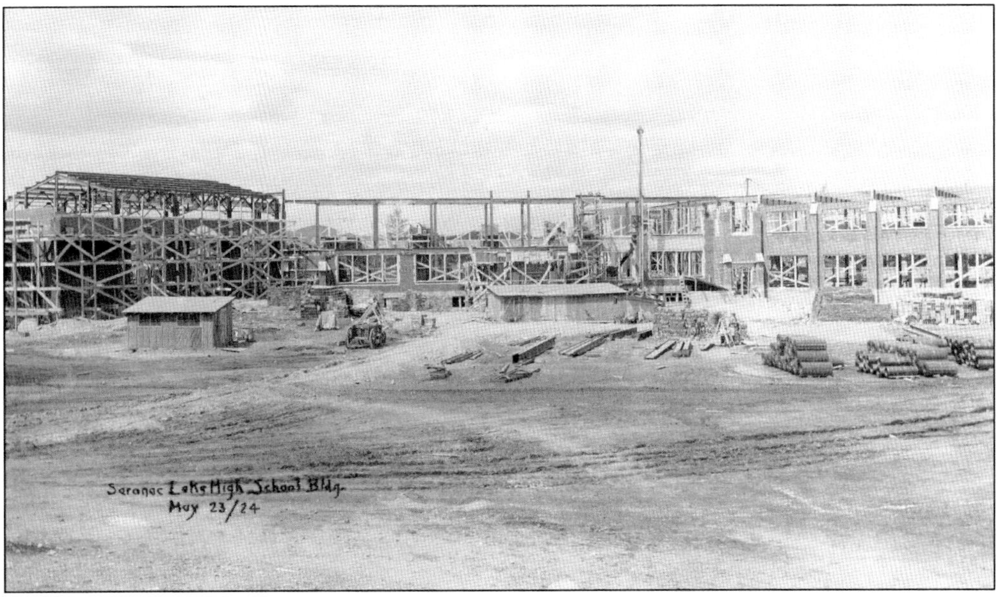

The Petrova School is still under construction in this picture taken on May 23, 1924. The school opened in September 1925, and housed kindergarten through 12th grade.

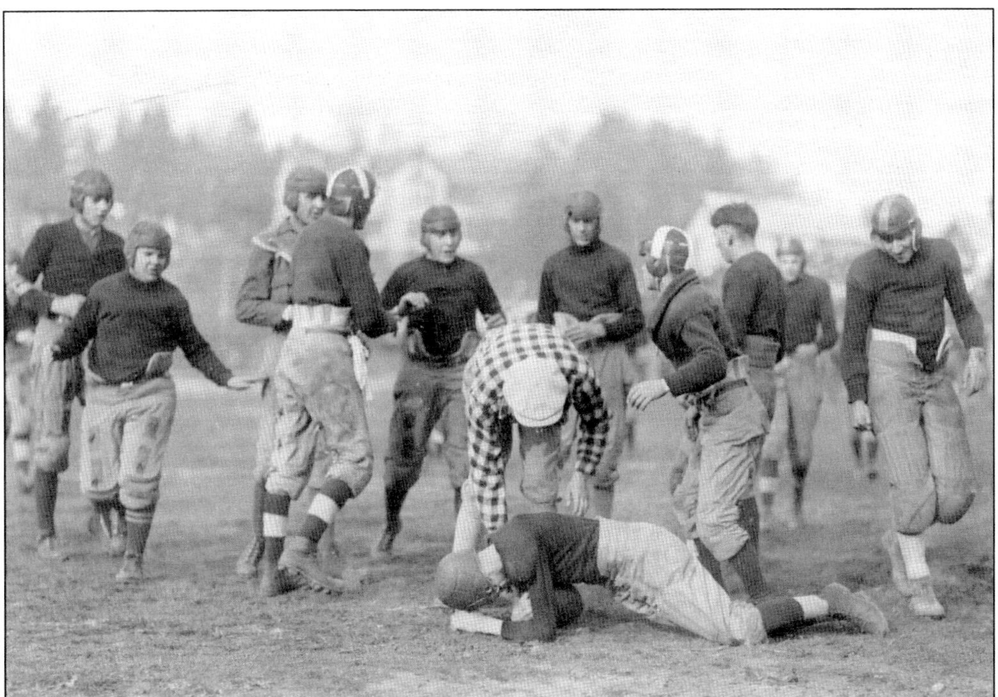

The Saranac Lake High School football team is on the field around 1930. The official has a checkered shirt instead of the striped shirts worn today, and players' uniforms have also changed.

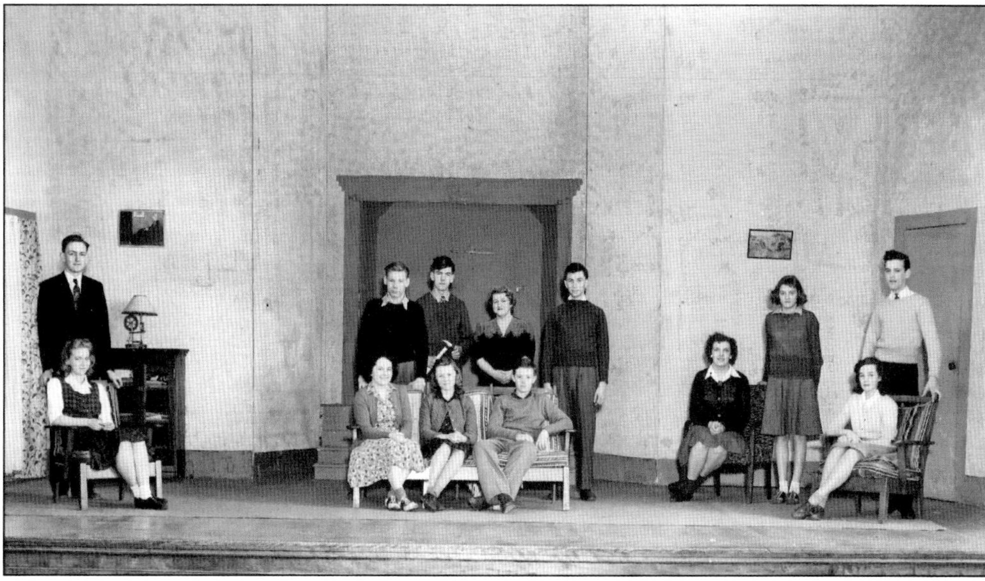

This is a photograph for the 1943 Saranac Lake High School Junior Class Play. Pictured, from left to right, are (far left) Carlton Hyde and Florence Mace; (center, standing) Jack Peightal, Bob Cheeseman, director Ruth Forth, and Herbert Turner; (center, sitting) Patricia Como, Mary Utting, and Benjamin Muncil; (far right) Irma Preston, Catherine Perry, Kathryn Ober, and Fred Carter.

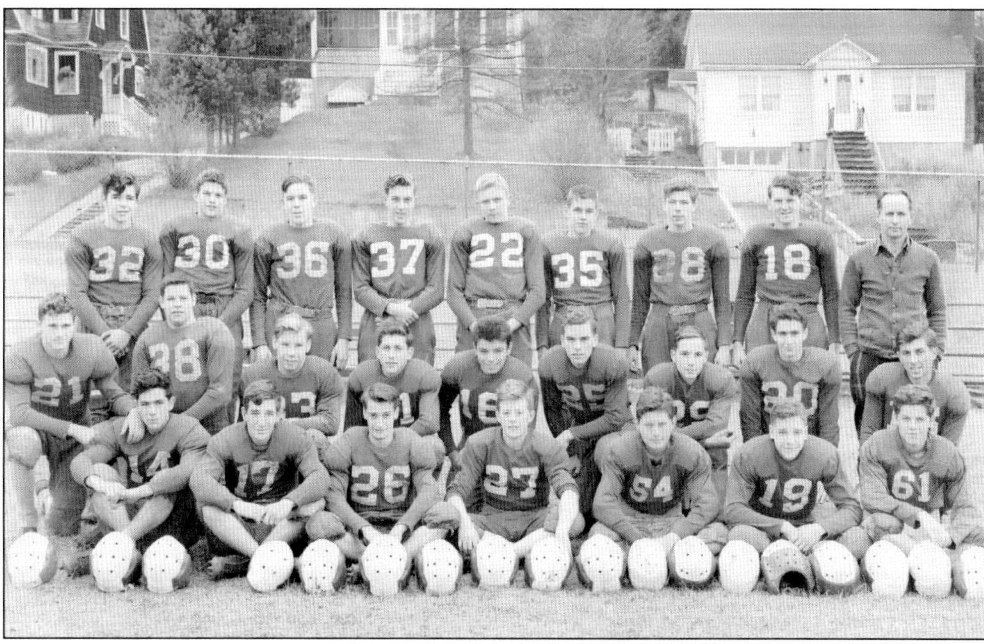

This is the 1944 Saranac Lake High School football team photograph. From left to right are (first row) George Garrant, Timothy Sweet, John Harrigan, Benjamin Muncil, Edward Mullen, Wayne Sweet, and Francis Pelkey; (second row) Austin Gowan, Robert Dupree, Jack Peightal, John Fitzpatrick, Nathaniel Oddy, Raymond Cassavaugh, Richard Newell, Clyde Baker, and Herbert Turner; (third row) William Hall, William McGrain, Phillip Hammond, Robert Pederson, Howard Harvey, George Rankin, William Mulflur, Gordon Tyler, and coach Ken Wilson.

Eight

Winter Carnival

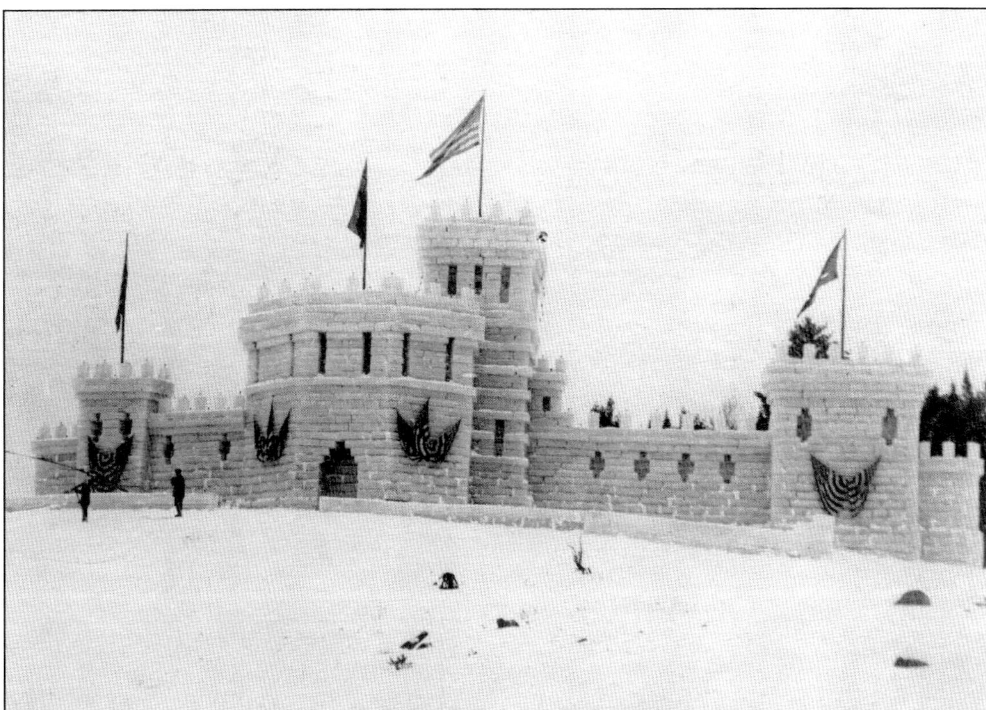

The first Ice Palace was built for the 1898 Winter Carnival. The Ice Palace tradition continues to current times. This is the 1909 Ice Palace.

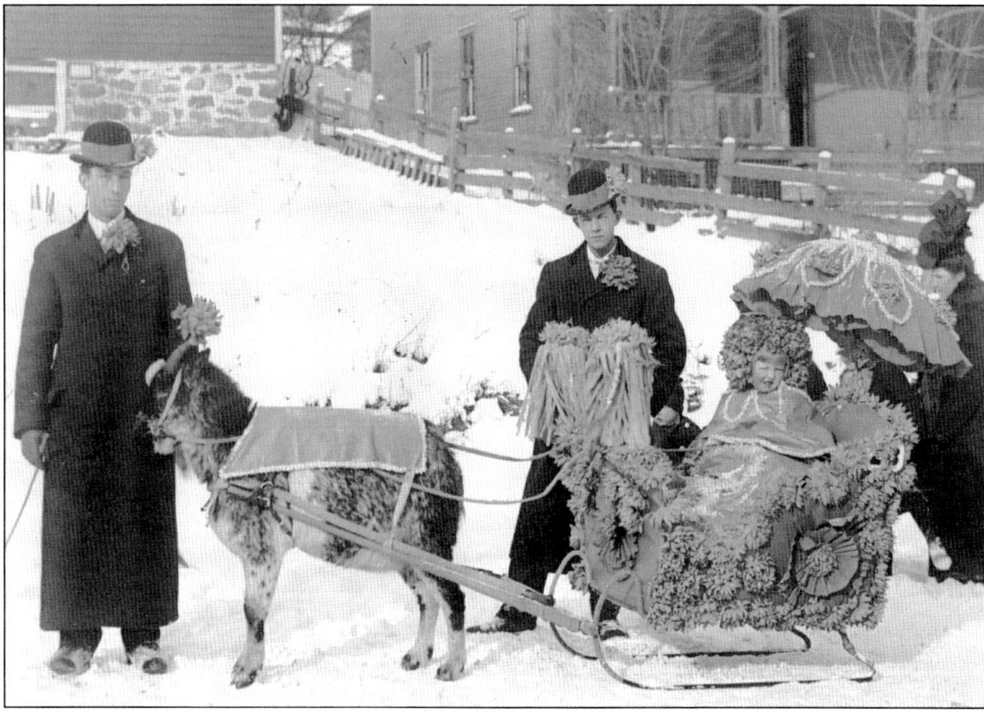

A family has their sleigh decorated for a parade in the 1890s. (Courtesy of Paul Smith's College.)

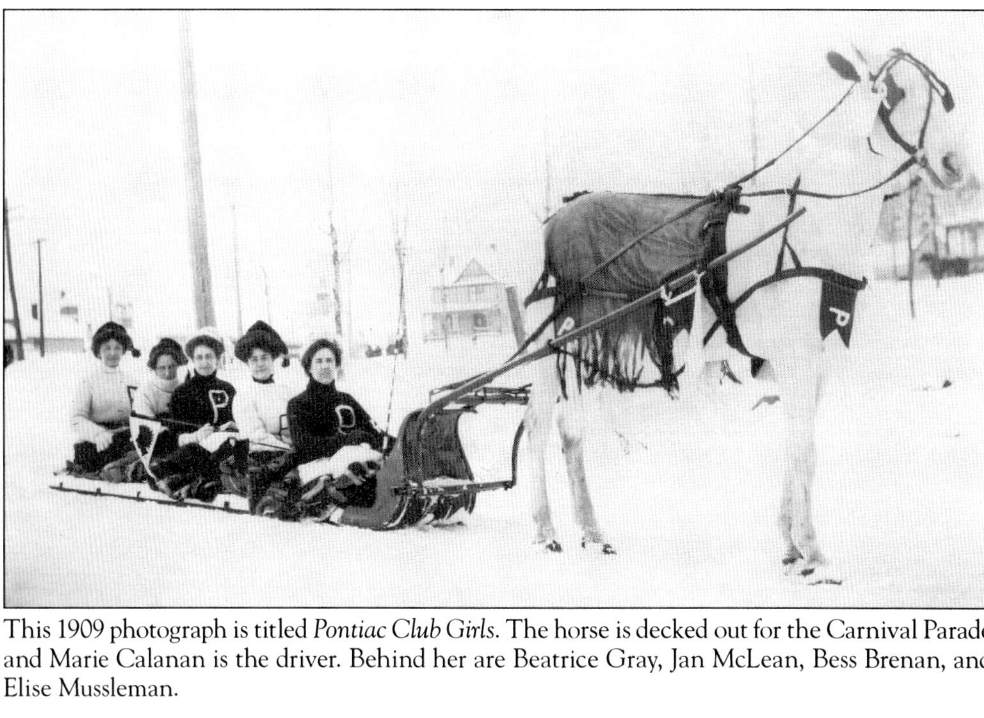

This 1909 photograph is titled *Pontiac Club Girls*. The horse is decked out for the Carnival Parade and Marie Calanan is the driver. Behind her are Beatrice Gray, Jan McLean, Bess Brenan, and Elise Mussleman.

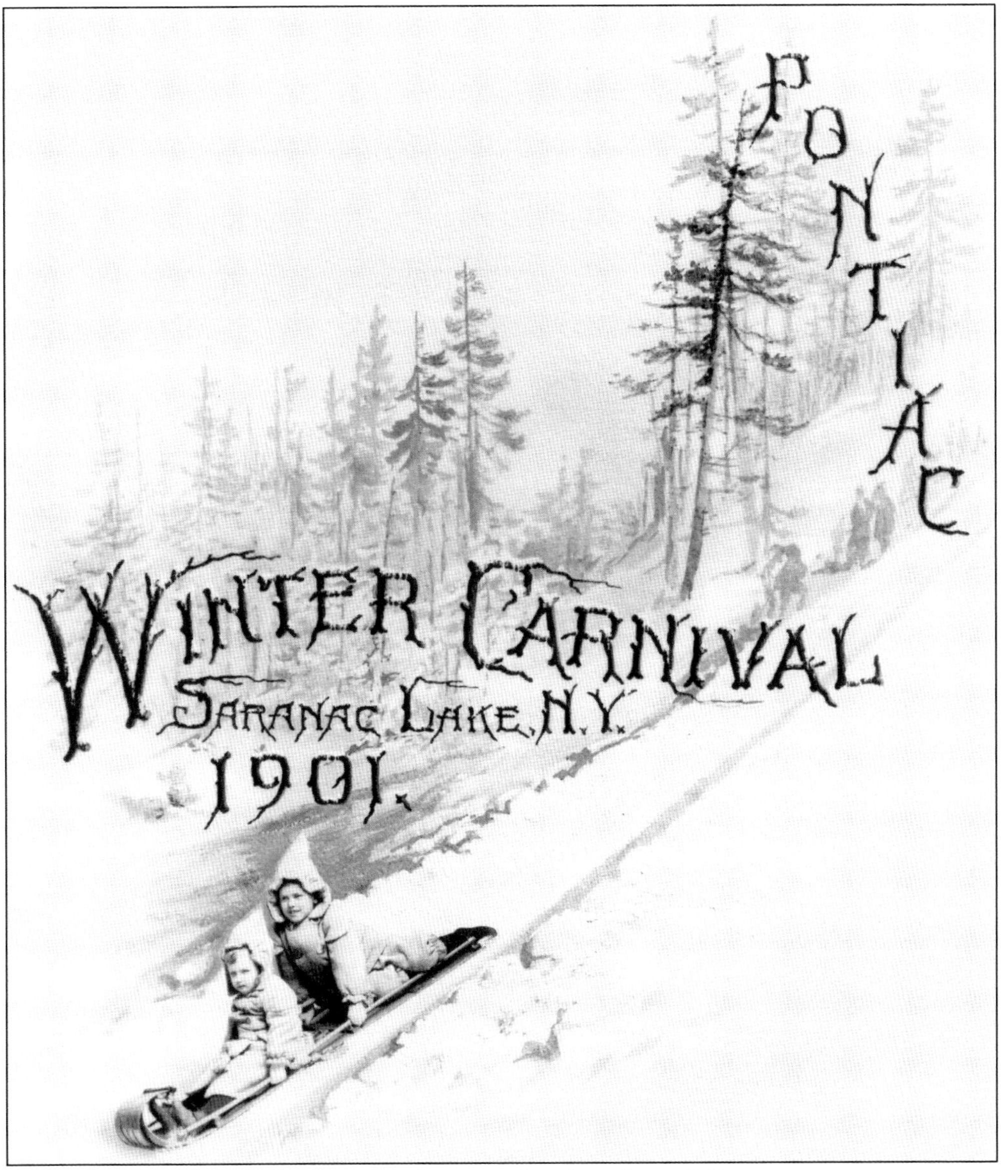

Here is the front page of the carnival advertising brochure from 1901.

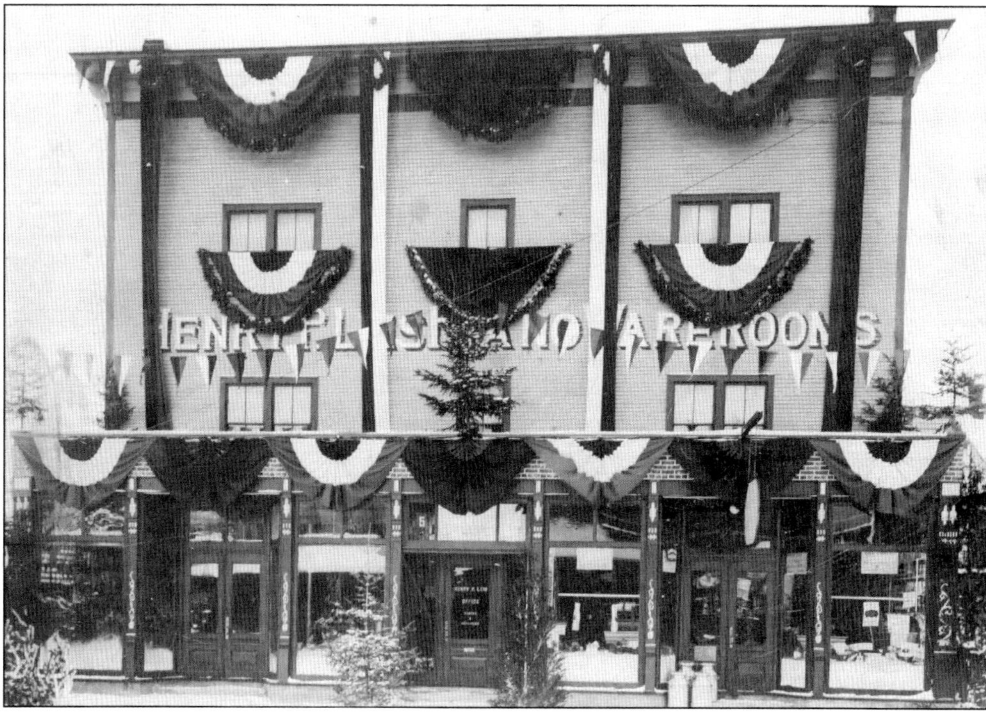

Henry P. Leis Piano Warerooms, which is now 12 Bloomingdale Avenue between the current Sturdy Supply building and the corner parking lot, is decked out for the carnival around 1920.

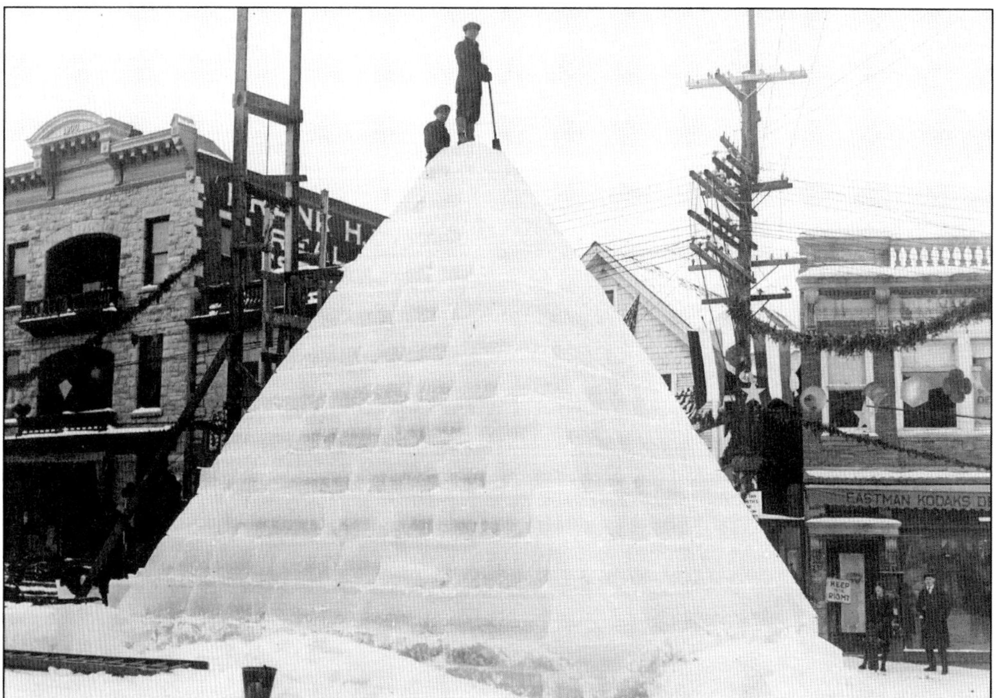

Building an ice pyramid at the intersection of Main Street and Broadway was a Winter Carnival feature in the early 20th century. These men are working on it in 1920.

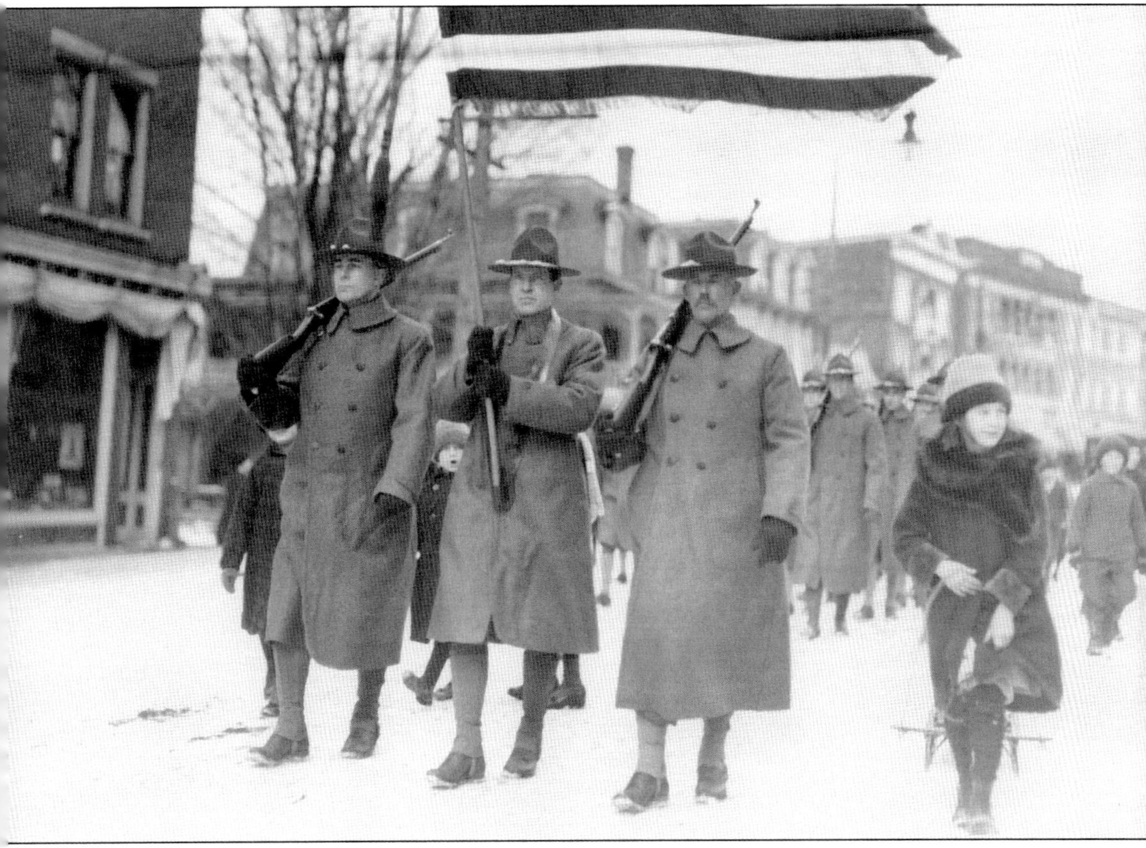

Local children joined the soldiers in this World War I–era parade.

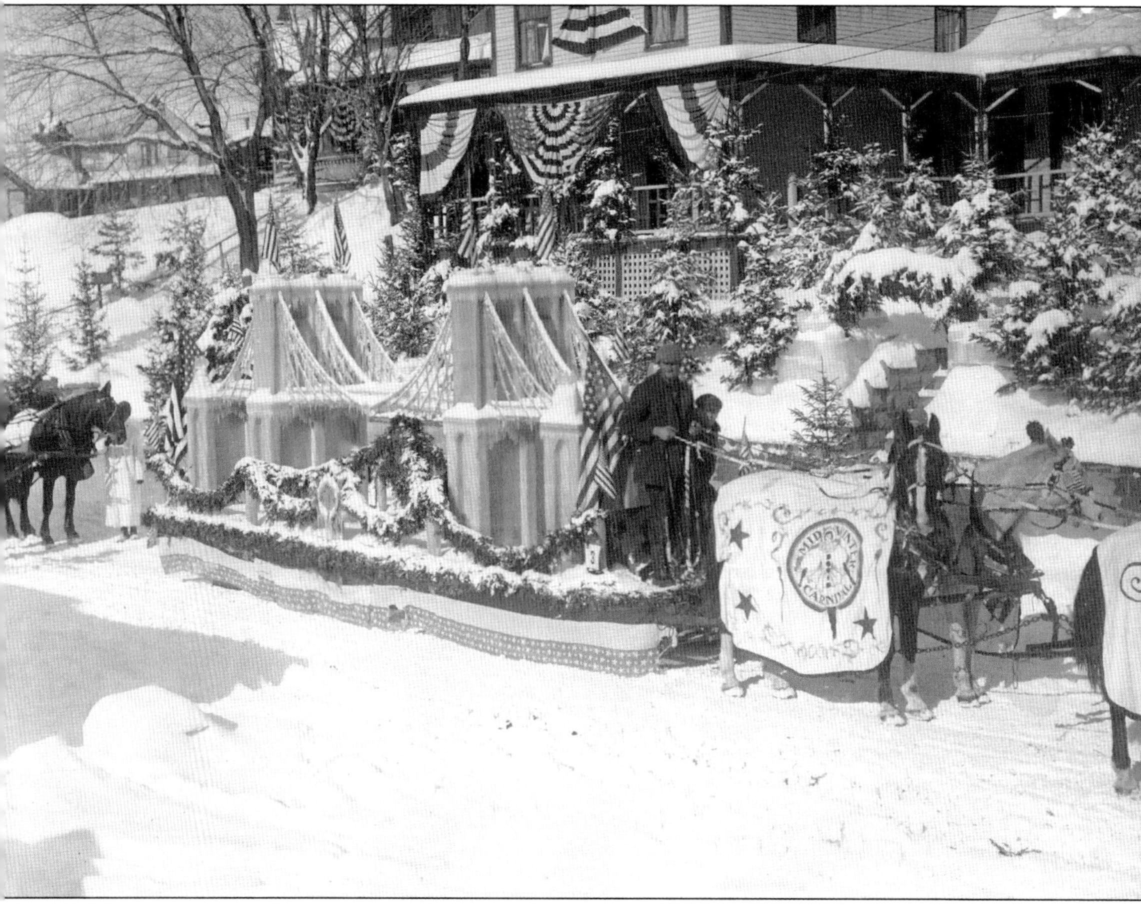

This float is a sculpture of the Brooklyn Bridge made entirely from ice. It was entered by the Paul Smith's Hotel Company and won the award in 1915 for being the best in the parade. The covering on the horse reads "Mid-Winter Carnival" around a picture of a female clown.

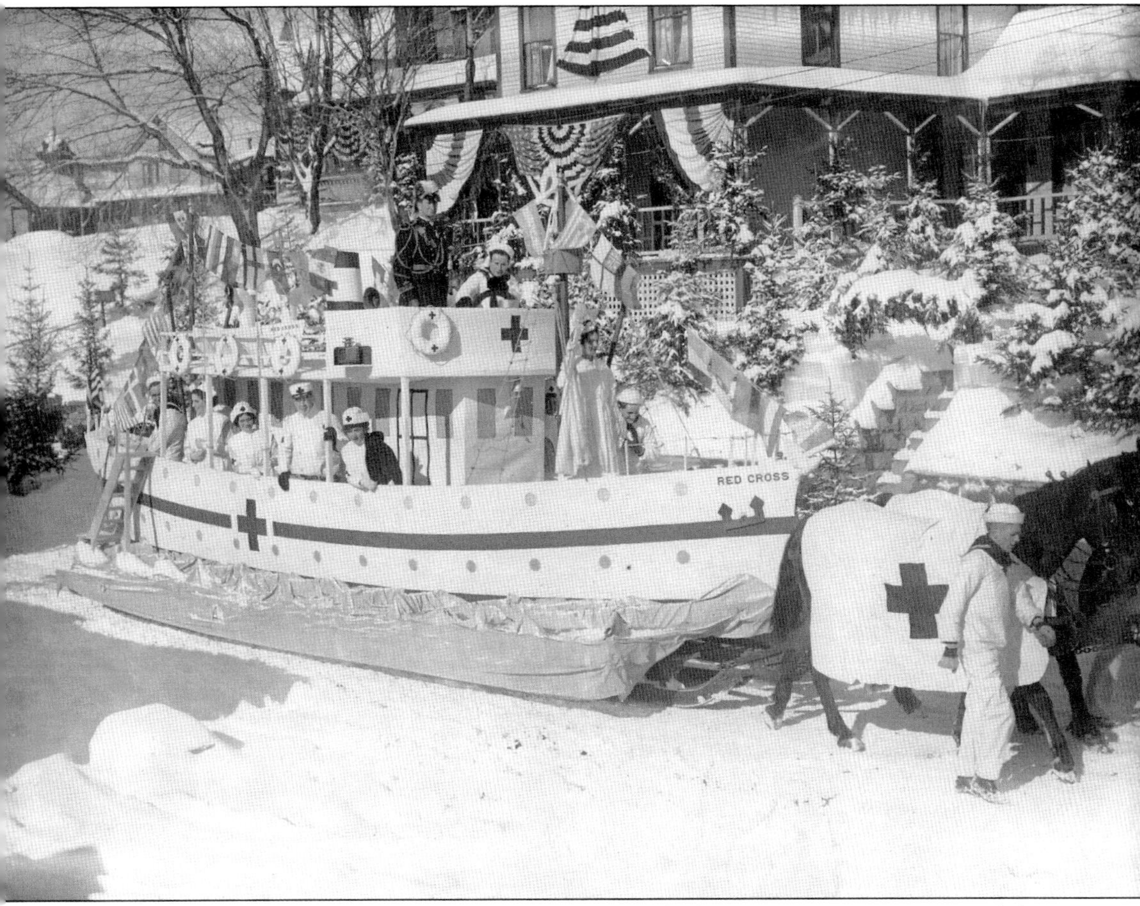

Here is another prizewinning float from 1915. The Adirondack Cottage Sanitarium entered this float, and the women on board are sanitarium nurses. It is titled "Red Cross Ship."

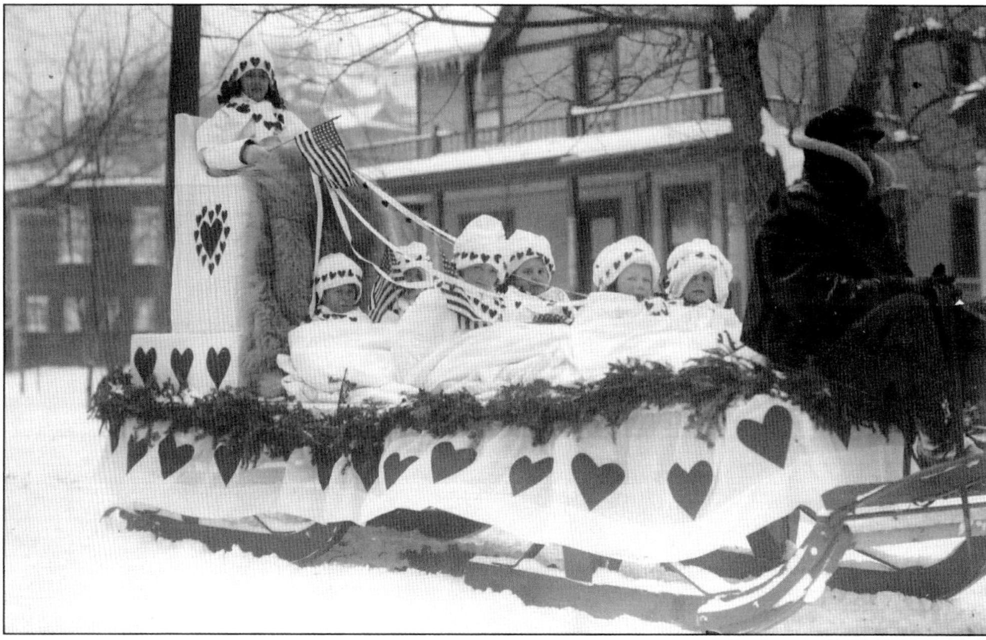

This undated early float was titled "The Queen of Hearts and Her Court." It was entered by Eaton Goldthwaite and won first prize in the children's division.

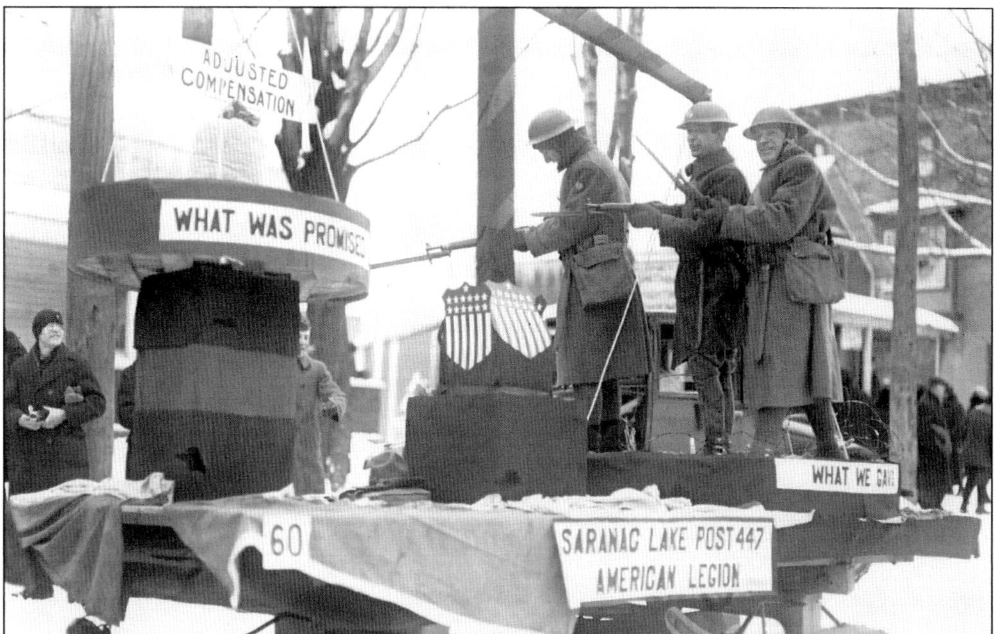

The American Legion entered this float with a political theme in 1924. The World War Adjusted Compensation Act was being debated in Washington, DC, that winter. The act would give all World War I veterans a cash bonus based on time served. The Legion strongly supported this bill. The float shows a scale with the small amount of money promised in the bill, "What Was Promised," weighed against the lives risked by the fighting men represented by, "What We Gave." The bill finally passed in May 1924.

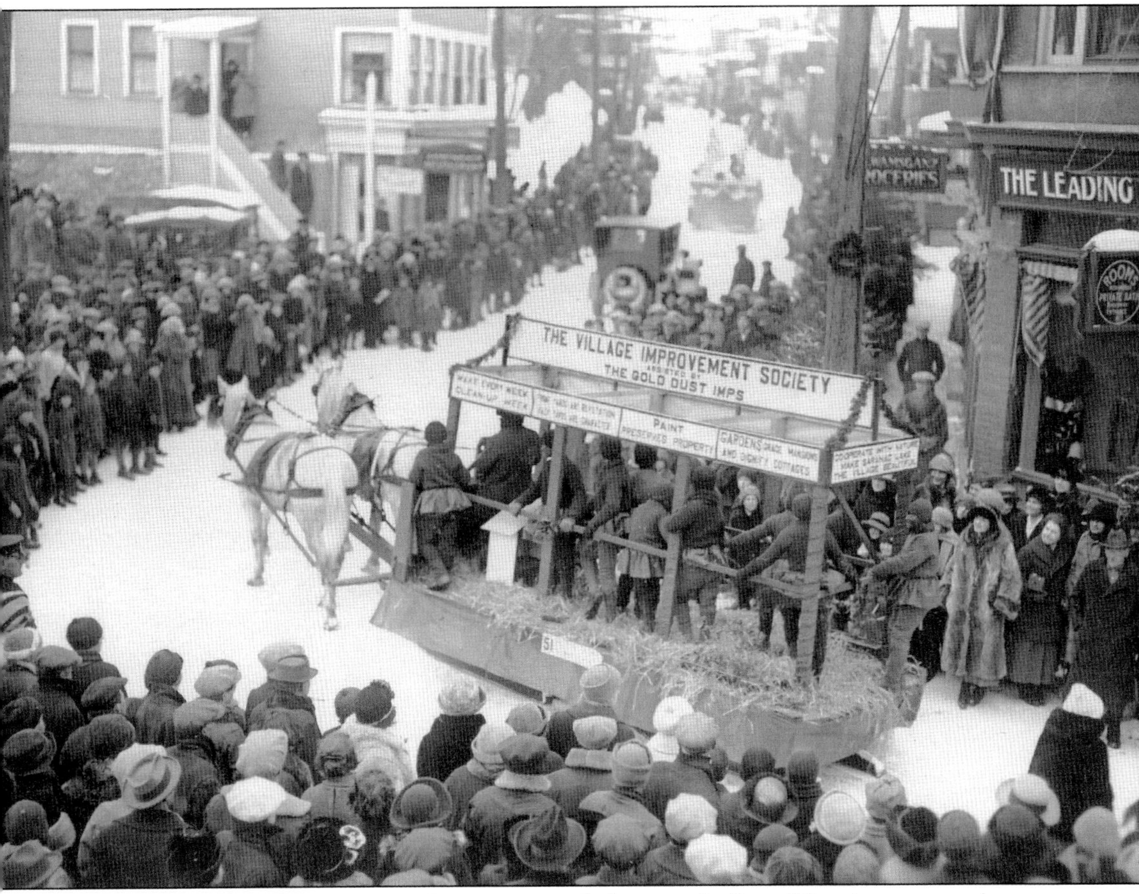

In 1924, the Village Improvement Society entered this parade float. The signs across the top encourage parade watchers to beautify the village in a number of ways: "Make Every Week Clean-up Week," "Front Yards are Reputation, Back Yards are Character," "Paint Preserves Property," "Gardens Grace Mansions and Dignify Cottages," "Cooperate With Nature," and one sign that could still be the organization's motto: "Make Saranac Lake the Village Beautiful."

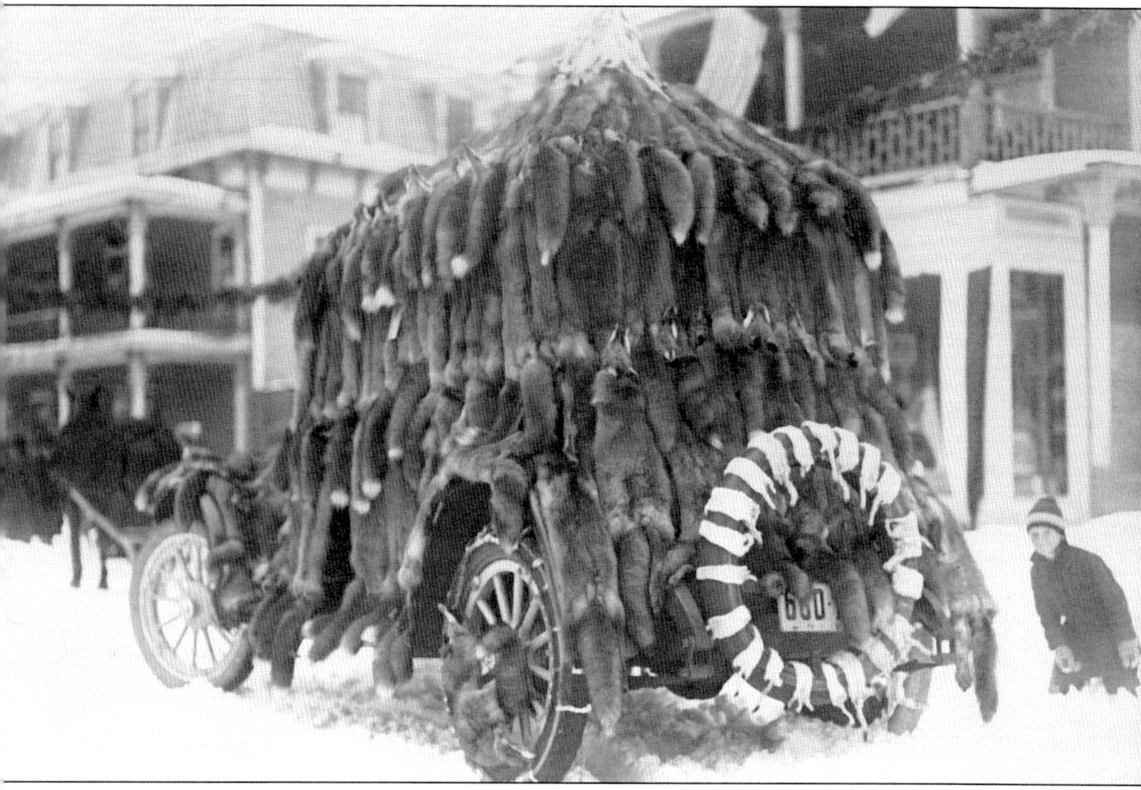

Trapping was an important local industry when this car was covered in animal pelts for a 1920s carnival parade. Fox skins cover the body and ermine skins surround the spare tire and the point built up at the top of the car.

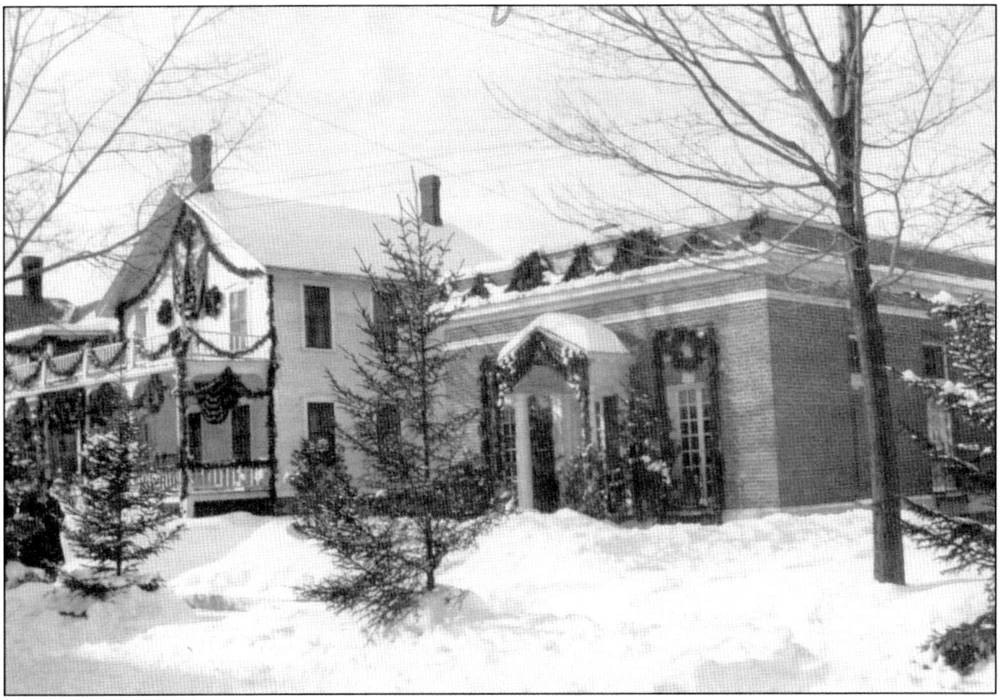

The Guild House and the library are decorated for a Winter Carnival in the 1940s. The Guild House was the home of the Saranac Lake Study and Craft Guild, which began in 1936. The Guild provided education, job training, and enrichment for the many patients who came to Saranac Lake hoping to recover from tuberculosis. The house was demolished to make way for a library expansion.

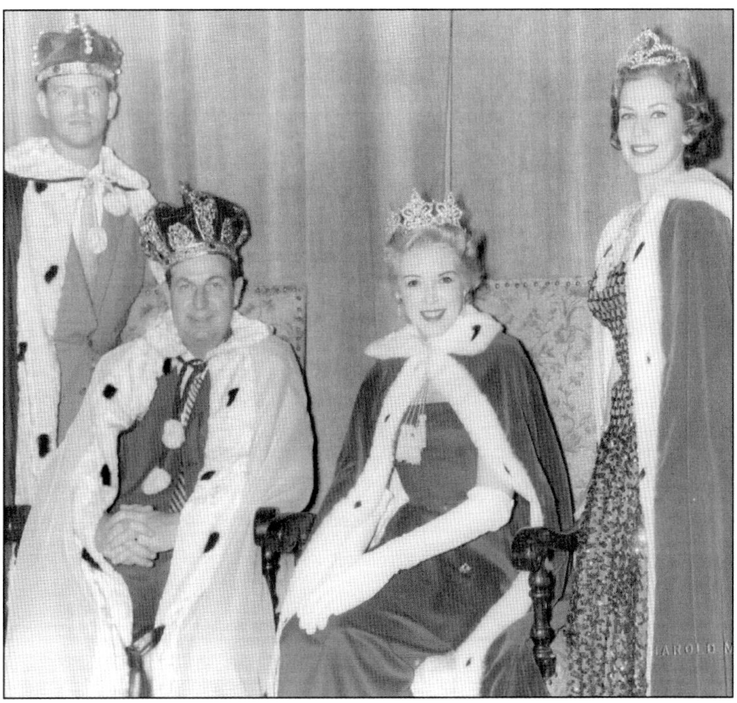

For a period beginning in the mid-1950s, national celebrities were brought to the village to reign as carnival royalty. In 1957, it was King Don McNeill and Queen Fran Allison (seated) and Prince Dick Noel and Princess Betty Johnson. They brought the excitement of the broadcast of McNeill's popular radio show *The Breakfast Club* live from the Pontiac Theatre. *The Breakfast Club* aired from 1933 to 1968.

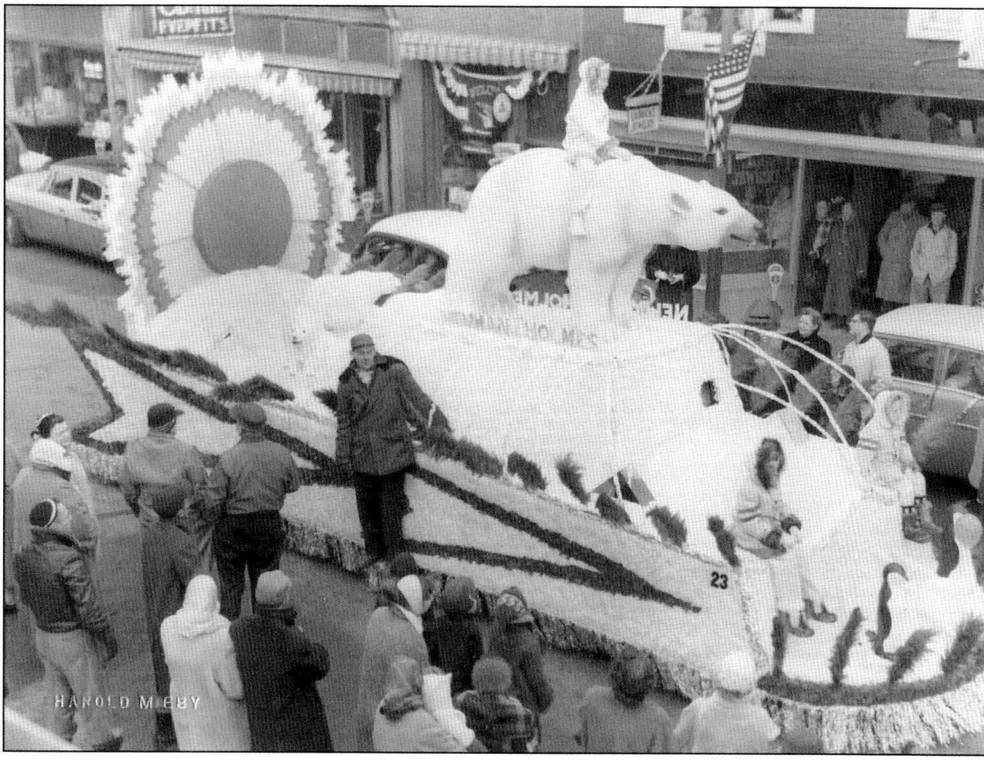

Newman & Holmes won a prize for this float in 1957. At that time, many floats were built on top of—and completely covering—the cars or trucks that moved them.

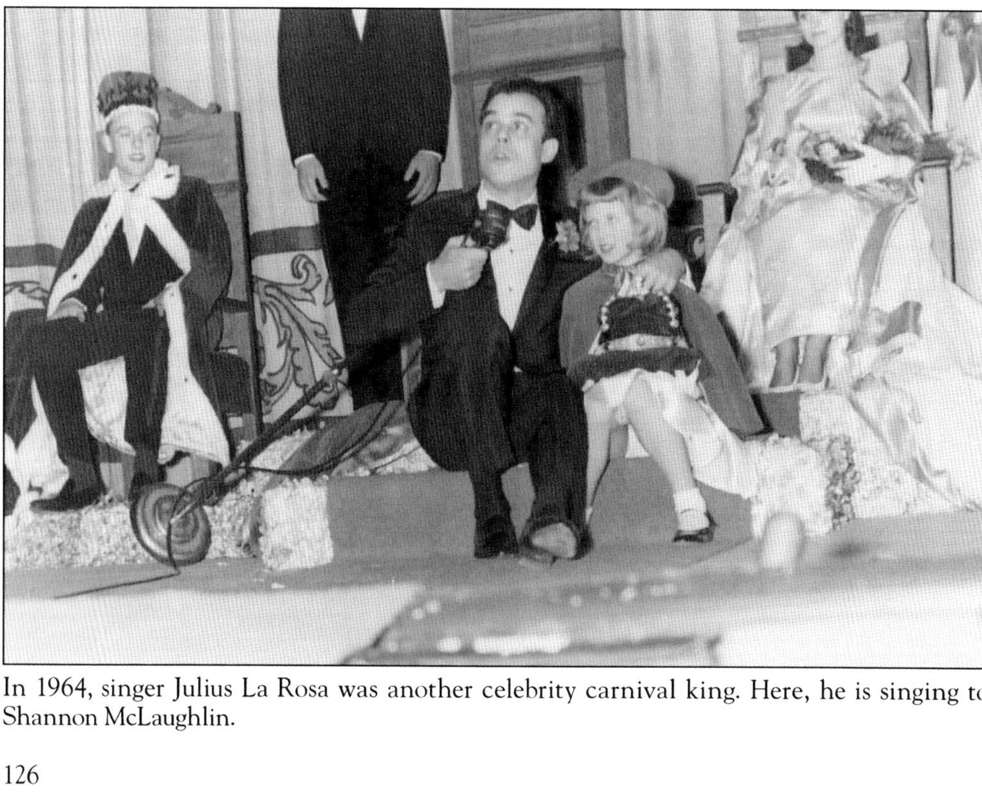

In 1964, singer Julius La Rosa was another celebrity carnival king. Here, he is singing to Shannon McLaughlin.

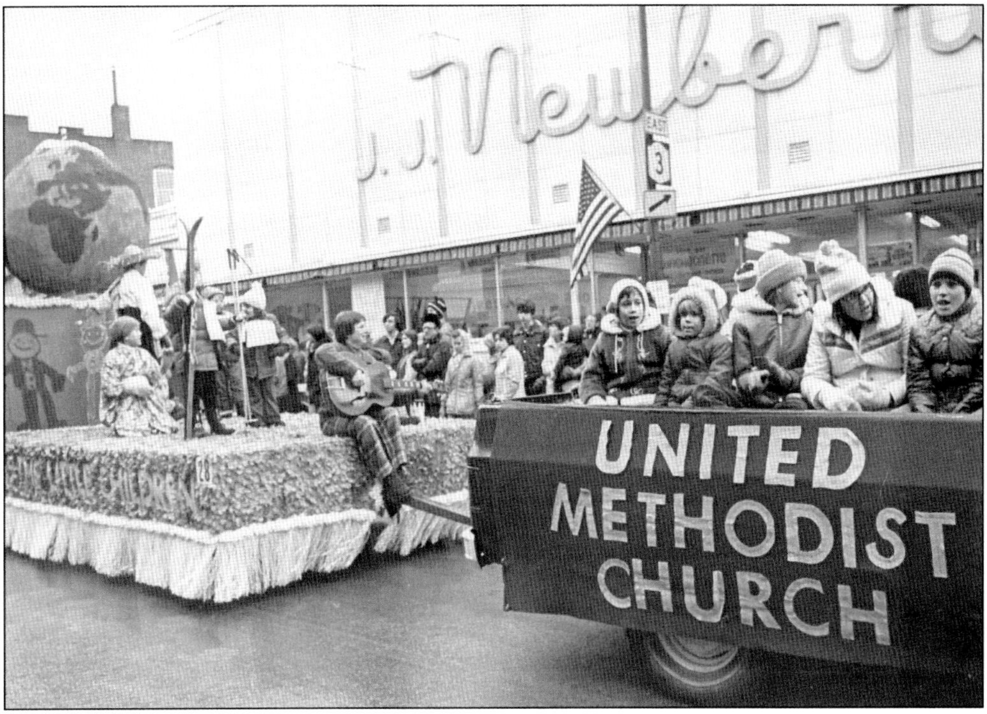

The United Methodist Church float is passing in front of the Newberry's storefront in 1977. The storefront was installed in 1962, but was torn down and the original brick front restored some years after Newberry's had gone out of business.

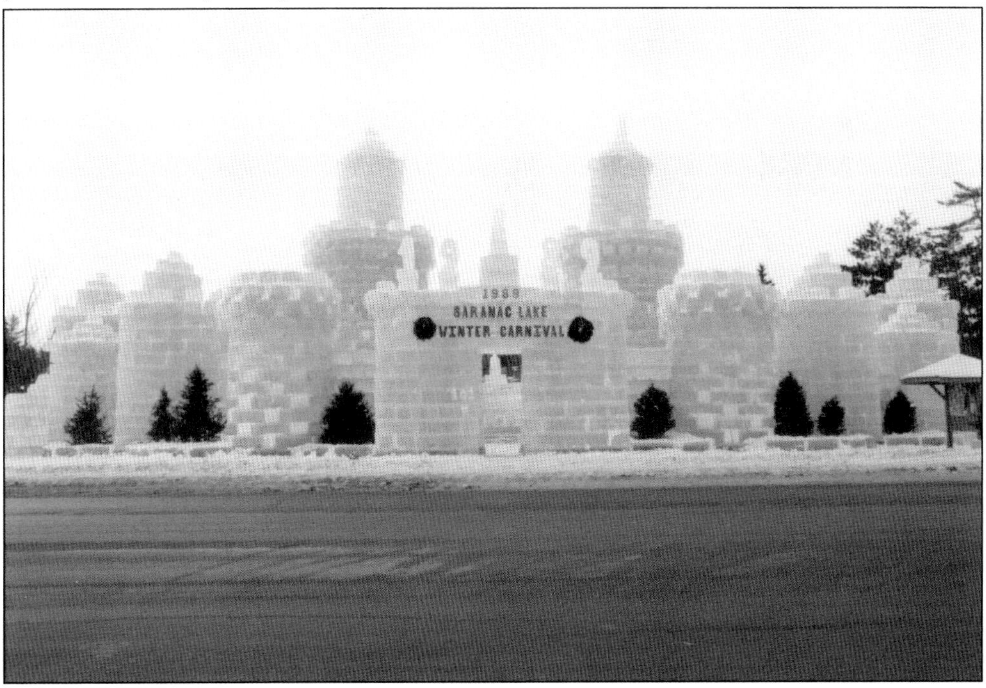

The 1980s saw a resurgence in Ice Palace architecture, as can be seen in the 1989 Ice Palace on the shore of Lake Flower. This trend has continued to the present day.